CANADA

Years of Challenge

To 1814

Elspeth Deir
Paul Deir
Keith Hubbard

Holt, Rinehart and
Winston of Canada,
Limited, Toronto

Canadian Cataloguing in Publica-
tion Data
Deir, Elspeth, 1947-
Canada: years of challenge
For use in grade 7.
ISBN 0-03-920171-6
1. Canada-History. I. Deir, Paul,
1947- II. Hubbard, Keith, 1940- III.
Title: Canada: years of challenge.
FC170.D44 971 C80-094361-9
F1025.D44

Acknowledgments

The authors would like to thank
Sheldon Diamond for his contribu-
tion to the planning of this text. As
well, special thanks go to Professor
W.A. McKay, Scarborough College,
University of Toronto, for his
comments on the early manuscript.

Holt, Rinehart and Winston of
Canada, wishes to thank the follow-
ing educators for their evaluations
of the manuscript and helpful
advice: Ken Osborne, University of
Manitoba; Bruce Hill, Brant County
Board of Education, Brantford,
Ontario; Marvin Longboat, Dun-
dana Public School, Dundas, Onta-
rio; David Flint, A.Y. Jackson
Secondary School, North York,
Ontario; Terrence Punch, Fairview
Junior High School, Halifax, Nova
Scotia.

Editor and Photo Researcher: Gary
Michaluk
Art Director: Barry Rubin
Design: Jim Ireland
Illustrations: Simon Harwood,
Deborah Drew-Brook, and Bill
Kimber
Maps and Posters: James Loates
Assembly: Jeanne Gray

Printed in Canada
1 2 3 4 5 85 84 83 82 81

Contents

Contents

Unit One
THE NATIVE PEOPLES

Chapter 1

THE NATIVE PEOPLES: THE FIRST CANADIANS

Who Are They?

Who are the Indians? Who are the Inuit? Who are the native peoples of Canada?

Most of us know something about Canada's native peoples—Indians and Inuit. But how much do we really know? Look at the pictures on pages 2 and 3.

3.

1.

4.

2.

5.

6.

9.

7.

10.

11.

8.

1. Which pictures do you think are of Indians and which are of Inuit?
2. List the things that helped you to make your decision. You might consider:
physical appearance (what they look like)
clothing
activities (things they are doing)
3. Are there any pictures where it is difficult to decide if the person is Inuit, Indian, or neither?

Let's Find Out

Here is a list of the people shown in the pictures. Don't look at it until you have tried to answer the questions.

1. Buffy Sainte-Marie is a Cree from Saskatchewan. She is well-known as a singer and composer. She is a regular performer on the children's television program "Sesame Street." She was educated at the University of Massachusetts.

2. Pierre Trudeau is not Indian or Inuit. The prime minister of Canada was presented with this headdress during an election campaign by some Indian supporters.

3. Chief Dan George is a chief of the Coast Salish tribe of British Columbia. As an actor, he has appeared in many television programs and films. He has also written about being an Indian in Canada today.

4. Norval Morriseau, an Ojibwa artist, was born in Thunder Bay, Ontario. Morriseau's paintings are like visions that tell stories about people and nature. His paintings have been shown in galleries across Canada.

5. Jay Silverheels (on the left) played Tonto, the faithful friend of the Lone Ranger (actor Clayton Moore) on television. A Mohawk, Silverheels was born on the Six Nations Reserve near Brantford, Ontario. His original name was Harold Jay Smith.

6. Dr. Howard Adams is a professor of sociology and an author. He is a Métis from Saskatchewan. A Métis is someone of mixed Indian and European background. The man in the poster behind Adams is Gabriel Dumont, a leader in the 1885 Rebellion of the Métis.

7. Stevie Collins is an Ojibwa from Thunder Bay, Ontario. Stevie, as a fifteen-year-old, competed for Canada in the 1980 Olympics and later won the World Junior Ski Jumping Championship.

8. Daphne Odjig Beavon is an Odawa artist from Manitoulin Island, Ontario. She is one of many Indian artists who are painting pictures that show stories from their people's rich heritage of myths and stories.

9. Grey Owl was a famous writer and a conservationist during the early 1900s. A scandal was raised when it was discovered that he was not an Indian as he claimed. He was really an Englishman named Archie Belaney.

10. Joan Kalaserk is an Inuit working for the Canadian Broadcasting Corporation as an announcer in Keewatin.

11. Paul Quassa is an Inuit working for the Canadian Broadcasting Corporation as an announcer. He is preparing for "Tusayaksat," CBC Keewatin's weekday magazine program.

Was it as easy to spot the native people as you thought it would be? How did you make your decision?

Stereotyping

Many people have definite ideas of what Indians and Inuit are like. Books, movies, television programs, and stories they have heard or seen have helped form these impressions. In some cases, these ideas may not be completely accurate. For example, mistakes have been made in describing the present life of native peoples. Some people believe that all Inuit live in igloos. This is not true. In fact, many Inuit living in the North today have never seen an **igloo** because the traditional skill of igloo building has almost completely disappeared.

The practice of making conclusions about a group of people from incorrect or incomplete information is known as *stereotyping*. People who think that everyone in Holland grows tulips and wears wooden shoes are stereotyping Dutch people. Stereotyping can lead to misunderstandings and problems. These problems are based on people's *prejudice* and *discrimination*. Prejudice involves the judging of a person or situation with the use of little or incorrect information. Discrimination is the unfair treatment of a person or group of people.

igloo: snow house

4

Discrimination or Not?

Another cartoon which appeared in a daily newspaper in Ontario showed a man in a big limousine passing by an Indian family. The man said to his chauffeur, "You'd think they'd have the decency to stay out of sight during Canada Week."

The newspaper later published several letters to the editor criticizing the cartoon. An editorial explained the intent of the cartoon was to show that too many Canadians are like the man in the limousine.

1. Write a letter to the editor explaining why you think the cartoon is an example of discrimination.
2. Write an editorial in which the newspaper editor defends the cartoon.

What's in a Name?

Misunderstandings about the native peoples are nothing new. The Italian explorer Christopher Columbus first used the word "Indian" to describe the natives of the Americas. When he arrived in the West Indies in 1492, he was sure that he had reached the East Indies. In actual fact, he was on the other side of the world from where he thought he was.

The name "Eskimo" was created by a French priest in 1611. He had heard the name "Eskimantsik" used by an "Indian" guide to describe the people living in the most northern parts of North America. The names mean "eaters of raw meat."

Neither the "Indians" nor the "Eskimos" called themselves by those names. They had a number of different names for themselves and for the other groups or tribes they knew. Here is a list of some of these names with their meanings:

Assiniboin:
people who use stones to cook
Beothuk:
man or human
Dené:
the people
Eskimantsik (Eskimo):
eaters of raw meat
Inuit:
the people
Haida:
the people
Iroquois:
poisonous snakes
Kutchin:
the people
Micmac:
allies or friends
Mohawk:

Is this cartoon an example of stereotyping? Explain your answer.

5

man eater
Naskapi:
rude people
Ottawa:
traders
Salish:
the people
Sarcee:
not good
Sekani:
people of the rocks
Tlinkit:
the people
Tsimshian:
people inside the Skeena River

These are only a few examples of the names of Canada's native peoples.

Many of these names were picked by the groups mentioned. At other times, groups were given names by different people who might be either their friends or their enemies. Sometimes the same people might be known by more than one name such as the Inuit who were also called the Eskimantsik.

1. Which of these names do you think were picked by enemies of the people named? Why?
2. Which names were selected by the friends or allies of the people named? Why?
3. Which names were probably picked by the people named themselves?
4. The most commonly used meaning for a group's name is "the people." What does this tell you about the way these groups thought of themselves?

values: those ideas that most people agree are important to them and their society

A Sense of Identity

A sense of who people are often comes from the ideas, **values**, and common beliefs of those people. While there have been and continue to be many differences among the native peoples of Canada, they also share common beliefs and values.

Many natives valued the world of nature. One of the main ideas shared by almost all native peoples before the arrival of the Europeans was that people should live in harmony with

An Inuit carver decorating a walrus tusk. The carvings tell a story such as a successful seal hunt.

nature. Native peoples believed that all living things played an important part in the world and should therefore be respected.

Many native peoples shared food, possessions, and land. Land was something that belonged to everyone and could not be "owned" by one person any more than the sky could. It was meant to be shared by all.

Other important native values included co-operating in hunting, fishing, and other tasks requiring large numbers of people. Respecting the authority of older members of the tribe was also considered to be important. It was expected that individuals would be loyal to their group, even if it meant personal hardship or sacrifice.

These values developed over a long period of time for a number of reasons. In the remaining chapters of this unit, you will see how these values played an important role in the lives of native peoples before their way of life was changed through contact with Europeans.

1. *What are the values mentioned above? Which ones do you think are accepted and followed by Canadians today?*
2. *Which of these values do you feel are important? Why?*

A dog totem in Kitwanga, British Columbia.

Indian child dressed in a highly decorated costume attending a ceremony. The decorations include beads and shells. Can you see where each material has been used?

These slate carvings represent a Haida shaman.

Carl Ray's painting called "Shaking Tent Ritual." The picture is about the dreams or visions experienced by Indian shamans (medicine men). What are the creatures shown in the picture?

A painting by Norval Morriseau entitled "Artist's Wife and Daughter."

Native Identity Today

For many years, Canada's native peoples had difficulty preserving their own sense of identity. At times their religious ceremonies were outlawed. Changing conditions prevented them from living the same sort of lives that their ancestors had lived. Many of their customs and beliefs were discouraged by outsiders who did not always understand them.

Today many of Canada's native peoples are turning back to their culture with pride. They are rediscovering their identity in their art, history, values, and beliefs. Canadian Indian and Inuit art illustrates their cultural heritage. Often these works of art are based on native myths and legends. Sometimes they are presented in traditional forms such as the carving of totem poles. At other times, they are presented in the new styles of artists such as Norval Morriseau. Many natives like this art because it gives them a sense of pride and identity. A large number of Canadians, who are not themselves natives, are also interested in this art work.

1. List the subjects that have been illustrated by the native artists.
2. Why is it important to have a sense of pride and identity?

IN SEARCH OF ORIGINS: PROBLEMS WITH THE PAST

Chapter 2

Ice-Age Hunters

When the caribou herds gathered for the fall migration, the people became restless. They too longed for their winter home. By mid-September the temperature had dropped to —32°C at night. The ground was frozen solid and covered with enough snow to make travel easy.

The tents were taken down and packed on the sleds. The willow poles and other camp equipment were stored for another summer's use. The people separated into a number of small hunting groups and departed. Each headed toward its own territory.

One group was made up of four families numbering twenty-three people in all. These stocky, short people were dressed in mittens, double-layered parkas, trousers, and thick skin boots all made of caribou fur and hides. The people's black hair shone above their brown faces with thick eyebrows, slightly slanted eyes, and strong mouths. Five adult hunters were with

the group, three of whom helped the women pull the sleds. Two older men led the way carrying nothing but spears on their shoulders.

After three days of travel they reached their new campsite. It had been chosen carefully. It was protected from the fierce arctic winds. Many thickets of willows along the nearby creek provided a source of fuel. The thickets were also feeding grounds for game, especially for mammoth and moose.

Another reason for the camp location was its closeness to a mountain that had a **Dall sheep** population of over fifty animals. They could be driven over the south cliffs, if necessary. The mammoth and caribou were difficult to follow and sometimes very dangerous to hunt. The Dall sheep were fairly tame. They could provide food for at least three months if all else failed.

The men helped the women set up camp. They had enough dried meat

Dall sheep: a variety of wild sheep native to the mountains of Alaska, the Yukon, and British Columbia

The hunters set out in search of game.

9

from the summer camp to last more than a month, but everyone was hungry for fresh meat. They decided to hunt for mammoth.

The hunters left the next day. They travelled until they saw the mammoths. The wind was still from the north and the men decided to use it for driving the game.

The woolly mammoth averaged three metres in height. It was a short stocky animal with a large head, great curved tusks, small ears and tail, and a woolly coat of rough thick red hair.

The herd was spread in a horseshoe formation. Some of the animals were resting. The herd was mostly cows and calves, but there were two young bulls. Bulls were easier to kill than cows who tended to charge when being hunted. It was one of the bulls that the hunters selected.

The men hid and spread into a semi circle. One of them crept forward. He carried a short spear with a long bone point. He would try to wound the animal and then separate it from the rest of the herd hoping to drive it toward the camp.

The huge reddish bodies stood out against the snow. The great shaggy forms shifted. The men waited patiently for a long time until one of the bulls moved to the side of the horseshoe. The hunter quickly crept close, approaching from the rear. He lifted the spear. He lunged forward and upward in one quick motion driving the weapon into the animal's belly with all his strength. He broke away in

an instant and ran back.

The wounded animal thrashed around. The herd stood in confusion unable to locate the danger. After a while, the herd moved down the valley. The crippled bull eventually fell behind. Now the hunters came closer. Shouting and threatening, they drove the bull closer to their camp. It lay down and died five hours later. When the bull's hind leg stiffened with the foot raised off the ground, the hunters knew it was dead.

They went forward and touched the mighty head. They prayed and thanked the animal for the gift of its body. To them the animal was a creature on the same level as themselves. The animal had made itself available as a sacred gift. Proper killing was a sacrifice. Wasteful slaughter was punished by animal spirits and gods.

First the soul had to be released before any butchering could begin. The men went to the river and got stones that they chipped into cutting and scraping tools. A small cut was made across the animal's neck which would free its soul.

Since dark was falling, they only opened the belly and pulled out the heavy pinkish intestines. They cut pieces from the liver and ate hungrily. It was the first they had eaten all day. Big clumps of fat scraped off the intestines and the rest of the liver were wrapped up and put on one of the sleds. Tomorrow they would return with the whole camp for the butchering.[1]

1. Why didn't these ice-age people use one campsite all year round?
2. How did these people know where to set up a new campsite?
3. What evidence is there to show that these people worked together in order to survive?
4. Why did these people have spiritual respect for the animals they hunted?

The woolly mammoth was a first cousin to today's elephant. The ancient remains of mammoth skeletons, with the bones split to expose the marrow inside, are strong evidence that the first natives hunted them.

Sources of Information

The events described in the story of

the ice-age hunters took place at least 20 000 years ago. There are no written accounts left by these people. How, then, do we know what happened that far back in the past?

Actually, we don't know exactly what happened. The story you just read is the result of carefully piecing together a number of clues. Some of the information comes from the work of archeologists. These scientists study the remains of bones, tools, campfires, and other relics from the past. From their careful study, archeologists can tell us where the earliest ancestors of the Indians and Inuit came from and how they lived. Unfortunately there are still more missing pieces to the puzzle than discovered ones. Because of this, archeologists often are unable to prove what they think happened really did happen.

At this point, most archeologists are only able to form hypotheses about their evidence. Hypotheses can be described as educated guesses that are believed to be true but cannot yet be proved. If further evidence is discovered, the hypotheses may be shown to be true, or they may have to be changed.

Archeologists may turn to other scientists for help. Anthropologists study the way people live and act in different places and at different times. By comparing the known behaviour of people elsewhere who lived by hunting, anthropologists can offer further clues about the probable behaviour of the ice-age hunters.

1. In the story of the ice-age hunters, what evidence was probably provided by archeologists?
2. What evidence was probably provided by anthropologists?
3. List one hypothesis from the story.

Where Did They Come From?
One of the great puzzles of history has been the origin of the Indians and the Inuit. For centuries scholars have produced a variety of theories to explain native peoples' presence in the New World. Some claimed they were the descendants of ancient Egyptians who sailed the Atlantic in reed boats. Others believed they might be the Lost Tribes of Israel, mentioned in the Bible, who disappeared in ancient times. Other theories included the idea that they had escaped from the lost continent of Atlantis which was thought to have existed somewhere in the Atlantic Ocean before it sank out of sight. Most of these theories were based on very limited evidence. Few people today take them seriously.

Mystery of the Land Bridge
What is the answer to this mystery? Our first clue is that about 13 000 years ago, during the last ice age in North America, great **glaciers** held much of the ocean's water. As a result, the water level was low, and the ocean floor was exposed in shallow places. In one particular spot, between present-day Siberia and Alaska, the bottom of the Bering **Strait** became dry land called Beringia. It served as a bridge between Asia and North America.

glaciers: huge moving masses of ice on land

strait: a narrow waterway between two land masses

The Land Bridge to the New World

Archeology: Searching for Clues to the Past

By the year 1650, the Neutral Indians, living in what is now southern Ontario, were wiped out by a combination of disease and war with the nearby Iroquois. The Neutrals were a peaceful tribe of traders with few skills in fighting.

All traces of their settlements and burial grounds slowly became lost among the trees and vegetation of the surrounding forests.

For over 300 years, the Neutral Indians were forgotten by everyone except for a few historians and archeologists.

In the mid-1970s, Walter Kenyon, an archeologist with the Royal Ontario Museum, received a phone call from Lawson Allez of Grimsby. Mr. Allez told the archeologist that he had dug up a few broken bones and a complete skull.

Walter Kenyon continued the digging started by Lawson Allez and eventually discovered that the site in Grimsby was a Neutral Indian burial ground. The graves contained over 300 bodies and many different beads and shells which were traded to the Neutrals by the Europeans.

Another site in Thorold has been discovered about forty kilometres away from the first burial ground of the Neutrals.

Evidence suggests that this new site may have been the capital of the Neutral Indians and the last complete Neutral village.

The remains of longhouses suggest that there may have been 1000 Neutral Indians living at this village. Archeologists use the number of fire pits found on a site to estimate the number of people living there. Normally there is one fire pit per family. Families averaged about five people each.

Complications

The Grimsby site quickly became a centre of controversy as well as a source of new information. Within a few weeks of the discovery, Dr. Kenyon was placed under arrest and charged with breaking into historic grave sites. The charges were laid by Delbert Riley, formerly research director of the Union of Ontario Indians. Delbert Riley stated:

The **intrusion** into graves of pioneers of that period is considered **desecration** and is illegal. Indians are likewise protected by the law ... or should be.[2]

The Royal Ontario Museum and Dr. Kenyon wanted to take the skeletons to Toronto to be studied and displayed. The Indians wanted them to be reburied with dignity.

The skeletons were reburied in the middle of a park in Grimsby.

1. Why did Dr. Kenyon want to study the skeletons? What was he placing value on?
2. Why did Delbert Riley want the skeletons to be reburied? What was he placing value on?
3. Do you think the decision to rebury the skeletons was the correct one? Why?

intrusion: breaking into

desecration: an action that lacks proper respect

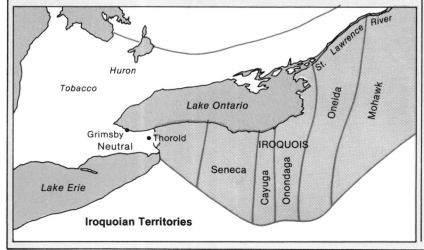

Huron
Tobacco
Lake Ontario
Grimsby
Neutral
Thorold
Lake Erie
IROQUOIS
Oneida
Mohawk
Seneca
Cayuga
Onondaga
St. Lawrence River

Iroquoian Territories

Dr. Kenyon directs the digging at the site. "Because we had arrived on the scene before the pot-hunters were able to rally their forces, we were in a position to protect an important and little-known segment of the history of Ontario. I decided, therefore, that I would not return to Toronto as planned, but would remain in Grimsby to protect the site."[3]

(Dr. Kenyon)

What are "pot-hunters"? What equipment is being used by the archeologists?

Tracks in the Snow

Over thousands of years, Beringia changed into a rolling plain with many plants and trees. The vegetation attracted large mammals from Asia such as the ground sloth, the big horned bison, and the giant beaver. These now extinct animals moved in search of food. At the same time, ice-age hunters from Siberia roamed about looking for prey. They followed the mammals onto the land bridge.

During the winter months, the animals travelled further inland. The valleys and forests in present-day Alaska and the Yukon were milder places to live until the spring came. The hunters followed the animals across the land bridge. As a result, these ice-age people became the first settlers of North America.

Over thousands of years the temperature became warmer and the glaciers melted. The water from the huge masses of ice flooded the land bridge. It never appeared again. The hunters were trapped in the new land.

A caribou shinbone made into a scraper with a serrated tip.

clan: a group of people who are closely related

A Clue

At least, that is the theory of the land bridge. It is based on reliable information concerning the rise and fall of the ocean's levels in the past. Where it is weak is in physical evidence to show that people actually crossed the bridge.

There is some tempting evidence. In 1973 a caribou shinbone was found in the Yukon. It showed definite signs of having been used as a tool, probably to scrape animal hides. Tests showed the scraper was about 27 000 years old. It shows that people were in the Yukon then, but does it show that they crossed the land bridge?

Unfortunately, the necessary evidence probably lies at the bottom of the Bering Strait protected by freezing water and thick deposits of sediment.

For the present, at least, the theory remains just that—a theory.

1. What is the Beringia land-bridge theory?
2. What is the strongest evidence to support the theory?
3. Why can't the theory be accepted as proved?

What Do the Native People Believe?

One of the problems of trying to sort out the distant past of Canada's native peoples is caused by the lack of written records. None of the groups living in what is now Canada developed a written language. Thus, there are no early written documents that help us to understand the past.

Most native peoples had rich traditions of story telling. These stories often helped to explain the important questions that people have.

One important question asked by all people is "Where did we come from?" The following stories tell us how two tribes explain their presence in North America.

The Creation of the Crane Clan of the Ojibwa

The Great Spirit created two cranes, a male and a female, in the upper world. He lowered them through an opening in the sky to the lower world and directed them to make their homes here on earth. They were told when they had found a suitable place to fold their wings close to their bodies as they landed on their chosen place, and they would be changed to a man and a woman.

The pair flew down to earth and spent a long time looking over the various parts which might make them a good place to live. They flew over the prairies and tasted the buffalo. Although it was good, they were afraid it would not last. They visited all the great forests and tasted the flesh of the deer, elk, the beaver, and many of the other animals. They found the taste very pleasing but were again afraid the supply of food from these sources would someday fail. After flying all over the Great Lakes and tasting the various kinds of fish which abounded in the water, they came to the rapids at the outlet of Lake Superior, where they saw great numbers of fish making their way through the rough water. They also discovered that the fish were easily caught and the supply seemed **inexhaustible**. They said to each other, "Here is food forever; here we will make our home."[4]

1. What concerned the two cranes when they looked for a suitable place to live?
2. Why did the two cranes choose the outlet at Lake Superior for their home?
3. What evidence is there to support the idea that the crane clan relied heavily on fish as a source of food?

The Creation of the North Pacific Coast Tribes

Feeling lonely in the world which was almost empty, **Raven** one day moved down to the sandy beach and there he wandered all alone. A sound came out of the wet sand at his feet from a clam that was half buried. The clam began to open its valves and out of it came a noise like a sigh. Raven stooped forward, listening, and a small face, the first of its kind, with two round eyes, burst forth, and then with fear, drew back.

"Whah," called the Raven in a whisper. The tiny face moved out a bit, stretched its neck and looked up. It withdrew back into the shell. As the Raven continued to listen he heard another voice coming from the shell. Soon, the second little human face, with wonder in its eyes, burst forth and then pulled back in fear.

More voices came out of the half-opened clam shell, and then human faces appeared one by one, in a row. A few had eyes gazing, necks slowly lengthening and unfolding and spreading out. The remainder simply appeared, smiling. And a **horde** of tiny people—men, women, and children—finally stepped out of the open valves and spread around the island. Raven looked on and sang a new song, for he was well pleased with his work. He had brought forth the first people on the island.[5]

1. List the words in the story which show that these tribes lived near water.
2. Why was Raven unhappy? What changed his attitude?

Myths

Stories like these are called myths. Most societies developed such stories before the invention of writing. The ancient Greeks had myths about gods and heroes such as Zeus, Herakles, and Aphrodite. The Romans copied many of the Greek myths only changing the names to Jupiter, Hercules, and Venus. In Northern Europe several thousand years ago, tales of the exploits of gods such as Thor and Woden were told. We still recall some of these ancient gods in our names for the days of the week (Thursday is Thor's Day, Wednesday is Woden's Day).

Myths serve many purposes besides the obvious one of entertaining people. They were sometimes used to teach the young how to behave. Often they provided an explanation for the values and customs of a tribe. They were also a sort of oral history of the people.

The Mystery Deepens

Since myths are one kind of oral history, we might expect at least one group's myths to include something about travelling across a land bridge to North America. Careful examination of the myths of both Indians and Inuit has failed to uncover any such myth.

History really is a puzzle with many missing pieces.

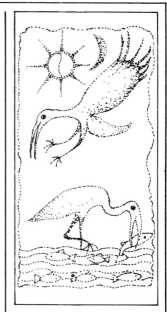

The Great Spirit created two cranes.

horde: a large group

inexhaustible: a supply that won't run out

Raven: a symbol of creation

Raven and the creation of the human race.

15

Chapter 3

THE NATIVE PEOPLES AND THE WORLD OF NATURE

The Setting

Canada contains some of the harshest extremes of climate and terrain to be found anywhere in the world. Most of us would have a great deal of difficulty surviving without the products of our technology such as furnaces, automobiles, and supermarkets. Yet for thousands of years the native peoples not only survived but developed creative ways of life to take advantage of the resources that were available.

The People

The native peoples are usually divided into six main groups:

1. The Inuit lived in the arctic region in the extreme north. Living in snow houses called igloos during the long winter months they survived by hunting caribou, seal, and walrus, and by fishing.

2. The Eastern Woodlands Indians occupied a stretch of territory from Newfoundland in the east to northern Saskatchewan in the west. They lived in heavily forested areas, hunting the rich variety of game found there. Some tribes began to practise agriculture as well.

3. The Prairie Tribes occupied the flat grasslands of western Canada. Their culture was the direct result of their skill as buffalo hunters.

4. The Subarctic Tribes lived in the area south of the arctic tundra. They followed game including caribou and moose across the vast territory that was home to them.

5. The Plateau Tribes lived in the mountains of southern British Columbia. They managed to survive by taking advantage of all sources of food available to them.

6. The Northwest Coast Tribes enjoyed the highest standard of living of any native peoples in Canada. They were able to harvest an abundant and constant supply of food from the sea. The cedar forests provided them with the raw materials for their homes, boats, and art work.

Dwellings

Examine the pictures of native dwellings carefully.

An Inuit igloo made of carefully shaped blocks of snow. When the cracks between the blocks were filled with loose snow, an igloo was airtight. A simple source of heat such as an oil lamp kept the inside at a comfortable temperature.

A Tlinkit house made of cedar and decorated with the symbol of the raven, the clan's crest. The entrance is through the hole in the central post. The house was built to hold several families in comfort.

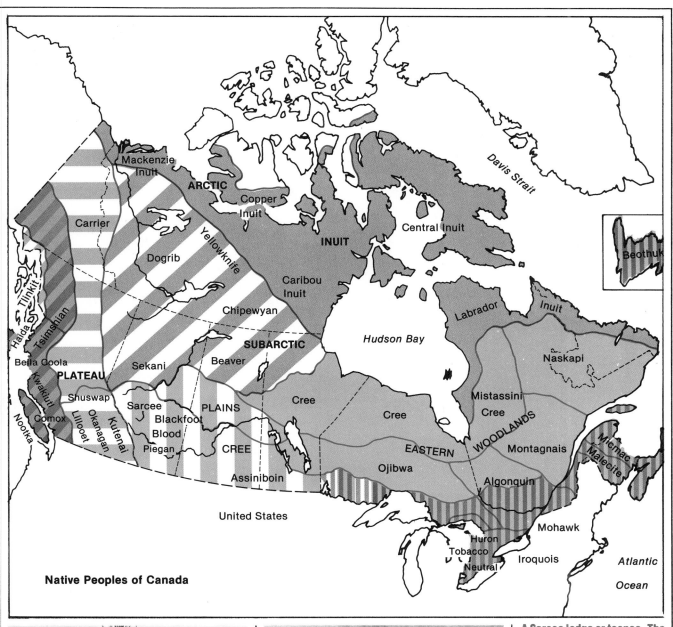

Native Peoples of Canada

A Sarcee lodge or teepee. The frame was made of lodge-pole pines which would be dragged from one location to the next by horses. The outer covering was originally of elk or deer hide though sometimes buffalo hides were used. It was light and easy to move.

The inside of an Algonquin lodge is shown here. Notice the snowshoes, animal hides, and pottery used by the Algonquins.

17

An Iroquois longhouse is one of a number in a farming village. The house was built of a frame of saplings covered with thick bark. In front of the longhouse is a painted false face and turtle shell.

This reconstructed wigwam shows the approximate size and shape of a Micmac dwelling. The wigwams usually had a framework of poles covered by hides or bark.

A large west-coast canoe with sails. Such canoes were used to hunt whales or for war raids against other tribes. The elaborate decoration on the canoes shows the love of art present among these Indians.

1. Which region does each dwelling come from?
2. How is each dwelling designed to provide protection from the climate where it is located?
3. How do the materials used in each dwelling make full use of what was available to the builders?

Transportation

As we have already seen, many native peoples were forced to travel from place to place following their food supply. People who live this way are known as nomads. Just as these people used their inventiveness to create portable shelters that could be easily taken apart, they also made use of available resources for transportation.

There were problems in getting from place to place. Then, as now, the main one was that of distance. Before the horse was introduced to North America by the Europeans, the only animal used to help transport things was the dog. This meant that inventions like wagons or carts that depend on large animals to pull them were impossible. However, in some parts of Canada, there were rivers and lakes that could be used as roads. Unfortunately, many of these were interrupted by obstacles such as rapids and waterfalls. And then there was the problem of winter, lasting nearly seven months in the northern parts of the continent.

How well did the native peoples deal with these problems in designing methods for getting around?

Examine the means of transportation shown in these pictures.

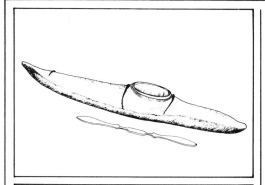

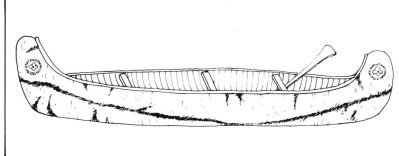

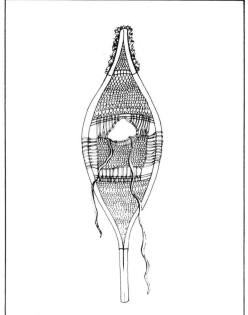

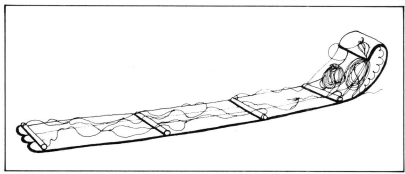

1. Under what sort of conditions would each of these have worked best? Which region or regions would they be useful in?
2. What materials were used to make them? How do you think they were made?
3. How well did the native peoples overcome the problems set by geography and climate in designing these objects?

The kayak was invented by the Inuit. Over a frame of bone or driftwood, a cover of sealskin was stitched. The boat was watertight when properly sealed.

Canoes came in a variety of shapes, sizes, and materials. Those used on coasts had to be heavier and more sea-worthy than those used on rivers where they had to be carried over portages.

Snowshoes made walking on deep snow possible.

The toboggan was made of thin pieces of wood. It was designed to be pulled over snow, either by dogs or humans.

Plains Indians using travois to travel. The travois was a pair of poles with a frame lashed to them. Objects were tied to the frame. The first travois were pulled by people or dogs.

Hunting

Obtaining food was often one of the most difficult and important tasks for the native peoples. They had not tamed animals as a permanent food source. Few of them were farmers. This meant that the game of the plains and forests and the fish and creatures of the sea were the main sources of food for them.

In most native groups, the skills of the hunt were highly prized. Those hunters who had the greatest success were regarded as great men. Young boys would try to imitate them in their games. Since the animals to be hunted varied in different parts of Canada, the skills used also varied from place to place.

The Seal Hunt

Few peoples have chosen an area as unfriendly and dangerous in which to live as the Inuit. While arctic summers are warm and pleasant, for more than half the year, the region is a winter wilderness. Snowstorms can blow up with sudden speed. Temperatures drop quickly. Ice can prove to be treacherous and unsafe.

Unlike the Indians of the Pacific coast who had many sources of food for most of the year, the Inuit had a narrow margin for error if they were to survive. The very careful steps taken by a seal hunter illustrate this. To be careless or impatient could lead to failure.

This account of a seal hunt is taken from *The White Dawn*, a novel of Inuit life, written by James Houston. The characters are his creations, but the details are accurate. While James Houston is not Inuit, he has lived with the Inuit for a number of years closely observing their traditional customs.

Taking a stand directly above the hole, I opened my hunting bag and took out a square of thick white bearskin, and placing it on the snow, stood upon it. I then **lapped** it up over my feet and tied a piece of line around both my ankles so that it held the bearskin bound like a warm single boot around my feet. In this way I also prevented myself from taking one step or making any sound on the snow. I drew out a bushy white foxtail and stuffed it in the neck of my parka so that the warm air of my body would not creep out and leave me trembling with cold. Beside the hole I placed two small notched pieces of driftwood upright in the snow so that I would have a place to rest my harpoon. I then fitted the sharp head onto the end of my harpoon shaft and lashed it tight with a skin line to the shaft. Quietly, I placed the harpoon on the stick rest. Then, drawing a thin wooden wand from my hunting bag, I probed very gently through the snow. ... I moved it around gently until I felt the seal's true breathing hole in the ice. ... I left the flat part of the probe floating just inside the eye-shaped opening, and taking out a soft goose-down underfeather, dampened its quill and instantly froze the feather to the upper end of the probe. This was to be my alarm.

I bent double, comfortably resting my elbows on my knees, making myself as small and compact as I could against the deadly cold that surrounded me. ... As time passed, I forgot the cold, the stars grew bright and there was only me staring at the thin wand upright in the snow, nothing else in the whole world.

All day and night I waited, knowing that the seal was feeding in the dark waters beneath me, cautiously breathing at each of the other places, never once coming to the one I had chosen. Perhaps he knew that I was there. A dozen times my mind commanded me to leave this useless breathing hole and move to the other three that the seal still used. But patience is the true art of the hunter, and I watched and waited until the first white streaks of dawn. Then I had a feeling as though I sensed someone listening, and the pains of cold and hunger rushed back

lapped: folded

to me, awakened me.

I saw the feather tremble and start to rise on the end of the wooden wand. I reached down silently, took up my harpoon and held its sharp point above the hole. Of course, I could see nothing, but I knew something alive was there beneath my feet. I politely allowed the seal one breath. Then I drove the harpoon straight downward through the snow into the water and felt its point strike deep into flesh and bone. I flung the harpoon shaft aside, knowing that its sharp point was firmly set, and the harpoon line whipped downward through my hands. I drew the end of it around my body, using myself as an anchor against the animal's strength. The seal was almost as heavy as I was and fought desperately, but the harpoon's point had done its work, and slowly I felt the line grow slack. Then, ... I cleared away the snow that covered the small hole and chopped away a thin layer of ice. When the hole was large enough, I drew the dear dead beast up out of the water onto the snow.

It was my first seal of the winter, and to show my gratefulness, I cut away a small piece of lip flesh and placed it back into the water of the seal hole. Our people know that this allows the seal's body to grow again in the sea. When I removed the harpoon head from the seal, I took a wound pin from my bag and plugged it carefully in the hole to save the blood, for all food is precious in a time of hunger. I longed to cut the seal open and eat, for I knew the rich meat would be steaming hot and delicious, but I held back my hunger, for it is not the custom of our hunters to drag home half-**devoured carcasses** when others in the camp are hungry.

We reached the camp in the semi-darkness of midmorning, and many people came out to greet us. ... This was the beginning of the hunting on the ice, and this first day of good fortune was said to be a wonderful sign for the future.

A successful Inuit seal hunter. The photograph was taken in 1925 when traditional hunting methods were still widely used.

Of course, no hunter told the women who among us had actually harpooned a seal and who had not, ... Generations ago it was decided that it is best not to tell the women too much about success or failure. Now they scarcely try to guess, for they know that a hunter coming in with many seals may be simply hauling them for another person. Another man returning with nothing may have **cached** a walrus or even a small whale of such great weight that it could not be brought into the camp. So the women, like the men, share the meat without question, both in hungry times and in times of plenty. In this way we accept what is given to us.[1]

cached: hidden

devoured carcasses: eaten bodies of animals

1. What steps does the hunter go through in preparing to harpoon the seal?
2. What are the worst parts of the hunt for the hunter?
3. Explain the meaning of the hunter allowing the seal one breath and later placing a piece of lip flesh back in the water.
4. Why shouldn't the hunter eat some of the seal meat if he is hungry?
5. Why is the food shared by everyone?

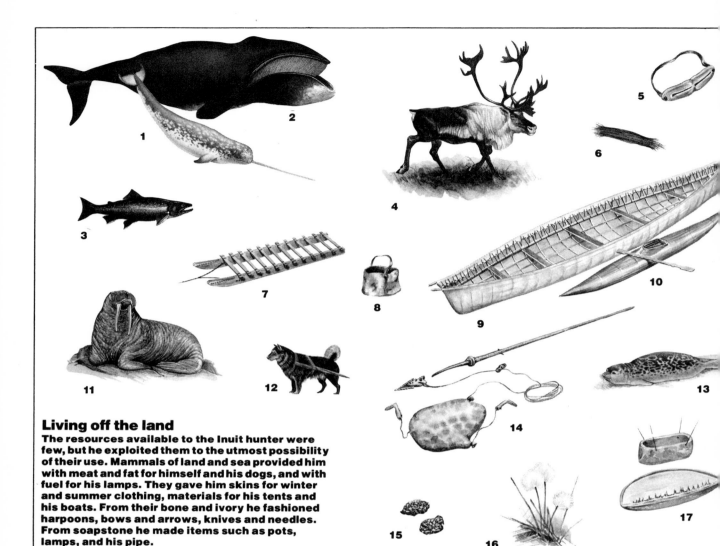

Living off the land

The resources available to the Inuit hunter were few, but he exploited them to the utmost possibility of their use. Mammals of land and sea provided him with meat and fat for himself and his dogs, and with fuel for his lamps. They gave him skins for winter and summer clothing, materials for his tents and his boats. From their bone and ivory he fashioned harpoons, bows and arrows, knives and needles. From soapstone he made items such as pots, lamps, and his pipe.

1. **Narwhal** "Unicorn" of the Arctic Sea; outer skin, muktuk, contains Vitamin C; ivory tusk made into harpoon shafts.

2. **Right Whale** Almost completely exterminated today, right whales once provided Inuits with meat, fat and building materials.

3. **Arctic Char** "The" fish of the arctic coast – so important to Inuit hunter that many fishing places were "holy ground".

4. **Caribou** "Supermarket" of the tundra – meat for food, skins for clothing, bones and antlers for knives, sinew for thread.

5. **Snow Goggles** Piece of antler or bone with two narrow slits.

6. **Caribou Sinew** From the back of the caribou came the sinew for use as thread.

7. **Sled** Made of wood obtained in trade with groups near tree line or from driftwood; basic mode of winter transport.

8. **Water Bucket** Made from skins of mammals.

9. **Umiak** The huge "woman's" boat, walrus hide over a driftwood frame used on whale hunts or for general transportation.

10. **Kayak** Sealskin or caribou skin over lashed driftwood frame.

11. **Walrus** Hide used for making harpoon lines, harness, lashings for sled.

12. **Husky** Harness fashioned from walrus hide.

13. **Ringed Seal** Basic food and fat source.

14. **Sealskin Float and Harpoon** Harpoon head was of ivory, with handle attached to float.

15. **Iron Pyrite** The classic fire starter.

16. **Cotton grass** Tufts were mixed with fat for lamp wick.

17. **Soapstone** Lamp and cooking pot.

18. **Wolverine** Fur of wolverine prized as trim for parka hood because ice and frost can be quickly beaten free.

19. **Ptarmigan** Meat as food, skin, and feather as towel, bones for needles, feet as toys.

20. **Black Guillemot** Provides the hunter with eggs and meat in late spring.

21. **Musk Ox** Hides used as covers on sleeping platforms of snow houses; cups and ladles were carved from horns.

22. **Needle** Made from ptarmigan bone.

23. **Ladle** Carved from soapstone

Bow Musk ox horn tough and sinewy; ideal for bow. Plaited sinew for string, caribou antler for arrow.

Spool Fish jigger was a standard part of hunting equipment of every Inuit.

Spoon Shaped from musk ox horn.

Sleeping Robe Heavy musk ox skin was used on sleeping platform.

Summer Dress Sealskin parka or old caribou-skin parka Sealskin trousers Sealskin boots Sealskin mitts Socks of bird or rabbit skin

Winter Dress Two complete suits of caribou skin – inner worn with fur next to body, outer with fur to outside; clothes light, airy and extremely warm.

30. Knives The snow knife, essential to Inuit survival could be made from a variety of materials.

31. Woman's Knife Ooloo, the woman's knife, for cutting and scraping.

32. Catkin tinder Shown in pouch.

33. Polar Bear Every part utilized except liver which contains too much Vitamin A, and is extremely toxic to humans.

34. Arctic Hare Meat is welcome food in winter months; fur makes excellent winter socks.

35. Ermine Of little use to Inuit hunter; of value to trapper for trade in store.

36. Ground Squirrel In times of starvation ground squirrels provided an alternate source of food.

37. Arctic Willow Provides tinder.

38. Arctic fox Almost worthless to Inuit hunter but source of approximately ninety percent of income of trapper.

1. List all of the sources of food used by the Inuit that are shown.
2. What other materials were used by the Inuit? How were they used?
3. What animal seems to have been most useful to these people? Why?
4. Which of the objects shown would probably have taken the longest time and greatest care to make? Explain the reasons for your choice.

The Caribou Hunt

Stretching in a giant arc across the map of Canada runs the band of northern woodlands. This was the home of a number of native peoples before the coming of the Europeans. The cultures of these peoples had many differences, but they shared one very important similarity. Their way of life and very survival centred on the annual caribou hunt. Although their diet might include other game and fish as well as roots and berries, they believed the annual migration of the great herds of caribou was a gift from the Great Spirit. They took part in a variety of ceremonies and rituals that they hoped would ensure the success of the hunt.

The following story describes a caribou hunt by the Beothuk Indians who lived in what is now Newfoundland. The Beothuks hunted the caribou by building long fences of felled trees that forced the herds into narrow funnels where they could be killed.

The Beothuks were among the first Indians encountered by Europeans. It is because of their habit of covering themselves with a red powder made from a mineral called ochre that Europeans called them "Red Indians." The Beothuks annoyed the French by their theft of articles and the French offered a reward for the head of any Beothuk killed. As a result of this bounty hunting by Europeans and their Micmac allies, as well as through the ravages of disease, the Beothuks were rapidly killed off. The last known Beothuk died in 1829.

Because of the destruction of the Beothuks, there are few written records about them. This story is not an eye-witness account. Instead, it is a skilful and imaginative story by a modern writer, Peter Such. The exact details, words and feelings contained in the story are creations of the author. However, the sense of mood, emotion, and drama that the story suggests are probably very similar to those experienced by the Beothuk.

First snow. Good killing weather .... The People gather, comfortable in new hide shoes and leggings, sheltered in their huddle of **mamateeks**. Shawnadithit with her spear stands tall. Longnon's boy runs from the woods and down the shore to join them. He's been out scouting.

—No. The lynx haven't come back. They left yesterday and haven't come back. The herds are coming for sure.

Last night wolves howled far away on the other side of the People's lake.

First snow. It muffles their voices. Good killing weather. Longnon's boy is eager. It's his first hunt as a grown man. Longnon sends him up to climb the lookout pine. Herd-scouts might come swimming across the channel.

mamateeks: shelters constructed of logs and brush, covered with earth

Spearing caribou.

They can catch three or four that way. A good start before the rest come in several **droves** over the next three days. ...

Longnon's boy shouts from the treetop—Hey! Hey! There's one out there already. A beauty. See him go.

Longnon calls him down—Come on, then. Here's your chance. Who'll go with you?

—Osnahanut. Osnahanut, will you paddle and let me draw?

Osnahanut grins at the boy. It will be the boy's first kill. And the first of the season too!

—Alright. If you think you can hit him square. You'd better take more than those two arrows though.

—What! I won't miss, cousin....

Nonosabasut is uneasy.

—Wait. Are you sure the deergod means this? If he's a particularly fine one maybe we should let him go. After all, ... last night the ceremony didn't seem to me to go as it should. ...

—Oh, come on, Nonosabasut. Let the boy shoot. It's obvious the god has sent it specially for him.

They wait. They can all see the stag now. His head is a floating bush. Grey sky, grey waters. His warm life bears his great crown calmly through thin swirls of snow over the chill lake.

Osnahanut says—This is the one we should feast on, Nonosabasut. I'm sure it's sent on purpose. ...

Nonosabasut **gestures** his permission. Osnahanut and the boy cast off. The People watch.

Close by, the stag sees them. He turns back into deeper water, his nose now high, his crown tipped backwards, swimming faster. A wake follows him. Osnahanut and Longnon's boy make the canoe lift with their speed. Close again. This time the boy draws and shoots. A miss. Osnahanut makes a quick turn, paddles hard, SHOOT NOW! Feathers of the second arrow show above the water. Its point is at the jam of neck and shoulder.

Longnon yells—Turn him! Turn him!

The animal is heading straight for shore away from the People. The boy paddles again. The canoe skitters about in its own length. Now they are right up to the stag's shoulder. Its antlers knock the bow. The boy leans and snatches. He hangs on. The canoe skids in crazy waters over the animal's back. Osnahanut stops them tipping. He could reach his spear and finish it in the spine but he gives the boy his chance.

The boy thrusts his weight down on the large head. Its neck is weakened by the arrow. A red stream is in its wake. Its nose tilts forward. The stag breathes water, coughs, jerks, boy hangs on. More water. It coughs again. Harder.

The stag will soon reach shallows. The boy pushes harder. Ah. It sinks. Its whole head sinks. Bubbles. Its motion weakens, stills. ...

Filled with summer fat its carcass floats just below the water. They tow it in. The People pull its hind legs up the bank. They're happy, shouting. Shawnadithit's mother bloods it with her mighty old stone knife.[2]

1. *Describe the method used by the Beothuks to hunt and kill the caribou.*
2. *On what does a successful hunt depend?*
3. *What evidence is there that the Beothuks were superstitious?*
4. *What significance is given to the first kill by Longnon's boy?*

The Buffalo Hunt

The Plains Indians relied on the bison (commonly called the buffalo) for their survival. In ancient times, they probably stalked the giant beasts on foot before attempting the kill with spears or arrows. Archeological evidence suggests that they may have stampeded herds over cliffs in order to slaughter them. It is likely that the Indians set fire to the prairie grasses in order to frighten the animals.

The introduction of the horse to the

droves: groups

gestures: waves

Prairies completely changed this style of hunting. Horses had existed in North America before the arrival of man but had become extinct. They were reintroduced by the Spanish in Mexico in the 1500s. Just how horses reached the Plains Indians is not clear, but within a century of the Spaniards' arrival, they were the prized possessions of the prairie hunters. With a well-trained buffalo runner, a skilled hunter could bring down a winter's supply of meat in a few days.

It was left to the women to butcher the buffalo and prepare the winter's supply of **pemmican**. The village was often moved to the site of the kill to make this easier.

After the kill, the tribe enjoyed the luxury of fresh meat. Feasting and celebrations took place, sometimes for days. It was not unusual for a hunter to eat three kilograms of meat per meal. The hump was considered to be a special treat.

If the hunt had gone well, the tribe might then look forward to a winter without starvation.

Some idea of the importance of the buffalo to the Plains Indians can be seen in this list of the uses made of different parts of the animal.

hide:
clothing, moccasins, war shields, teepee covering, bull boats, blankets

fat:
mixed with dried meat to make pemmican

tail:
paintbrush

leg bone:
tool to clean hides

stomach:
cooking pot

intestine:
container to hold pemmican

pemmican: a mixture of dried meat, grease, and berries

Hunting bison. Where is the hunter aiming? Why? How close does he get before shooting?

sinew:
bowstring, cord, thread
blood:
food, paint pigment
tongue:
hairbrush
skull:
altar in sun dance ceremony
brain, fat, and liver:
used to tan hides
horn:
drinking cup
bone:
needles, punches, fuel
dung:
fuel
head skin and horns:
headdress

1. Would the Plains Indians have been able to survive without the buffalo?
2. What advantage did the horse give the Plains Indians in hunting buffalo?

Fishing

Fishing was important to the survival of many native people. Some groups such as the Pacific coast Indians lived mostly on the fish taken from

the ocean and rivers. For others, fish was a source of food to be turned to when other supplies ran out.

Regardless of the amount of fish in their diet, the native peoples developed a variety of clever devices for catching fish.

Fish was preserved by different methods. Sometimes it was cut into thin strips and placed in the sun to

Blackfoot women preparing a meal. The meat has been cut in strips and hung to dry. What evidence is there in the picture that these Indians have traded with Europeans?

A painting by Paul Kane shows Menominees spearing spring salmon by torchlight. The fish were attracted by the light and rose to the surface where they were easily speared.

A Nootka Indian waits with fish spear in hand. He is probably after salmon on their way upriver to spawn (breed). What is his cloak made of?

Five Nations: in 1722 this became the Six Nations when the Tuscaroras joined

dry. Sometimes it was smoked over fires to produce a tangy delicacy. Oil was extracted from a number of species to fuel lamps. Fish eggs were regarded as a treat, the same way caviar is today.

1. In your opinion, was fishing harder or easier work than hunting?
2. What seems to be the most efficient method of catching fish shown? Why wasn't it used all the time?

Farming

Alone among the native peoples of Canada, the Iroquoians developed the ability to feed themselves from the crops they grew. The Iroquoians included the Hurons, Neutrals, and Tobacco tribes who lived north of Lakes Erie and Ontario, and the Senecas, Cayugas, Onondagas, Oneidas, and Mohawks (known as the Iroquois Confederacy or the **Five Nations**).

The discovery of farming gave these tribes advantages over their neighbours who lived by hunting and gathering. Iroquoian villages were large, well-constructed, and comfortable. Certainly, the villages of the Five Nations were safer, with their palisades of sharpened logs, barring entry to their enemies.

Iroquoian villages were not permanent towns as ours are today. They were usually occupied for ten to fifteen years and then left for a new location. One reason for moving was probably the gradual loss of fertility of the soil over the years. Another was the increasing difficulty in obtaining completely dead firewood for almost invisible fires. (It's interesting to note that a popular gift to an Iroquois bride was a bundle of firewood. Gathering it was one of the women's least-liked tasks.)

A fish weir. These were traps designed to capture fish as they swam upstream. They were used by both Atlantic and Pacific coast tribes. The weirs would be checked once a day and the catch removed.

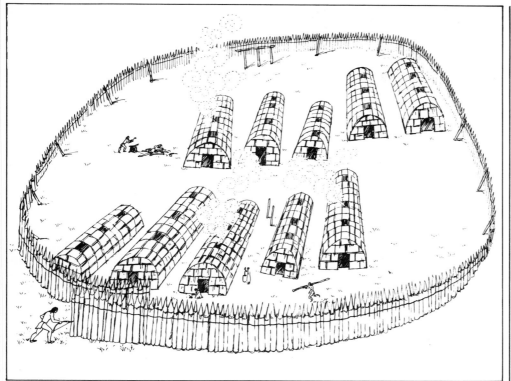

Examine this drawing of a longhouse village carefully. Can you suggest why the houses have been arranged in this way? How would you get in or out of the village? How might you go about estimating how many people lived in the village?

Although the Iroquoians hunted and fished regularly, much time was spent in expanding the cornfields around the village. Clearing trees was hard work, especially before trade with Europeans brought steel and iron axes. It was often easier to burn off trees than to fell them with stone axes. In either case, the stumps would be left standing. Clearing the fields in this way was considered by all tribes to be men's work. Hoes and mattocks made of sharpened stone, or the shoulder blades of deer, broke up the soil. Then the seeds of corn, squash, beans, and tobacco were carefully planted. This work was shared by both men and women among the Hurons. Among the Five Nations, only the women worked the fields.

1. What advantages did farming give to the Iroquoians?
2. What difficulties or problems would they face as farmers?
3. Can you suggest why no other groups of Indians developed farming the way the Iroquoians did?

4. Why did the Iroquoians refuse to burn wood that was not completely dry?

People and Nature

Native peoples tried to live in harmony with the world of nature. They thought of themselves as brothers and sisters to other living things. They did not believe that they were better than other creatures. They also did not believe that the world of nature existed for their exclusive use. All living things had an important place. All should be respected.

Conservation was practised by most natives. Rarely did they kill more than they needed at any one time. The idea of hunting for "sport" alone was unknown to them. Hunters were taught to kill only enough food for their needs. After a kill, it was usual for a hunter to pray to the spirit of the animal he had slain, asking for forgiveness.

The world of nature was one large family in which every creature had a particular role to play.

29

Chapter 4

THE SPIRIT WORLD

The native peoples of Canada shared a deep sense of their place in the world of nature. They commonly believed that all living things were similar to people and were to be respected. Most groups had developed a religion based on the worship of a great spirit who had power over the lives of all living things.

Inuit Magic

One group who did not develop a belief in a great spirit was the Inuit. The Inuit had no formal religion. Their idea of the spirit world was one of demons and monsters who could be driven off through the use of spells. They practised magic to bring about success in such things as the hunt, in producing a male child, or in defeating an enemy.

There were no formal religious leaders among the Inuit, but many groups did have figures who were recognized as **shamans** or medicine men. The shaman was believed to be able to influence the powerful forces that existed in nature. Through the casting of magic spells or the performing of special ceremonies, the shaman tried to act for his family and friends against the forces of evil and danger that surrounded them.

Some modern experts compare the role of the shamans in Inuit society with that of psychiatrists or psychologists. Both of these professions are concerned with helping people to deal with mental and emotional problems.

The Inuit concern with magic and the power of shamans is clear in the following myth which tells the story of a group of men who became stranded on an ice floe while hunting. Although they were in sight of land, they were unable to reach it. They remained adrift for an entire winter, according to the story. Among the hunters were two shamans. They were convinced that evil spirits were responsible for their problem.

Fortunately, the shamans knew how to stop the ... winds and currents. The shamans knew that the spirits who live on the ocean floor love metal objects. What could be done to please the spirits? Each hunter possessed a long-bladed raw copper knife—a weapon which never left his side. Without it a hunter on a long journey would risk hunger if not certain death. Perhaps their fortunes would improve if they were to make a gift of the knives to the spirits.

Thus the decision was made. One after another each man sacrificed his knife.... Still all this was in vain and the men and their ice pack continued to drift....

One knife still remained, that belonging to Qingalorqana.... Motioning to his friends to gather around, he held the knife over the surface of the clear water. When it left Qingalorqana's hand the hunters were astonished to see this solid copper weapon float for a long period of time. Eventually, it disappeared from sight. Everyone took this to be a good sign; the spirits must be pleased.

Just to be certain that all would be well Qorvik [one of the shamans] performed one more magic rite. Selecting a small block of ice which the ocean had washed onto their floe, Qorvik threw it in the direction of the land. As he did so he asked the spirits to return them safely to their homes. Shortly thereafter the wind changed direction

shamans: religious leaders — men who performed magic

and the men knew that they were now moving toward safety.[1]

1. What is magic?
2. Whom did the hunters blame for their misfortune? Why?
3. How did the shamans deal with the problem?
4. Can you suggest any other explanations for what happened?

Totems and Taboos

The word "totem" comes from an Ojibwa expression ototeman meaning "he is my relative." Totem refers to the bird or animal taken by a family as its own personal sign or emblem. Often there are detailed myths explaining how a particular creature came to become one group's totem.

In some tribes, it is believed that certain characteristics of the creature were passed on to the people having its sign. An example of this might be having the strength of a bear or the cunning of a raven.

Totems were common to many tribes. Usually a member of one clan or sign-group was not allowed to marry a member with the same sign. Similarly, members of a clan were often forbidden to kill the creature whose sign they held. Restrictions on behaviour such as these are called taboos. They were usually based on fear or uncertainty about the causes of events.

Among many Inuit, a house in which a person died was immediately abandoned and never used again. A common taboo prevented a man from being in the dwelling where a woman was giving birth.

Totems and taboos were two ways in which native peoples tried to deal with the many fears, dangers, and uncertainties in their world.

A shaman attempts to cure a sick man through ceremonies and magic spells. What creature is the shaman hoping will help the sick man?

West-coast Indian masks represent animal figures.

1. *Define totem and taboo.*
2. *Can you think of examples of anything similar to totems or taboos in our society today?*

The Cycle of the Seasons

Religion played an important part in the lives of the Iroquoian farmers. Their year was marked by the series of festivals and ceremonies that accompanied key phases in the growing season. These festivals differed from tribe to tribe. The following examples are typical of many of those that were practised.

Spring was the time of the Maple Festival. Following ceremonies of confession and thanksgiving, maple sap was collected and boiled down for syrup.

Summer was marked by the Planting Ceremony with offerings to the Great Spirit to ensure a good crop. The Strawberry Ceremony also took place in early summer. A feast of fresh berries and maple sugar highlighted this festival.

As the crop of Indian corn began to ripen in the summer sun, the Green Corn Ceremony was held. This was a four-day festival of dances, speeches, and feasts. A similar series of events marked the Harvest Ceremony in the fall.

The last major festival was the Mid-Winter Ceremony held in early February. This ceremony marked the end of the old year and the start of the new one. It was a time of confession of sins and purification or cleansing lasting seven days. Its symbol was the Burning of the White Dog. This was the sacrifice of a pure white animal which was killed without shedding blood or breaking bones by strangling. The animal was displayed and later burned.

It might happen that at this time a bear was killed, an animal having special religious significance for the Mistassini Cree. When a kill was made, a special feast must be held at which only bear meat and grease were eaten. First, the leader made an offering of some meat and grease to the ancestral spirits. At the end of the feast the men might drum. The bear's skull was saved and later erected in a tree in such a location that it looked out over the water. One of the leg bones would be prepared as a tool for **flensing** beaver. The other bones were carefully placed on a special bone cache rack. The hide was prepared by the women, the hair being left attached so it might be used as a sleeping mat, but it must not be used for one year out of respect for the slain animal. The chin skin was made into a charm.[2]

flensing: removing flesh from a skin or hide

Drum with beater, rattle, and decorated bear skull.

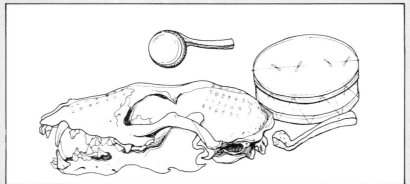

1. *How did agriculture influence the pattern of the year's activities for these people?*
2. *What was the purpose of the ceremonies that were practised?*

The Sun Dance

To the Plains Indians, the circle was a sacred symbol. The sun, their most powerful spirit, was a circle. The cycle of the seasons was seen as a circle as was the life of a person. They placed their lodges in the form of a circle. Once a year they took part in the most important of their religious ceremonies—the sun dance.

The sun dance was in honour of Wakan-Tanka—"the greatest sacred one." It consisted of a series of ceremonies, dances, and rituals over a period of several days. It was the one occasion other than war which brought all the members of a tribe together.

At the heart of the sun dance was the belief that every living thing had a spirit that was influenced by the great spirits. By appealing to spirits, by performing the necessary ceremonies, and by making the proper sacrifices, it was hoped that the spirits would come to one's aid.

The Plains Indians believed in the power of magic and attempted to make it work for them in a number of ways. Most Indians wore a charm or amulet around their necks designed to protect

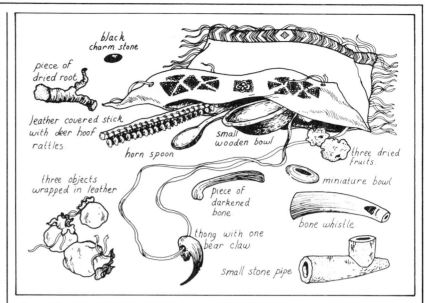

them from evil. The sun dance was a larger attempt to protect the tribe from the forces of evil.

The sun dance usually took place in early summer. The tribe gathered at the traditional site, and a special pole was selected to form the centre of the sun dance lodge. Offerings to the sun were tied to the pole and attached rafters. The ceremonies included a number of different dances, feasts, and rituals. Not all of them were religious in nature. Some were social events.

Medicine Bundles

The most awesome events of the sun dance involved the opening of the medicine bundles. These bundles were often very old and were believed to have great magical powers. They contained a wide assortment of different objects.

The main object in every Medicine Pipe Bundle is the sacred Stem. Like exceptionally long regular pipestems, they have a straight hole beginning at the carved mouthpiece and ending at the carved bowl-fitting. Sacred Pipes are very handsomely decorated with many black-and-white ermine tails, black-and-white eagle feathers, eagle plumes, other feathers, and beads, bells, and porcupine quills....[3]

Can you suggest why each of these objects has been included in this medicine bundle? If you were to create a bundle representing the things that you value and respect, what would you include in it?

Medicine bundles displayed on a tripod. They were believed to be very powerful against enemies or evil spirits. Why would these be placed outside the entrance to a lodge?

There were special songs and prayers for each object in the bundle. Only someone who knew them all was able to perform the bundle-opening ceremony.

The Sun Dance Torture Ritual

Among some, but not all, tribes, the sun dance might include self-torture rituals. This involved young men having slits cut in the muscles of their chests or backs and having thorns, eagle claws, or sticks attached to them. These objects were then tied to the ends of rawhide thongs which were suspended from the central pole of the sun dance lodge. The ritual required the individual to tear himself free.

The following song was sung by young men as they performed the self-torture ritual.

SUN DANCE TORTURE SONG

They say a herd of buffalo is coming.
It is here now!
Their blessing will come to us.
It is with us now!

The Sun, the Light of the world,
I hear Him coming!
I see His face as He comes.
He makes the beings on earth happy,
And they rejoice.

O Wakan-Tanka, I offer You
    this world of Light!
This sacred day You made the
    buffalo roam.
You have made a happy day
    for the world.
I offer all to You!

Wakan-Tanka, be merciful to me.
We want to live!
That is why we are doing this.[4]

1. What was the purpose of the sun dance for the Plains Indians?
2. Why might the sun have been regarded as "the greatest sacred one" by the Plains Indians?
3. What were medicine bundles?
4. Why did young men perform the self-torture ritual at the sun dance?

The World of the Dead

There was no general agreement among native peoples as to what happened after the death of an individual. Among the Inuit, the person simply seems to have disappeared, although the spirit might return to haunt the living unless precautions were taken. Some tribes like the Ojibwa may have believed in the rebirth of an individual in a new life. Others seem to have believed there was a life after death

The sun dance ritual.

34

since they placed a number of objects with the body. Some groups made sure that the dead person's memory would live on by giving the same name to a new baby.

Burial customs differed greatly as well. The Inuit often left the body in a sealed-up hut or igloo. Some tribes buried the dead carefully in the earth. Others wrapped the bodies and placed them in caves or trees. The Plains Indians erected platforms for the dead. Some tribes practised cremation. Some west coast tribes built "spirit houses" for the dead and their valued possessions.

One of the more complicated rituals involving the dead was that of the Hurons. It was called the Feast of the Dead. When a person died, the body was placed in a temporary grave. Every ten or twelve years, a Feast of the Dead was held at a special location. The bones were removed from their temporary graves and decorated. They were then taken to the special location where they were all placed in a fur-lined grave and reburied.

1. What do burial customs indicate about a group's attitude to life after death?

2. Why were so many different burial customs followed by the native peoples?

People and Beliefs

There were many different beliefs and ceremonies among the native peoples, and they shaped their lives in a wide variety of ways. However, all native peoples shared similar hopes and fears about life.

A west-coast Indian grave marker.

The Huron Feast of the Dead.

35

Chapter 5

MAKING RULES: HOW SOCIETIES WERE RUN

No group of people can exist for long without some sort of rules and some way of enforcing them. However, the type and number of rules in use can vary greatly. So can the way in which they are enforced.

Think for a moment about each of the following "societies":

your family
your friends
your class
your school
your town or city

Who sets the rules in each of these cases? What sort of rules are they? What happens if people don't follow them? Who enforces them? How?

Now you have some idea of the different kinds of rules that can operate in different situations. Among the native peoples there were wide differences in what rules were made and in how they were made, obeyed, and enforced.

An Inuit family sets out on a winter hunting expedition. They are using the traditional sleigh called a "komituk" pulled by dogs.

Inuit Society

Inuit society was the simplest for a number of key reasons. In the first place, the number of people living and working together as a unit was never very large. In most cases, they would be closely related as well. Finally, they all shared the common concern of surviving in one of the harshest regions in the world. All of these factors tended to keep their social organization simple.

The social unit was led by a headman. In Inuit, the title for this man translates as "he who knows best." He was picked by the members of the group for his skill as a hunter and problem solver. He would make such decisions as where the group would move to next to hunt seals or caribou.

The headman had few special privileges from the other members of his group. The title was not passed on to his son automatically. When a headman died or became unable to carry on, the members of the group would select a suitable replacement.

Since the Inuit lived together in very close quarters, they had simple ways of solving problems. Someone who refused to share with others would be ignored or forced to leave the community. Someone who committed murder would have to be killed to revenge the dead person and protect the rest.

Conflict between individuals was sometimes settled by wrestling. The most common means of solving conflict, however, was through song duels in which the people involved sang insults at one another until one dropped out.

Here are some of the insulting songs by two men who were childhood enemies. One will sing:

Whom then have you married?
Whose fragile daughter is she?
As for myself, I made a good
  marriage!
My wife is tall, my wife is beautiful!
And the other answers:
Now my turn! Oh, this enemy!
His kayak is made of bad boards!
Now my turn!
His hut is made of rotten wood
And bad skins.
Now my turn!
He cannot kill the seal
For he does not know one
When he sees one!

Aja, aja, hai! answers an excited audience. The musical duel is not ended after the first night. It often lasts for years, during which period, the opponents meet many times. Between the meetings, each of them invents more horrors about his rival:

You who always tremble,
You are a coward!

You come for your revenge,
Miserable little nothing!
You dare to come here!
Challenge me to a drum duel. ...
Come here in your poor sled![1]

Inuit singer and drum. Do you think he is taking part in a song duel?

1. Why might the Inuit try to avoid open arguments between members of the group?
2. What sorts of insults are exchanged in these songs?
3. What do the insults suggest were highly valued personal qualities and possessions to the Inuit? Can you suggest why they would value them?
4. How was the Inuit social organization well-suited to the conditions of life in the Arctic?

The Subarctic Tribes

The organization of most tribes of subarctic Indians was only slightly more complicated than that of the Inuit. They shared a similar concern for surviving in difficult surroundings. Thus, they too had a headman who was selected for his ability as a hunter.

These tribes tended to come together in groups of up to a few hundred people during the summer months. They would break up into smaller groups, usually a few families each, for the winter. They regarded their nearest neighbours as a form of insurance. If they ran out of food they expected to be helped out. They in turn

An Assiniboin hunter travelling with his dogs. What is he using the dogs for? How is he armed? What might he be hunting for?

would assist others in time of need.

The headman had few definite duties. Settling conflicts over hunting grounds was probably the most important one.

1. Why did the subarctic tribes have a simple sort of social organization?
2. Why was sharing regarded as a duty among these people?

The Plains Indians

The life style of the Plains Indians was largely determined by the buffalo hunt. They lived in small bands for most of the year, only coming together in large groups during the summer. This was the time of the sun dance ritual. It was also the time for war with traditional enemies and the buffalo hunt.

Leaders among these tribes were selected for their skill as hunters and warriors. The competition was great. Many young men were anxious and willing to display their courage, cunning, and boldness in the hunt, horse-stealing raids, and battle.

Most Plains Indians belonged to at least one society. These societies existed to take part in dancing, feasting, religious ceremonies, and war. Some societies were for men only, some for women and others were mixed. An individual could belong to more than one of these. The more societies one belonged to, the more status or importance one had.

Because of the loose organization of these tribes and their large numbers, the societies came to play key roles. War societies not only acted as an army for the tribe, they were also a sort of police force dealing with internal disturbances.

War

Within a war society, an individual's status was largely set by the number of coups he had counted. Counting coup was the practice of touching an armed enemy with a bare hand or coup stick and then riding away from him. This was thought to be a far braver act than killing an enemy.

If a chief was thought to be losing his courage, or if he became too old or feeble to continue hunting and fighting, his young braves would leave him.

War among the Plains Indians was a serious matter involving honour, skill, and status. There were traditional hatreds such as those between the Bloods and the Crows or between the Crees and the Sioux that could lead to a long series of acts of violence between them. There was also a series of alliances such as those involving the Blackfoot Confederacy, which included Bloods and Piegans. When

Blackfeet meet at their summer encampment. Are they prepared for hunting? For war? For both?

war was declared, it was not demanded that all men go, although most young ones did. Similarly, young men might join a war party of a neighbouring tribe, especially if there was a chance of obtaining horses. Indian wars usually were brief in length and involved only a few warriors. Wars might be fought over hunting grounds, especially in the late nineteenth century when buffalo were becoming scarce. Wars might also be matters of revenge and honour, such as repaying the death of a fellow tribesman. They also might take place because there had not been one for some time, and the young men who had not counted coup were anxious to do so.

In addition to the chiefs who were responsible for wars and the hunts, the Plains Indians also had holy leaders. These were respected leaders believed to have special favour with the spirits. Some leaders were both war leaders and holy leaders.

1. What problems were there in the social organization of the Plains Indians?
2. What seems to have been the purpose of war for the Plains Indians?
3. Why might some men choose not to go to war?
4. Why does it seem unlikely that there would ever be a long period without war among the Plains Indians?

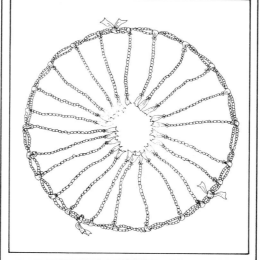

The Iroquois Confederacy

The Iroquois Confederacy was unique as an organization among North American native peoples. It was a union of five (later six) tribes that were related, but had traditionally fought with one another. The union is believed to have taken place in 1570 as the result of a vision by a prophet named Deganawidah. The Iroquois name for the league of Five Nations was Hodinonshonni.

The Iroquois Confederacy was governed by a council of sachems or wise men. There were fifty sachems. When one of them died, his replacement was named by the women of the clan the

The illustration shows the traditional wampum circle of the sachems of the Iroquois Confederacy. The word "wampum" comes from the Algonquin word "wampumpeag" meaning "white strings." It was made from the shell of the quaog sheel, an extremely hard clam. Wampum was used by most Indians in eastern Canada, but it was particularly popular with the Iroquois. Strings and belts were arranged in patterns so that they could be "read." As such, they could be used to record laws and important statements.
A sachem of the Onondaga tribe was the official keeper and reader of the wampum in the confederacy.

sachem had represented. If a sachem failed to perform his duties properly, he would be warned three times by the head woman of the clan. If he still did not change, he was removed, and the women named a new sachem.

The chief sachem was known as the Pine Tree. He was picked for the job because of his courage and success in war. The Iroquois were frequently at war and had the reputation among their enemies as fierce warriors. The name Iroquois means "poisonous snakes" and was given to them by enemies.

Warfare

Iroquois warriors prided themselves on their skill, bravery, and cunning in warfare. They attacked unexpectedly from hiding places, often after having travelled long distances without being detected. They preferred hand-to-hand fighting with war clubs and tomahawks to the use of bows at greater distances. Those enemies not killed would be taken captive and returned to the Iroquois camp. Many captives underwent torture at the hands of the Iroquois. Even women and children might be tortured.

The Iroquois admired a captive who faced torture with courage. A captive was not supposed to cry out in pain at any time. The captive was either to remain silent throughout, or sing out his scorn and defiance of his tormentors. On some occasions, the Iroquois apparently ate the hearts of particularly brave captives. This may have been an attempt to obtain some of their captive's bravery.

In a long series of wars, in which they finally destroyed their ancient rivals the Hurons, Iroquois warriors displayed military courage, skill, and resourcefulness second to none.

Despite the stories of the torture of captives, many of those taken prisoner by the Iroquois were adopted into one of the Five Nations to replace Iroquois losses. These captives were not treated as slaves, as were similar vic-

tims captured by the Pacific coast tribes. Instead, they became full-fledged members of the tribe, usually by being adopted by a mother, wife, or other relative who had lost a member of his or her family.

The Status of Women

The Five Nations were unique among native peoples in the influence held by women. As was true in most tribes with clan systems, one's clan, such as bear or turtle, was the same as one's mother's. Individuals with the same totem or clan sign could not marry one another. When a marriage took place, the couple moved into the family of the bride's longhouse. If necessary, an addition was added to the dwelling.

All property was inherited through the women. The longhouse, the garden plots, and the tools were all owned by them. An Iroquois woman could divorce her husband and still keep her property. The ex-husband would have to leave the longhouse. No other native women enjoyed as much authority and power.

1. How was the social organization of the Iroquois unique?
2. What was the advantage of having the sachems elected by the women of the clan?
3. Why was the chief sachem picked for his skill as a warrior?
4. Account for the success of the Iroquois in their wars.

The Northwest-Coast Tribes

Social Structure

The most complex social order of all Canada's native peoples was found among the tribes of the northwest coast. They were headed by great chiefs who commanded the respect of thousands of followers. Below the chiefs were nobles who enjoyed considerable wealth and status. Then

came the commoners. Finally, the slaves, usually captives taken in war, completed the structure.

A sense of the complex nature of these societies can be seen in the following description. It is from a history of the Haida people called *Raven's Cry*. The author, Christie Harris, is an expert on west-coast tribes. The passage describes the feelings of a Haida named Yatza at being selected as Chief Edsina, the most important chief of his clan.

Now that he was Chief Edsina, Yatza was lord of one mighty family, overlord of a dozen others. ...

Like a Haida house, a Haida family held large numbers of people together. Family affection, the central fire, warmed countless cousins, aunts, uncles, grandparents, and in-laws as well as father, mother, sisters, brothers. Family responsibility—the strong posts, beams, and planks—sheltered the whole kin connection. Family traditions and emblems enriched and decorated the entire **lineage**.

Loyalty was a blood relation; security was a blood alliance.[3]

Great chiefs like Yatza were closer to European kings than they were to most other Indian leaders. They had immense power. This power was based on the wealth of the tribe and on the skill and daring of the fierce warriors who manned their mighty war canoes.

Natural Resources

Unlike many parts of Canada, the west coast provided food in abundance and offered a relatively mild climate. The west-coast tribes rarely faced the constant struggle for survival that was common elsewhere. The regular harvest of the sea—salmon, halibut, cod, whale, eulachon (noted for its oil), porpoises, seals, and sea otters—meant that villages did not have to be relocated at frequent intervals. In fact, the deposits of clam shells over seven metres deep in front of some ancient village sites, suggest that the villages were occupied for centuries.

lineage: family tree

In addition to the abundance of food, the coast also provided magnificent cedar trees for the construction of houses, canoes, and totem poles. Because of the lush growth of the forests, and the often rocky heights behind the shoreline, few tribes went far inland. When they did go, it was to hunt mountain goats for their meat and wool or to seek minerals such as jade, which was used for arrow- and spearheads as well as works of art.

Slavery

Many tribes had large numbers of slaves who had been captured in war. These slaves might make up as much as one-third of the population. They were well-treated, though it was not unknown for a chief to kill several slaves during a potlatch, to show his scorn for their worth. The existence of this class meant that many of the hard and unpleasant tasks that usually fell to the women were handed over to slaves.

Art and Culture

As a result of these conditions, the coast Indians had the opportunity, the time, and the resources to develop in other areas. This may be seen in the

A chief displaying his copper during a potlatch. Note the elaborately designed blanket he is wearing as well as the intricately carved poles behind him. What impression is he trying to give?

splendour of their large cedar houses overlooked by brilliantly painted totem poles. (Totem poles were not worshipped, nor did they tell a story in the traditional meaning of that term. They usually indicated some of the accomplishments of the clan.) There might also be crest poles on which only the clan's symbol appeared.

The culture of the coast Indians was reflected in their joy in beautiful objects. Even simple daily utensils such as spoons were intricately and lovingly decorated. Works of art specially made for potlaches were often magnificent.

Potlatches

The term "potlatch" comes from the Nootka word "pa-chitle" which means "to give." Basically a potlatch is a feast, but it could also be much more than that. It might be given to celebrate a marriage, or the naming of a child, to mark the death of a chief, or to announce the naming of a new one. A potlatch also served to show the wealth, power, and importance of the giver. For that reason, it was carefully planned. Whole families or clans might help the giver to prepare for it.

Each giver of a potlatch tried to outdo all others in the quality of food, dances, and gifts. The more he gave away, the more status he obtained.

The coast Indians had symbols for extreme wealth in strings of rare dentalium shells and in unusual objects called "coppers." These coppers were flat, hammered copper sheets which had been decorated with designs by skilled metal workers. The coppers had no practical use and only slight actual value. However, they were given an extremely high value by the Indians. (In the same way today, we assign a value to precious metals like gold, which has little relationship to the costs of producing it.) Thus, only very wealthy men could afford the luxury of owning a copper. Occasionally, a copper might be given as a gift to obtain great status for the giver. How-

ever, even more status could be obtained by deliberately breaking a copper and then giving away its pieces as gifts, or throwing the broken pieces into the sea.

The potlatch often became an intense competition, almost a form of war, as this potlatch song of a famous Kwakiutl chief named Qwaxila shows:

I only laugh at him
I sneer at him
Who empties (the boxes) in his house
His potlach-house
And the inviting-house that is the
  cause of hunger
All the house dishes are in the
  greatest house
Of our chief
Ya, ye, a, a!³

1. *What features did northwest-coast society have that were unique?*
2. *Why did chiefs like Yatza have so much power?*
3. *What was the purpose of potlatches?*
4. *What possible problems could potlatches create for these people?*

████████████████████

The Nature of Societies

The societies developed by the native peoples ranged from the very simple ones of the Inuit and the subarctic tribes, to the extremely complex ones of the Iroquois and the Haida. Each unique society developed in its own way as a result of the complicated relationship between people, the world of nature, and the climate of each location.

Ceremonial dances were an important part of potlatches. These dancers are dressed in costumes representing creatures from Northwest Indian myths. Can you identify any of the creatures shown?

Chapter 6

GROWING UP

What would it have been like to have grown up in one of the groups of native peoples that we have looked at? There was no standard way of raising children just as there is no commonly accepted way in our society. Each group tended to have different ideas of what children should learn and how. Some were stricter than others. However, there are a few generalizations that can be made.

Infants

Children received a great deal of affection among most groups. When they were very young they received constant attention. Many babies were raised in back cradles until they could walk. Dry moss was usually placed in the cradle with the infant to act as a diaper.

By our standards, children were usually not weaned until late. They might still be fed by their mothers when they were over two if a new baby had not come along. Of course by this time, they were also eating the same diet as the rest of the family. Children were often given the choicest bits of meat.

Rules

Most children were not put under strict rules. They were allowed to stay up as late as they wanted. Until the age of six or seven, they had few set chores. They were encouraged to watch their elders, to ask questions, and to listen. In this way, it was assumed that they would learn what they needed to know to play a successful role as an adult in their society.

Most tribes did not scold or punish children. The Iroquois, though, threw cold water on children who were behaving badly.

Girls and Boys

Girls seem to have been expected to do more actual work than boys. Common tasks for them included fetching firewood and water, sewing moccasins, and minding younger children. Boys had few set duties. It was expected that they would imitate their elders in learning the necessary skills for survival.

Stories

As part of their education, children were frequently told stories, especially around the evening fire. These stories helped to pass the long nights but they had other purposes too. The survival of the nomadic hunters depended on the young acquiring not only the skills of the hunter but also the attitudes and values that had been developed over a long period of time. The skills of the hunt were taught by older hunters and, as these skills were

Deerstalking. Describe the thoughts going through the hunter's mind at the moment shown.

Making fire with a bow drill. Why was this an important skill for a boy to learn?

mastered, the young boys were allowed to participate in the hunt. The first attempts were probably limited to snaring hares or shooting birds. At the same time, the traditional beliefs and values of the tribe were passed on through the telling of stories. The following is one such story.

Games

Native peoples enjoyed playing a variety of games. Both adults and children took part in many of them. Some of them could be played alone, such as the stick-tossing game that was common all across North America. The game involved a pierced object tied by a short cord to a stick. The object was tossed in the air. The trick was to insert the stick into the hole before the object fell.

Other games involved more than one person. Many were contests between individuals or teams. Throwing the snow snake was usually done by teams. Long highly polished sticks, shaped something like a snake, were thrown along a path in the snow. The idea was to make the stick go farther than anyone else's.

Perhaps the most famous Indian game was lacrosse or baggataway, as it was called. There were several versions of this game. All involved a hard ball and sticks with a webbed pouch at the end that could be used to carry or throw the ball. In some versions each player had only one stick, in others he had two. The game was played by

Lacrosse. Can you estimate the size of the playing field being used? How many players seem to be involved in this particular game of lacrosse? Is there a referee?

Throwing a snow snake. How is the man aiming his "snake"? What muscles is he using to give strength to his throw?

45

The mocassin game. What is being bet here? Do you know which moccasin is the winning one?

with the sticks used to break heads and arms.

A popular pastime among native peoples was gambling. Some tribes had a reputation for gambling on anything at any time. A common form of gambling was the moccasin game where an object was placed in one moccasin. Several empty moccasins were also used. The gambler had to select the moccasin with the object to win.

Children apparently copied their elders in these activities, just as they did in other things.

Children also played with dolls, tops, noisemakers, whistles, and other toys that were not very different from those we are familiar with.

1. Why would games be popular with all ages of native peoples?
2. What skills could be developed from playing these games?

teams of varying sizes as well. There are reports of games becoming so heated that they turned into battles

Hunter of Eagles

"Never do as the Hunter of Eagles did in the long past," warned the eastern Woodlands' storyteller, as he began this tale. ...

"This is what he used to do. From his grandfather he had received the gift of being able to call the beasts and birds to his hiding place, so that he could use his bow and arrows to shoot them easily. This ... was a very bad thing to do, unless in time of bad famine. He was warned that the Great Spirit would surely punish him for these bad deeds, unless he changed his way of life.

He did not listen to these warnings. He would still call the eagles down from high in the sky by promises of much meat to take back to where they nested and sometimes had baby eaglets. To kill eagles at these times was very bad, but Hunter of Eagles still tempted them down from the sky and shot them for their splendid feathers.

Then one day the huge mother of eagles swooped down from the skies to protect the baby birds of all eagle

talons: claws

mothers. Hunter of Eagles saw her coming and had just enough time to creep inside a hollow log. ... The great eagle seized the big log in her strong **talons** and flew away with it. Even though she flew very fast, many hornets and ants and other biting things inside the log tortured the hunter by stinging him all over his body. The mother of eagles dropped the log on the big ledge where her nest was, then flew off to hunt food for her three young. The hunter quickly wriggled out of the log and saw that he could not possibly escape from the high ledge. He had to think quickly of how he was going to escape death from the talons and savage beak of the eagle mother.

His strong bow and arrows had been left behind, but he still had his thin, strong leather carrying thongs, which he used to carry small animals and birds that he shot. Quickly he undid the thongs and tied one around the beak of each eaglet. Soon the mother bird returned carrying a rabbit. When she saw what the hunter had done, she was going to kill him, but first she tried to remove the thongs from the

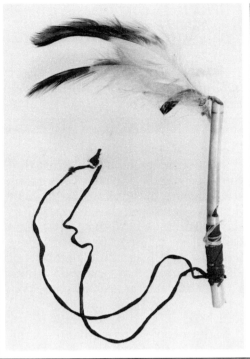

How has this doll been dressed? What materials has it probably been made from?

What practical use might this bone whistle have?

beaks of her babies. That she could not do, though she tried hard and long with both beak and talons. Night came and went twice, while she struggled to release her children, but she could not do so.

Then she was glad that she had not killed the hunter when she arrived back at her nest, because she hoped to make him release the thongs. Through his magic power, she was able to talk with him. She promised not to tear him to pieces if he would vow to do three things: first, to unfasten the thongs from the beaks of her babies; second, never to kill more deer than were needed for food; and third, the most important vow of all, never to kill an eagle without first getting permission from his totem spirits.

When he promised these things, the eagle mother told him that she would carry him back unharmed to where she had found him. Nearly starving, and with wonder filling his mind about the goodness of the great bird, he agreed to do everything that she had asked. ... Hunter of Eagles had changed so much because of his adven-ture with the mother of eagles that he begged all of the hunters of his tribe to spare all deer and eagles whenever they could, and even to feed them when the winds of winter blew and snow covered the ground like a great white blanket.[1]

An Assiniboin hunter asking forgiveness from the spirit of the eagle he has killed.

47

Coming of Age

Most societies have some test that young people have to pass before they are accepted as adults. The ancient Hebrews developed the bar mitzvah as such a ceremony. Young Jewish men still follow its requirements before being accepted as adult members of their religion. In our society, obtaining a driver's licence is seen by some people as a sign of maturity and adulthood.

Native peoples had similar tests and ceremonies. Among the Woodlands Indians, a boy did not become a man until he had killed a bear or a moose by himself. In Inuit society, a boy was accepted as a hunter when he killed his first seal. In theory, these accomplishments meant that the successful hunter could now survive on his own.

Special ceremonies usually followed such a kill. The animal slain was cut into small pieces so that as many people as possible might share in it. Among the Inuit, the new hunter was not allowed to eat any of the kill himself.

Such occasions were marked by feasting and celebration.

For the Plains Indians, a similar mark of adulthood was participation in a successful war party or a horse raid. The following story is the account of one such raid against a Crow camp by a young Blood named Eagle Plume and his friends.

Eagle Plume's Story

Sun went to his island home. Night came, and we sneaked down into the valley and through the timber to the river, and drank plenty of water and ate of our dried meat. I then led my companions to the point of timber, a little way below the camp, that I had selected for our gathering place, and there we remained in the camp, until visiting, feasting, smoking, dancing, and singing ceased and the lodge fires all died out and the people slept. ...

The night could not have been better for our raid. Clouds hid Night-Light, above us, yet it was not too dark.

A buffalo runner like those sought by Eagle Plume and his friends. How can you tell that this rider is proud of his horse?

48

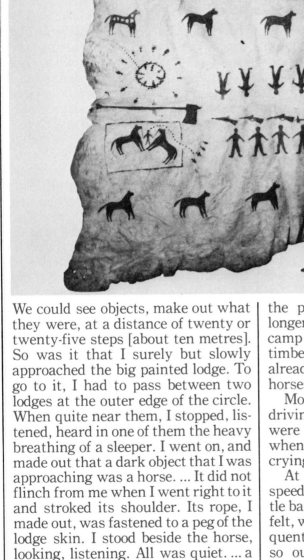

We could see objects, make out what they were, at a distance of twenty or twenty-five steps [about ten metres]. So was it that I surely but slowly approached the big painted lodge. To go to it, I had to pass between two lodges at the outer edge of the circle. When quite near them, I stopped, listened, heard in one of them the heavy breathing of a sleeper. I went on, and made out that a dark object that I was approaching was a horse. ... It did not flinch from me when I went right to it and stroked its shoulder. Its rope, I made out, was fastened to a peg of the lodge skin. I stood beside the horse, looking, listening. All was quiet. ... a sleeper within began dream-talking, not loud, a few words at a time. I didn't like that. People who talk in their sleep wake up. This one might awake, hear the horses moving off, and come out. I was very uneasy. I led the horse still more slowly, and at last came to the other one. I cut his rope at the right length for leading him, and then I went on with the two, backing away from the painted lodge until I could no longer see it. ... I went out from the camp and at a faster pace to the point of timber. Several of my companions had already arrived there with their horses. ...

Mounting, ... I led off, the others driving the loose horses after me. We were not out of the [valley] bottom when we heard great shouting and crying back in that enemy camp.

At that, we went on with all the speed that we could make with our little band of loose animals. But that, we felt, was fast enough, for we could frequently change on to fresh horses, and so outride any who might pursue us. ... We made the long way back to our People without trouble, and got praise for our success. ...

Kyi! I end my tale.[2]

1. Why did Eagle Plume and his friends go on a horse-stealing raid?
2. What characteristics were needed to be a successful horse thief?
3. How could these be learned?

What Did Young Women Learn?

While young men were learning the skills of the hunt, war, and raiding, young women were learning from their mothers the skills they would need as wives and mothers. Everyone's roles were clearly understood. Rarely did anyone try to change them.

The training of an Inuit girl is typical of that of many young women

belonging to nomadic groups of hunters.

A woman's role was to cook, make and repair clothing, and raise the young children. She would probably marry at an early age—thirteen to fifteen—although this varied from place to place. Marriages were rather informal and were often arranged by the parents as early as the birth of the children. A young woman who could make sealskin boots with seams tight enough to keep out cold arctic waters was a valued bride. Her husband's survival depended on her skill with a needle and sinew just as hers depended on his skill as a hunter. They were equally dependent on one another. There were few unmarried Inuit. Widows and widowers usually remarried as soon as possible.

A wife had to keep the tent or igloo clean. She had to ensure that the cooking pot was kept full and simmering so that anyone who was hungry could dip into it. She had to keep the seal-oil lamps burning properly, not smoking so the igloo became dirty. She prepared

What are the Inuit women doing in these pictures?

the hides of seal, walrus, or caribou that would make the summer tents or cover the kayak frame. She constantly mended boots, mitts, and clothing that had worn thin or been snagged on sharp ice. Among all the native peoples, only the Inuit had custom-tailored clothing. The climate demanded it. In winter both men and women wore cleverly designed double parkas, trousers, and boots. The fur would face in on the inner garments to keep them warm and out on the outer layer. The air pocket between acted as a layer of insulation.

1. What skills were important for young women to learn? Why were they considered important?
2. In what way did the roles of men and women prevent them from being completely independent?

Marriage

As we have seen with Inuit women, marriage often came at an early age to the native peoples. When we realize that the average life span of these people was only about thirty years, we can understand why.

Marriages were frequently arranged by the parents of the couple, often years before the event. Among the Iroquois, the mothers usually arranged things. A bride was chosen by the young man's mother. The two mothers settled the details. Gifts were exchanged between families and the couple were married. The young man went to live with and work for the girl's family.

Before the Europeans Came

Before the arrival of Europeans in Canada, the native people lived in communities, forming laws and adopting different religious beliefs. The meeting of European and native cultures would take place on the plains, mountains, and forests where the native peoples had lived in harmony with nature for centuries. The words of Black Elk, a member of the Sioux, may best explain what Indian life was like before the arrival of Europeans in North America.

Even the seasons form a great circle in their changing, and always come back again to where they were. The life of a man is a circle from childhood to childhood and so it is in everything where power moves. Our tipis were round like the nests of birds and these were always set in a circle ... a nest of many nests where the Great Spirit meant for us to hatch our children.[3]

Unit Two
NEW FRANCE

Part 1

Chapter 7

NORTH AMERICA: DISCOVERY AND EXPLORATION

The First Europeans on Our Shores

The fair-haired ones sailed cautiously along the rocky coast. They looked for a place to land, build houses, and settle. They were Vikings. Originally from Norway, Vikings came to this forbidding coast from Iceland and Greenland. They sought riches, adventure, and good farmland. Instead they found a land of glacier-covered mountains and large flat stones. They named it Helluland and then sailed farther south. They came to a wooded land and named it Markland. Finally their boats were beached at Vinland, a beautiful place where cattle could graze outside all year and grapes grew

A Viking ship.

abundantly. Other ships brought men and women who worked together to build a village. Their settlement was short-lived. In a few years, the Vikings were forced to return to Greenland after some unpleasant encounters with the natives of Vinland, called Skraelings. So the stories say.

The "stories" are the Norse sagas—tales of the Vikings and their history, tales filled with a blend of fact and fiction. Historians, anthropologists, explorers, and archeologists have spent 100 years trying to separate the facts from the fiction. The exact locations of the lands named in the sagas are still being debated. Modern experts feel that Helluland refers to Baffin Island, and Markland to the Labrador coast. Vinland has never been pinpointed, although the Cape Cod area is often chosen as the most likely site. Viking relics have been found at L'Anse-aux-Meadows in Newfoundland. Whatever may be the true details about the Vikings and their voyages, there is no doubt that there were Norsemen in North America about the year 1000—nearly 500 years before Columbus.

Other legends have told the story of monks who sailed across the Atlantic Ocean from Ireland. Their leather-hulled boat carried St. Brendan and his seventeen followers to the Promised Land, according to the legend, around the year 600. This date would have been 400 years before the Vikings' voyages.

In 1976 a small group of adventurers built a leather boat called the *Brendan* and sailed it from Ireland to Newfoundland. Their long voyage was sometimes dangerous, but usually boring. However, it was successful! The *Brendan*'s skipper wrote:
She may have looked more like a floating bird's nest than an ocean-going vessel, but she had brought us safely through fog, ice, gale, and calm, across some of the world's most unforgiving waters. She had proved beyond doubt that the Irish monks *could*

have sailed their leather boats to the New World before the Norsemen and long before Columbus.[1]

Find a map of the North Atlantic and follow the route of the Brendan *to: Ireland, the Hebrides, the Faroes, Iceland, and Newfoundland.*

To Find a Route to Asia

In the fifteenth century, Europeans risked the known and imagined dangers of an Atlantic crossing in order to find a way to India and China. They sailed from England, Spain, Portugal, Denmark, Italy, and France. Their heads were filled with myths and superstition. They feared the huge monsters that lived in the seas, waiting to swallow their ships. They feared sailing across the equator for they had heard stories of boiling seas. The Arctic offered as many dangers—huge icebergs to crush their ships and numbing cold. Navigation was very primitive because of the lack of reliable instruments, accurate maps, or a knowledge of latitude and longitude.

A diver exploring the remains of a sunken Basque galleon, the San Juan, that was lost in Red Bay, Labrador, in 1565. Current underwater research by Parks Canada will teach us more about the Basque whaling expeditions and settlements in Labrador. What kind of problems might this diver face, in searching for remains of the ship? Find out why whale oil was so valuable in the sixteenth century.

55

Early sailors preferred to stay within sight of land. That way they were less likely to become lost, or fall off the edge of the world. Many expected this disaster because of the widespread belief that the earth was flat. Despite the terrors of venturing into the unknown, courageous explorers sailed across the Atlantic to find the Orient.

Christopher Columbus was not the first European in the New World, but his 1492 voyage inspired many others. John Cabot, an experienced Italian mariner and map maker, sailed from Bristol, England, in 1497. His aim was to find a route to Asia for the king of England and to "sail to all parts, regions and coasts of the eastern, western, and southern sea, to find, dis-cover, and investigate whatsoever islands, countries, regions, or provin-ces." Cabot could not go south—Spain and Portugal had already claimed the territory of present-day Mexico and Central and South America.

Cabot's crew of eighteen men must have found their ship, the *Matthew*, slim protection against the dangers of the North Atlantic. Their voyage took them to the world's greatest fishing grounds, the Grand Banks of New-foundland. Cabot's report on the abundant fishing was a spur to coun-tries all over Europe that were looking for new sources of cod. His discoveries were also evidence that Columbus had not found India. Others would have to continue the search.

John Cabot prepares to sail from Bristol, England, in search of the riches of the Orient. He found instead the riches of the Grand Banks of Newfoundland.

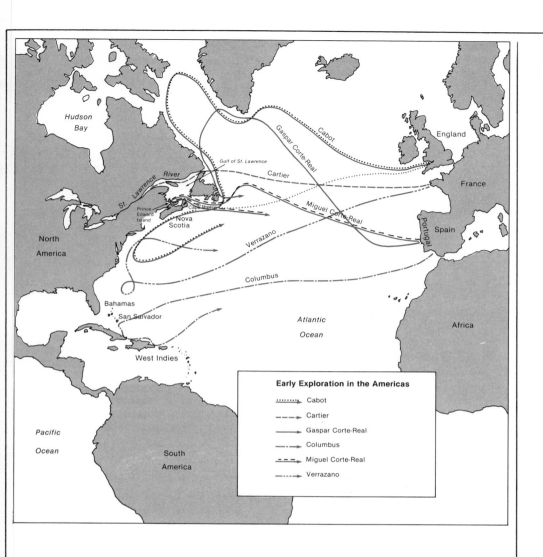

Early Atlantic Explorers

Name	Date	Country	Discoveries
Christopher Columbus	1492	Spain	San Salvador, Bahamas
John Cabot	1497	England	Nova Scotia
Gaspar Corte-Real	1500	England	Cape Breton
Miguel Corte-Real	1502	Portugal	Prince Edward Island
Giovanni da Verrazano	1524	France	West Indies
Jacques Cartier	1534	France	Gulf of St. Lawrence

None of these men reached his goal: a route to the Orient from Europe across the Atlantic Ocean.

None of these men reached his goal: a route to the Orient from Europe across the Atlantic Ocean.

1. List the known and imagined dangers of sailing west from Europe to the Orient.
2. What importance does Cabot's voyage have? Why did Cabot not sail to the south?

A Northwest Passage

First came the winds, whipping up blizzards. Then the ice formed, with pressure so strong that a ship's hull could be crushed. Finally the darkness of the arctic winter closed in. Men spent months suffering, without proper food, exercise, or medical care in tiny huts buried in snow. Disease and death were certain to attack many. An arctic explorer wrote about his crew's misfortunes:

The cold was as extreme this month [February] as at any time we had felt it and many of our men complained of

Henry Hudson, shown here, sailed up the Delaware River. He is thought to have perished in the icy waters of the bay that bears his name, the victim of his mutinous crew.

sore mouths, all the teeth in their heads being loose. Others complained of pain in their heads, weakness in their backs, aches in their thighs and knees.

The 2nd of May it did snow and blow.

We were continually, till the 22nd of July, pestered and tormented with ice.

We returned to England on the 22nd of October. We all went to church and gave God thanks.[2]

Thomas James's experiences during his 1631-32 winter in the Canadian Arctic, were similar to those of many others. James may even have fared better, since fewer of his crew died than was usually the case. Despite these hardships, determined explorers continued to set out from Europe, driven by the winds and a desire to find an arctic route to the riches of the East.

1. List the problems faced by Thomas James and his crew. Find the route of their voyage on a map.
2. Was James the first British explorer to visit the Canadian Arctic? How and what might he have learned from the experiences of others?

What did the explorers seek? Spices such as cloves, nutmeg, pepper, and cinnamon were needed in Europe to preserve food in an age before refrigeration. Beautiful fabrics such as silks and velvets were luxuries that were highly valued. Thus companies in Europe spent a great deal of money to outfit ships that would carry the goods of the Orient more quickly and cheaply than existing overland methods. An arctic-water passage seemed an easy way for no one knew the vastness of North America. In fact, nobody knew that North America was a continent. Europeans felt it was perhaps a groups of islands. A short trip through a strait would surely bring them to Asia. Many people lost their lives in the frigid Canadian Arctic before it was realized that a passage above

Early Arctic Explorers*

NAME	DATE	COUNTRY	DISCOVERY
Martin Frobisher	1576	England	first beyond Greenland
	1577		Frobisher Bay
John Davis	1585	England	Davis Strait
Henry Hudson	1609	Holland	Hudson River
			Hudson Strait
	1610	England	Hudson Bay
Henry Button	1612	England	follows Hudson
William Baffin	1616	England	Baffin Bay
Jens Munk	1619	Denmark	Hudson Bay winter
Luke Foxe	1630	England	Hudson Bay, Hudson Strait
Thomas James	1630	England	James Bay

Of course, Vikings had sailed the arctic waters long before the voyages of Martin Frobisher.

North America was much more than a short cut to the Orient.

Something else took people into the North's unknown hazards—greed. Spanish explorers following in the wake of Columbus had discovered, conquered, and plundered the gold and silver of the Aztec and Incan empires. The Spanish sought further riches in Central and South America. Other Europeans, envious of the ready wealth the Spanish had found, began their own search for riches. A route across the Atlantic seemed necessary in order to reach the wealth of Asia.

Attempts to find a passage across the Canadian Arctic ceased after Thomas James and were not renewed for more than 150 years. The first successful voyage through the Northwest Passage did not take place until 1906. It was a long time coming!

1. Why did so many men try to find the Northwest Passage?
2. Explain in a paragraph why you would or would not like to have accompanied Thomas James or some other arctic explorer.

3. How had the Spanish helped to spur the exploration of North America?

Some Long Inuit Memories

Martin Frobisher first sailed to the Arctic in 1576. His dealings with the Inuit on his three voyages were unpleasant and unfriendly. Frobisher kidnapped one of the Inuit. The natives of Frobisher Bay replied by shooting at Frobisher and his crew. There were several other encounters between the explorer and the area's natives. All were tinged with conflict.

Two hundred and eighty-six years afterwards, an American arctic explorer encountered a group of Baffin Island Inuit. They told of Europeans who had come to their land for three years in a row to dig up the ground. Their stories were accurate accounts of Frobisher's activities (he was digging up ore) 286 years later!

1. How could the American explorer prove that Frobisher had been there?
2. How would the story of the Europeans and their activities have been preserved and passed on by the Inuit?

Part 2

Chapter 8

NEW FRANCE: THE EARLY YEARS, 1534-1632

THE KINGDOM OF THE SAGUENAY

The sentry stamps his freezing feet. His breath forms a cloud around his head. His hands are stiff with the cold.

Where is Pierre anyway? It's his turn to take over. The Indians from the nearby village of Stadacona are becoming more threatening as this terrible winter drags on. Many of the crew have suffered from scurvy. Of the 110 who sailed here last summer with Jacques Cartier, only 3 or 4 have avoided the disease—and 25 have died.

The ice and snow are so deep that dead bodies have to be left unburied until spring. The three ships have been locked in the ice of the St. Lawrence River since November. It's now the middle of February, 1536. Will this cruel winter never end?

Why were these French colonists shivering through a Canadian winter so far from home?

In 1534 Cartier received permission from King Francis I of France to

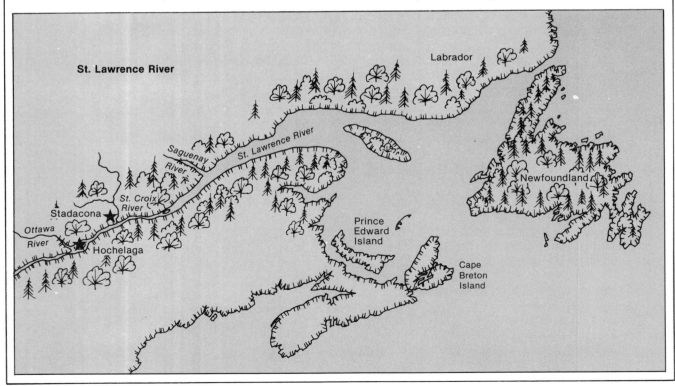

search for a new route to the Orient. Cartier also hoped to find new lands full of riches, such as the Spanish had found in the Aztec and Incan kingdoms.

On Cartier's first expedition, he sailed along the coasts of present-day Labrador, Newfoundland, and Prince Edward Island. He was especially impressed with the beauty of Prince Edward Island.

The Indians who were in the area on a fishing trip had been friendly as they traded their furs for the knives and axes brought by Cartier and his crew. They watched as Cartier's crew erected a huge wooden cross on the Gaspé shore. They gave a noisy farewell to Chief Donnacona's two sons, who returned to France with Cartier. These Indians were from somewhere in the interior, and Cartier planned to train the chief's sons as valuable interpreters and guides.

While in France, Donnacona's two sons told Cartier of a river that led to the place where they lived. They also told him of a kingdom they called Saguenay.

The Search for the Saguenay

The next spring, Cartier's ships again appeared on the river, which he named St. Lawrence. They sailed as far as Stadacona (Quebec City). Cartier was determined to explore more of this mighty river, and to travel to the village that the Indians called Hochelaga.

Cartier's boats received a warm welcome from the villagers at Hochelaga in early October, 1535. Cartier described Hochelaga as a village surrounded by a ten-metre wall:

In many places about the enclosure are galleries with ladders for mounting to them with rocks and stones for the defence and protection of the place. There are some fifty houses in this village, each about fifty paces [thirty-eight metres] or more in length, and twelve or fifteen [five or six metres] in

width, built completely of wood and covered up with large pieces of bark. And inside these houses are many rooms and chambers; and in the middle is a large space without a floor, where they light their fire and live together in common.[1]

Cartier climbed Mount Royal and listened excitedly as his Indian hosts described a wonderful Kingdom of the Saguenay, where "the natives go clothed in woollens like ourselves;

These two pictures show Cartier meeting the Indians during his first voyage in 1534. What differences are there between the two pictures in the way that the Indians are shown? In the landscape? What reasons could there be for these differences? List the items being traded.

Jacques Cartier. Very little is known of Jacques Cartier and his life except for the records of his three voyages. This portrait, drawn after his death, shows what Cartier might have looked like.

Cartier finally managed to obtain a valuable piece of medical advice from the Indians. He recorded the event in his journal:

Two squaws brought nine or ten branches. They showed us how to grind the bark and leaves and to boil the whole in water. Of this one should drink every two days, and place the dregs on the legs where they were swollen and affected. According to them this tree cured every kind of disease. They called it in their language "annedda."[3]

The remedy worked; most of the suffering men were cured, and that spring Cartier's ships returned to France.

there are many towns and tribes composed of honest folk who possess great store of gold and copper."[2]

Gold! Riches! A fabulous kingdom waiting to be explored. Cartier planned to find this glorious place. Instead he found a bitter Canadian winter.

1. What did the Indians call the "kingdom" that Cartier was searching for?
2. What is scurvy? What is the cause? What are the symptoms? (You may need to do some research.)
3. Do you think that Cartier was more concerned with finding a new route to the Orient, or finding a new kingdom of riches? Explain your answer.

Cure for Scurvy

The health of Cartier's crew worsened daily. Cartier was afraid that the local Indians would learn of the scurvy epidemic. If the Indians attacked, Cartier and his men would have had little chance to defend themselves. The situation became so desperate that Cartier had his men rattle and pound on the sides of the ships to create the impression that they were all well and working.

Fool's Gold

In 1541 Cartier was given another chance to find the Kingdom of the Saguenay. The French expedition was led this time by the Sieur de Roberval. Cartier sailed with five ships and a number of colonists, many of whom had been taken from prisons in France. They spent another harsh winter at Stadacona and returned to France excited about the "gold and diamonds" Cartier had found.

Disappointment followed, for Cartier's treasures were only "fool's gold" and quartz. Interest in sending colonists to New France diminished, and the area was visited only by fishermen who sometimes traded with the Indians for a few furs. It would be sixty years before another group of French colonists endured winter in Canada, or enjoyed a Canadian spring.

1. Was it true or false that Cartier found gold and diamonds in the Kingdom of the Saguenay?
2. Cartier's voyages were successful. Do you agree or disagree? Why?
3. Why do you suppose Cartier himself did not get scurvy?
4. Why would prisoners from France be sent as colonists to the New World instead of other people?

The first prescription in Canada, 1536. Cartier's crew recovered from the scurvy that plagued them after drinking a "tea" recipe prescribed by the Indians.

How the Fur Trade Started

Cartier's activities on the St. Lawrence River were not restricted to searching for copper and gold. He also traded on the side as we read in an excerpt from a book called *The Great Canadian Skin Game*:

The fur trade in Canada started in the Gulf of St. Lawrence in 1534 when Jacques Cartier, in the process of discovering the Bay of Gaspé, also discovered a tribe of Indians who "made frequent signs to us to come on shore, holding out to us some furs on sticks." Cartier bartered for these furs, which turned out to be beaver robes, and thus initiated Canada's fur trade.

Cartier reported that the Indians he met were very happy to trade, and were leaping and dancing in their canoes when he left. He also reported, somewhat unnecessarily, that they were a small tribe. Any tribe that practises dancing in canoes is bound to be small.

These early furs were not beaver pelts as we know them today, but beaver robes, which the Indians were wearing as clothing, fur side in. They consisted of five to eight pelts trimmed into rectangular shape and sewn together with bone needles and moose sinews. Under constant wear, the guard hairs wore off, and Cartier describes them as being "well-greased, pliable, yellow in colour, and downy."[4]

Meeting between Cartier and the Indians at Stadacona, with the cross that he had erected, in the background.

Stretching the Truth

Not all of the talk between the French and the Indians was completely honest.

The Indians soon found out that by giving information to Cartier, they would receive a gift of some sort. Would some Indians stretch the truth a bit in hopes of getting a special gift?

Their chief, Donnacona, hesitated when Cartier asked him about going to Hochelaga, a village farther up the river. Donnacona understandably didn't want to lose his position of advantage. At that time, Cartier depended on Donnacona for guidance and direction in the New World. If Donnacona made it too easy for Cartier to move farther upriver, Cartier would seek help from other tribes, and Donnacona would lose the gifts.

When Cartier and his men put up a large cross on the Gaspé shore, Donnacona objected. He thought that the French were claiming the land as theirs. Cartier explained that it was only a marker to help the ships find their way. What was Cartier's real reason?

On Cartier's second voyage, there was a struggle for the leadership of the Indians at Stadacona. Cartier became involved in the struggle, and after tricking Donnacona, he kidnapped the chief and nine Indians. He took them back to France and within a few years, all except one Indian had died.

Suppose you were one of the kidnapped Indians. Tell about your feelings toward (a) Cartier and his men and (b) going to France.

Fish and Furs

The news that John Cabot took back to England in 1497 contained some hope. He had failed in his attempt to find a route to the Orient, but he did discover an ocean area near Newfoundland that was "teeming with fish." Cabot had come upon one of the greatest fishing areas in the world to this day—the Grand Banks.

In many European countries in those days, fish was very important. The church did not allow people to eat meat either on Fridays or on other days of fasting—and that amounted to a large number of days in a year. On those days, people ate fish instead of meat.

News of the fabulous fishing ground spread through Europe, and soon fishermen were making trips each summer to catch the codfish. They put the fish in the holds of their ships and salted them very heavily to keep them from spoiling on the trip back. These fishermen gradually learned all about the shores and harbours of Newfoundland.

Some fishing fleets, especially those of England and France, soon began to use a different method of keeping their fish catch from spoiling. They took their catch ashore, and after cleaning the cod, laid the fish out on racks (called "flakes") to dry. They still had to use salt on the fish when they were put into the hold of the ship, but less salt was needed this way.

Along with the racks, the fishermen also built sheds for storage and shelter. Some of the men from the ship spent the summer ashore drying the catch.

The Indians soon came in contact with these Europeans. The Indians were eager to have some of the knives, axes, and kettles that they saw. The fishermen were willing to give up these items in exchange for the beaver skins that the Indians wore as robes.

Fur pelts were expensive in Europe, and the fishermen soon realized that they could profit from taking back as many of these furs as they could. It became so profitable that in time men would come to the New World to fill their ships' holds with furs instead of fish.

About the end of the 1500s, felt hats became very fashionable in Europe. It was discovered that beaver fur made excellent felt. What better place to get the pelts than in the New World? The supply was plentiful, and the Indians were glad to trade them.

The fur trade soon became the main reason for Europeans to come across the Atlantic to the New World. It was to remain the principal reason for many years to come.

1. Why was fish such an important part of the European diet?
2. Explain the different methods that were used for preserving the fish catch.

They Called It Canada

The two sons of Chief Donnacona, whom Cartier had taken to France to train as interpreters, returned with him on his second voyage in 1535.

When Cartier's ships entered the Gulf of St. Lawrence, the chief's sons began to recognize the country. They told Cartier that the body of water that he named St. Lawrence was in fact a long river that led to the Kingdom of the Saguenay and then to "Canada." Soon map makers applied the name Canada to all of the country then called New France.

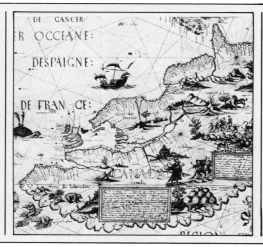

This map was drawn in 1550 by a Frenchman named Desceliers. Do you recognize the area? (Try turning the map upside down.)

Chapter 9

CHAMPLAIN AT PORT ROYAL

An artist's romantic view of Samuel de Champlain.

Tadoussac 1603

Samuel de Champlain took the pipe from the chief seated on the ground beside him. He would have to appear to enjoy the smoke. All those at the feast expected the French visitors to get as much pleasure from tobacco as they did. He took a puff of the smoke and quickly passed the pipe to his friend Jean de Poutrincourt. The noise from the Indian drummers and singers made conversation difficult.

Thousands of French fishermen and traders had been coming to Tadoussac since the days of Cartier, and even before. Champlain, Poutrincourt, and their captain, Pont-Gravé, were thankful for the safe Atlantic crossing and the warm welcome given to them by these Montagnais Indians. Soon the feast would end, and the trading would begin.

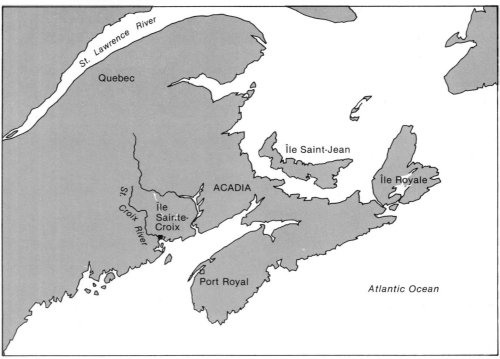

Acadia included present-day Nova Scotia plus part of New Brunswick.

Champlain's first visit to Canada in 1603 promised excitement and adventure. He had been invited by the leaders of this fur-trading voyage to sail with Pont-Gravé to see the country and learn as much as he could about the New World. His previous experiences with drafting and as a map maker and geographer made him a welcome addition to the crew. Later he would be able to provide King Henry IV of France with important information about Canada.

Champlain looked forward to travelling up the majestic St. Lawrence River. The fur trading would last two weeks, time enough for him to explore some of this wonderful new land.

When the trading was over for another season, the French returned home with their ships full of fish and furs. Champlain returned to France with his head full of dreams. His two weeks of exploring had convinced him that Canada was a perfect land for colonizing. There were rich furs for trading, good soil for farming, friendly Indians, and good transportation on the many rivers. Surely a route to the riches of the Orient lay somewhere in this vast and unknown New World. Champlain was determined to be a part of any further ventures in this exciting New France.

How did Champlain's "dream" for the New World differ from Cartier's? In what way was it the same?

St. Croix 1604

In the spring of 1604, when de Monts had led his expedition of three ships of settlers to the New World, the future had looked bright. King Henry IV had granted de Monts a fur-trading **monopoly** in New France. In return, de Monts had promised to take 100 settlers to Canada. He would be able to support the colony with his profits from the fur trade.

De Monts decided to build his settlement in Acadia on the Atlantic coast,

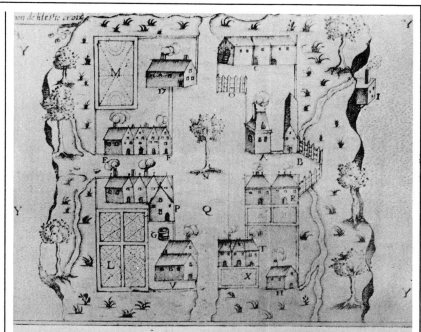

CHAMPLAIN'S VIEW OF THE SETTLEMENT ON ST. CROIX ISLAND.

A Dwelling of Sieur de Monts.
B Public building where we spent our time when it rained.
C The Storehouse.
D Dwelling of the Swiss.
E The blacksmith shop.
F Dwelling of the carpenters.
G The well.
H The oven where the bread was made.
I Kitchen.
L Gardens.
M Other gardens.

N Place in the centre where a tree stands.
O Palisade.
P Dwellings of the Sieurs d'Orville, Champlain and Champdore.
Q Dwelling of Sieur Boulay, and other artisans.
R Dwelling where the Sieurs de Genestou, Sourin, and other artisans lived.
T Dwelling of the Sieurs de Beaumont, la Motte Bourioli and Fougeray.
V Dwelling of our curate.
X Other gardens.
Y The river surrounding the island.

in hopes of escaping the harsh winters he knew occurred at Tadoussac. He had chosen a lovely little island, which the French named Île Sainte-Croix, in the St. Croix River.

In the summer it seemed like a perfect spot, so the crew set to work building a storehouse, houses for their leaders and themselves, a chapel, a kitchen, and a forge. They prepared and planted gardens. That autumn Champlain explored the coast of the area that is now called Maine. He made friends with the local Micmac Indians.

Champlain and the seventy-nine colonists quickly learned that winter how unwisely they had chosen the site for their settlement. Floating ice in the channel made the short trip to the mainland impossible. They were cut off from getting a supply of firewood, fresh water, and game. They were stranded, a perfect target for a harsh Canadian winter.

Champlain's view of the settlement on Île Sainte-Croix. The shelters were constructed hastily and poorly. The icy winds of winter easily found their way through the cracks in the walls.

monopoly: exclusive trading rights

Worst of all was the scurvy. Of the seventy-nine men, thirty-five died and more than twenty were near death. Only eleven remained well. They knew of the cure for scurvy that Cartier had used, but were unable to find the secret ingredient, the annedda. Their cure would have to be the coming of spring and the arrival of fresh supplies from France.

Port Royal 1605

In the spring, the search began for a better place to settle. Champlain explored part of the Atlantic coast as far south as Cape Cod, but the Indians there were not friendly. De Monts finally chose a spot across the Bay of Fundy from Sainte-Croix. The place they called Port Royal was well protected from the wind and had a good supply of fresh water, firewood, and game.

This time the workers built a more compact "habitation," with the buildings around a central square, rather than scattered about. Now that they knew of the problems the winter could cause, they made the buildings far more weatherproof.

The 1605 winter turned out to be abnormal. It was very late in arriving, and much less severe.

Their friends, the Micmacs, helped to keep the people healthy, bringing fresh fish and game to trade. That year only twelve died of scurvy—still too many, but an improvement over the last winter.

The next summer, de Monts and his ships arrived with fresh supplies and a new load of colonists. Things were improving.

Champlain again explored the Atlantic coast to the south, but the trip was cut short when four of his companions who were camping on the shore were killed by Indians.

Disaster struck Port Royal in 1607 with the news that the king had cancelled the fur-trading monopoly. Sadly the colonists packed up and left for France. Without the profits from the fur trading, de Monts could no longer support the colony.

Further attempts to colonize Port Royal ran into great difficulty. Port Royal failed, but the lessons that Champlain had learned there would not be forgotten. He would use his skills in years to come in another part of the vast territory called New France.

1. List some of the things that contributed to the failure of Port Royal.

2. How was the granting of a fur-trade monopoly used as a way to colonize the new world?
3. Why had de Monts chosen Acadia instead of the St. Lawrence area for his settlement?
4. Why do you suppose Champlain and his colonists were unable to find the "annedda"?

The Order of Good Cheer, winter 1606. "In order to keep our table joyous and well provided, an Order was established which was called the Order of Good Cheer. Each man was appointed Chief Steward in his turn. Now this person had the duty of taking care that we were all well and honourably provided for. For there was no one who, two days before his turn came, failed to go hunting or fishing, and to bring back some delicacy in addition to our ordinary fare."[1]

In what ways is the habitation at Port Royal different from the Île Sainte-Croix buildings?

Chapter 10 | RETURN TO THE RIVER OF CANADA

Basques: inhabitants of a northern region in Spain

What became of the French efforts to settle along the mighty St. Lawrence River? After Cartier's disappointments there, interest was lost. Acadia became the target for exploration and settlement. In 1608, Champlain convinced de Monts to abandon Acadia and try the St. Lawrence area again. Their fur-trade monopoly had been returned to them for one year. Champlain had good reasons for preferring the St. Lawrence:

This region would be farther from competition from other European efforts and would be easier to defend.

The Indians there would be very helpful to the French.

They would be much closer to the major source of furs.

The river looked as though it might lead them to the route to the Orient.

Champlain led an expedition of three ships that arrived at Tadoussac in June of 1608. To Champlain's surprise, he found that **Basques** had already taken over the fur-trading activity in that area.

The French ships travelled farther up the St. Lawrence to a spot where the river narrowed at present-day Quebec City. Here Champlain decided to build his habitation. This one would be different—it would be built like a small fortress, complete with moat, drawbridge, and outer walls.

After the habitation was completed, some of the crew returned to France, while twenty-eight, including Champlain, stayed to brave the Quebec winter. Disease struck again that winter,

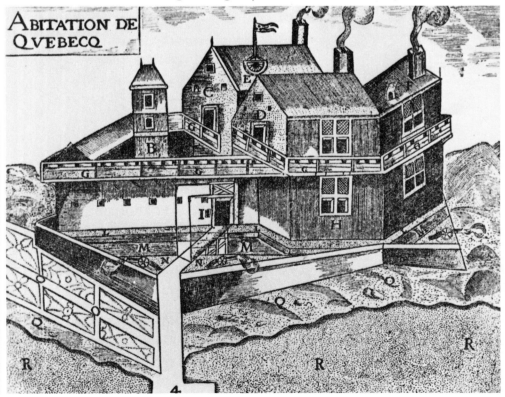

The habitation in Quebec, 1608-1624.

and unfortunately the Indians seemed to know nothing of the "cure" that Cartier and his people had been shown years earlier. Only eight survived until spring.

1. Why did Champlain decide to locate his colony on the St. Lawrence River instead of in Acadia?
2. How was the habitation at Quebec going to be "different"?

Iroquois Gone South

The Indians that Jacques Cartier had met when he wintered at Stadacona (Quebec) were the Iroquois. For some reason, probably because of attacks from their Algonquin neighbours, the Iroquois moved south of the St. Lawrence River and the Great Lakes. The Algonquin Indians moved into the area around the St. Lawrence that the Iroquois had abandoned.

By the time Champlain and his expedition arrived at Quebec, the Iroquois were gone. The Algonquins that Champlain met didn't seem to know anything about the tree that could cure scurvy.

Conspiracy

The building of the habitation at Quebec didn't take place without problems. A small group of colonists planned to take over the habitation after it was built. They intended to earn some money by turning it over to the Basques. One of these colonists was Jean Duval, a locksmith. Duval had survived a Port Royal winter and an Indian attack near Cape Cod in 1606. His luck was about to run out.

News of the plan reached Champlain's ears, and the colonists were brought to trial. Four were sentenced to die on the gallows, but three of them were sent back to France for punishment. Jean Duval, the fourth man, was hanged. His head was stuck on the top of a pole, in full view of all those who were building the habitation, as a warning against other conspirators.

Lescarbot Puts in a Word for Women

The French who organized the voyage to the St. Lawrence in 1608 thought that eating salted meat caused scurvy. For this reason they brought some cows and a bull to Quebec to provide fresh meat and milk. The plan failed, as colonist Marc Lescarbot described in his diary:

For want of some village housewife who understood taking care of them [the cows], they let the greater part die in giving birth to their calves. Which shows how necessary a woman is in a house, and I cannot understand why so many people slight them, although they cannot do without them. For my part, I shall always believe that in any settlement whatsoever, nothing will be accomplished without the presence of women.[1]

Explain Lescarbot's plan for helping the colony to survive.

The profile of this ship is similar to that of the ship used by Champlain.

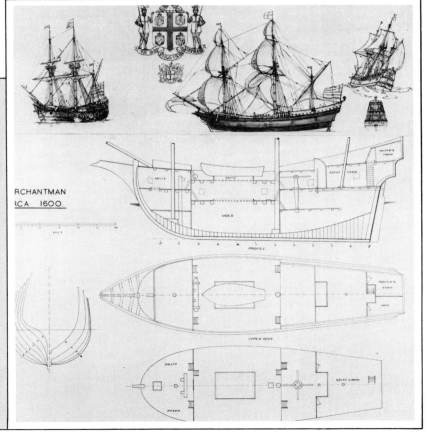

71

Chapter 11 | HOW THE FUR TRADE WORKED

The Early Fur Trade

The act of trading furs for knives, axes, kettles, and other European goods was quite simple. But this trading activity didn't happen overnight. It took many years of contact between the Indians and the French before the fur trade became big business.

Why didn't the French trap the furs themselves? The Indians knew how and where to trap the best beaver. Besides, why should the French go to all that work? The Indians carried the furs, often hundreds of kilometres, to the French and traded them at what the French thought (but didn't tell them) was a cheap rate. The Indians were very reluctant to let the French find out about the country where they trapped the beaver.

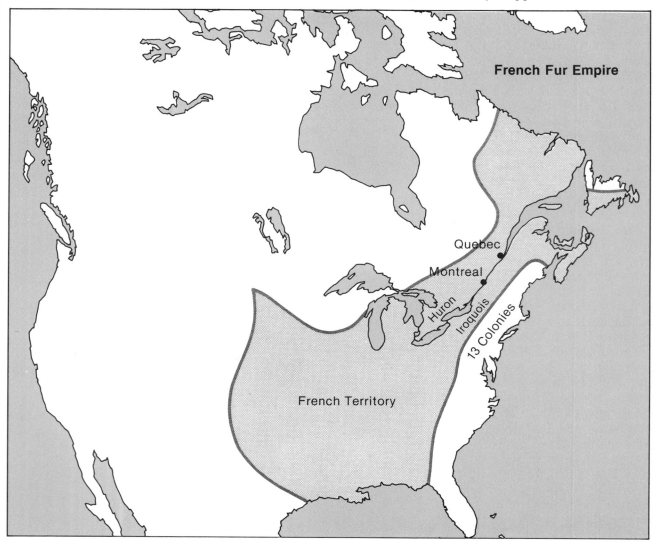

French Fur Empire

Quebec

Montreal

Huron

Iroquois

13 Colonies

French Territory

Wanted: Castor Canadensis (The Beaver)

—**length:** 1 m to 1.3 m (North America's largest rodent)

—**mass:** 13 kg to 27 kg

—**fur:** longer guard hairs cover softer inner hair (brown)

—**back feet:** are large and webbed to help in swimming

—**front paws:** are smaller—used for walking and carrying—five toes on each

—**tail:** broad, flat, and scaly—used as a rudder—considered a delicacy to eat

—**flesh:** oily but good to eat

—**teeth:** large chisel-like front teeth that grow continually—worn down by chewing trees

—**ears:** small—ears and nose have special valves that close automatically when beaver goes underwater—can stay submerged for fifteen minutes without coming up for air

—**food:** tender bark on small branches of aspen and poplar trees—cuts down trees to get at smaller branches (beaver doesn't climb)—the small branches are stuck in the mud bottom of the pond—this gives it food for the winter

—**home:** builds dams of stone, mud, and tree branches—this makes a protective lake—beaver builds its home in the middle of this lake—house is built with branches and mud—floor is just above water level, with entrance below the lake surface

—**young:** are called kittens—remain with parents for more than a year

73

Chapter 12

CHAMPLAIN FIGHTS THE IROQUOIS

In July of 1609, Champlain met the Huron Indians, who were the most important trading tribe in the Great Lakes area. These Hurons were eager to trade with the French. In order to prove their loyalty to the Hurons, the French were asked to venture into Iroquois territory to help attack enemies of the Huron nation. Champlain had little choice but to agree. The Hurons wouldn't come to Quebec to trade their furs if Champlain didn't prove his friendship.

Two of Champlain's men went with him. All three Frenchmen wore impressive steel breastplates and helmets—and they carried their **arquebuses.**

The Huron war party led them into Iroquois territory by way of the Richelieu River. They soon came to a long, narrow, beautiful lake that today is called Lake Champlain. In order to avoid being seen by the enemy, they travelled only at night, resting during the day. Champlain described the battle with the Iroquois in his journal:

As we were paddling along very quietly about 10 o'clock at night we met the Iroquois. Both they and we began to utter loud cries and each got his arms ready. We drew out into the lake and the Iroquois landed. They began to fell trees and they barricaded themselves well. When daylight came, my companions and I were still hidden getting our firearms ready, each in a canoe of the Indians. After we were armed with light weapons, we took, each of us, an arquebus and went ashore. I saw the enemy come out of their barricade to the number of two hundred and at their head were three chiefs. Our Indians told me that those who had the three big plumes were the chiefs, and I was to do what I could to kill them. Our Indians divided into

arquebus: a primitive rifle

This engraving was first published in Paris in 1613. It depicts Champlain's battle with the Iroquois in 1609. Match details in the picture with the description in Champlain's own account of the battle.

two groups and put me ahead and I marched on until I was within some thirty paces of the enemy, who as soon as they caught sight of me halted and gazed at me. When I saw them make a move to draw their bows upon us, I took aim with my arquebus and shot straight at one of the three chiefs, and with this shot two fell to the ground, and one of their companions was wounded, who died a little later. As soon as our people saw this shot so favourable for them, they began to shout so loudly that one could not have heard it thunder, and meanwhile the arrows flew thick on both sides. The Iroquois were much astonished that two men should have been killed so quickly. This frightened them greatly. As I was reloading my arquebus, one of my companions fired a shot from within the woods. Seeing their chiefs dead, they lost courage and took to flight. I pursued them and laid low still more of them. Our Indians also killed several and took ten or twelve prisoners.[1]

Champlain's victory was certainly decisive. This marked the beginning of ill feeling and violence between the French and the Iroquois that would last for many years.

1. Had Champlain made the right decision in choosing the Hurons as allies rather than the Iroquois? Did he really have a choice? Why did he need to have allies?
2. Do you agree or disagree that the tactics that Champlain used were unfair. Why?
3. Imagine that you were one of the Iroquois braves. Describe how you would feel about Champlain after the battle.

Problems in the Colony

In 1608 the Quebec colony had started off rather shakily, and things hadn't improved the following year.

The year 1610 held out even less hope to Champlain and his dreams. The Indians kept promising to take Champlain to explore the "northern sea" (Hudson Bay), but kept delaying the journey. They didn't want the French to know anything about the territory where they trapped the beaver.

No one had been granted a fur-trading monopoly that year, so all were free to trade as they pleased. There was so much competition that very few of the traders profited. The traders who were trying to support the Quebec colony did not do well.

The English were now occupying areas of North America that France claimed.

To add to all this misfortune, King Henry IV of France was assassinated. He had been one of Champlain's active supporters. The new king was only nine years old, and things were unsettled in France.

Champlain's colony at Quebec was in trouble. The fur-trading monopoly had been taken away, and without this support, the colony seemed doomed to failure.

Champlain spent much of his time for the next few years in France trying to convince merchants and government officials to back his plans. He had little success.

1. Why was Champlain so eager to find the "northern sea"? Why did the Indians not help him find it?
2. Suggest a plan to help the Quebec colony survive.

Champlain with Brûlé.

Champlain travelling by canoe. "They told me that if unfortunately my canoe should upset, since I did not know how to swim, I ought under no circumstances to let go, but keep hold of the small pieces of wood in the centre of the canoe, for they would easily rescue me. These tribes are so clever at shooting rapids that this is easy for them."[2]

Champlain Shoots the Rapids

In the spring of 1611, Champlain met the Hurons and Algonquins at the "Great Rapids" (Lachine Rapids), where the Ottawa and St. Lawrence rivers join. He hoped to outwit the rest of the fur traders who waited downriver.

After a successful trading session, Champlain asked to be taken down the rapids. Champlain got through safely, the only white man to do so besides young Brûlé.

The Story of Étienne Brûlé

Among the survivors of the winter of 1608 at Quebec was a young Frenchman name Étienne Brûlé. Champlain was impressed by the way this young man adapted to life in New France. Such a resourceful youth would be an ideal person to undertake Champlain's plan.

In the summer of 1610, Champlain sent Brûlé to live among the Hurons. Brûlé was to find out more about where they lived, their language and customs, and any other information that might be useful.

Brûlé became the first European to see the Huron territory as well as many other parts of the country. He quickly learned the Huron language and ways. He became an expert interpreter between the French and the Hurons.

Brûlé lived happily with the Hurons for many years. In 1632 the friendship suddenly ended, and the Hurons killed Brûlé. The reason for his killing is not known.

Why do you suppose Brûlé was killed?

The Riddle of the Northern Sea

In 1611, Champlain sent another young French colonist, named Nicolas de Vignau, to live with the Algonquin Indians. His mission was to try to find out more about the "northern sea" (Hudson Bay) that the Indians talked about.

On his return in 1612, Vignau told Champlain that he had gone up the Ottawa River and on to the "northern sea," where he had seen an English shipwreck. Vignau said that the English survivors had been killed by the local Indians.

Champlain set out in 1615 to travel up the Ottawa River to see this "northern sea" for himself. Part of the way up the river, he met the Algonquins. They said that Vignau was lying, and that he had never left their village. Vignau admitted to Champlain that he had lied, and Champlain's trip to the "northern sea" ended.

Did Vignau really lie? Historians disagree on the answer, but here is one theory that's interesting:
1. The Algonquins wanted to keep the French in the dark about as much of their country as they could for as long as they could. They told Champlain that Vignau had lied to prevent further discovery.
2. Vignau had in fact been to the "northern sea." He was afraid of the Indians, so he told Champlain that he had lied.
3. The "shipwreck" that Vignau claimed to have seen was that of Henry Hudson and eight of his men who had been set adrift in 1611. This followed a mutiny on board Hudson's ship.

Was Vignau lying or not? Why?

THE COLONY GROWS SLOWLY

In spite of Champlain's best efforts, the colony at Quebec was off to a very uncertain start. Part of the problem was that the fur-trade monopoly discouraged settlement in New France.

By 1614, the fur trade in New France was quite well established. A new company was formed to take part in the profits, and once again Champlain was involved in the agreement. He had plans to make the colony at Quebec a better place. He wanted to bring more farmers to New France to grow food, so that the colony needn't depend so much on the supply ships from France. Champlain also thought it was a good idea to teach the Indians about Christianity. He convinced the

WHY WOULD I WANT PEOPLE TO SETTLE IN NEW FRANCE WHEN I HAVE THE FUR TRADE MONOPOLY? 1.

NO SOONER WOULD THEY GET SETTLED THAN THEY'D START TRADING TO MAKE A LITTLE MONEY ON THE SIDE. 2.

AND THAT MEANS LESS PROFIT FOR ME! 3.

FURTHERMORE, I HOPE THIS RUMOUR ABOUT TAKING PRIESTS TO NEW FRANCE ISN'T TRUE. 4.

IF THE INDIANS DO BECOME CHRISTIANS AND GIVE UP THEIR OLD WAYS, WHO'LL TRAP THE BEAVER FOR US? 5.

AFTER ALL, WHAT'S MORE IMPORTANT— THE FUR TRADE OR SOME SILLY PEOPLE TRYING TO MAKE HOMES IN THAT FORSAKEN LAND? 6.

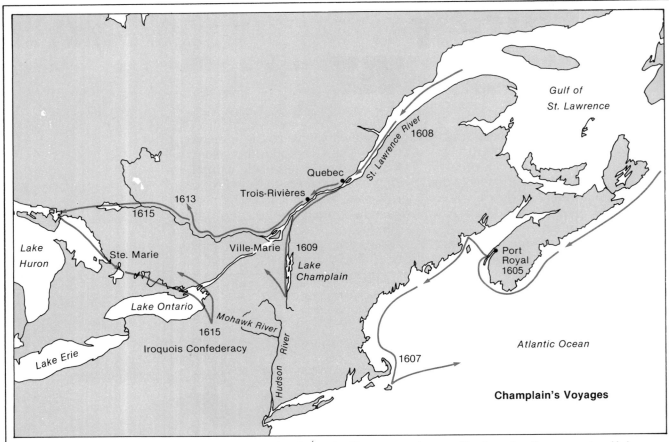

Map labels:
Gulf of St. Lawrence
1608
Quebec
St. Lawrence River
Trois-Rivières
1613
1615
Lake Huron
Ste. Marie
Ville-Marie
1609
Lake Champlain
Port Royal 1605
Lake Ontario
Mohawk River
Hudson River
1615
Iroquois Confederacy
Atlantic Ocean
Lake Erie
1607

Champlain's Voyages

Récollet order of priests in France to send some of their missionaries to Quebec.

Three ships departed from France in 1615, and among the passengers were Champlain and four Récollet fathers. They were headed for New France.

When the ships arrived at Tadous-sac, Father le Caron set off immediately for Huron country. He began trying to persuade the Indians to accept Christianity.

Champlain made his first visit to Huronia that summer, following the long canoe and portage route up the Ottawa River and across to Lake Huron. The 900-km trip took twenty-two days.

1. In what ways was settlement in New France discouraged by the fur trade?
2. What was Champlain's plan to improve the colony at Quebec?

Champlain's trip to Huronia by way of the Ottawa River required many portages. What other hardships besides the gruelling work of portaging would the travellers have to endure?

Iroquois Victory: A Turning Point

The Hurons informed Champlain that their Iroquois enemies had obtained guns from the Dutch in the Hudson River valley. These Iroquois were continually ambushing the

Huron and Algonquin fur-trading canoes along the St. Lawrence River. Champlain was asked to lead the Hurons in battle again in 1615.

A war party was eventually formed, and the group travelled into Iroquois territory south of Lake Ontario. Somewhere near Lake Onondaga, the French and their Indian allies came upon a fortified Iroquois village. This village was much like the one Cartier had described at Hochelaga.

The Iroquois defences proved to be too strong. Many of the attackers were killed, and Champlain was wounded. They were forced to give up the battle, retreating to Huronia carrying the wounded Champlain.

The Hurons refused to supply transportation to return Champlain to Quebec. They probably wanted the protection of his guns for their return trip. Champlain was forced to winter at Huronia. However, he made the best of his time by doing a lot of exploring in the area.

Next spring, Champlain went back to Quebec with the Huron trading expedition. Father le Caron went with him.

The battle of 1615 was a turning point for the Iroquois. It proved that the French, with their arquebuses and fancy outfits, were not invincible. From that time on, the Iroquois took the offensive, making more attacks on the St. Lawrence fur traders and colonists. They wanted to divert the fur trade from the St. Lawrence to the Hudson River region where it would be more profitable for them.

Louis Hébert

Louis Hébert was not a newcomer to New France when he and his family arrived at Quebec in 1617. He had been one of the colonists at the Île Sainte-Croix and Port Royal settlements in 1604-1607.

Champlain persuaded this French **apothecary** to bring his wife, three children, and brother-in-law to Quebec.

The Company of Canada, which then held the monopoly, made Hébert sign a contract. It was obviously made to discourage Hébert and other potential colonists, because the terms were very unfavourable. Hébert was to look after remedies for the sick people of the colony, and to farm only in his spare time. Anything that he grew was to be sold to the Company, at their prices of course. He was absolutely forbidden to trade with the Indians.

To add to Hébert's frustrations, he was given only three of his promised six hectares when he arrived at Quebec.

Hébert and his family were apparently very determined, because they managed to clear some land and build up a successful farm. They formed the backbone of the community that was struggling for its very existence.

Louis Hébert fell from scaffolding at Quebec in 1627, and that winter he died as a result of his injuries.

His wife, Marie, and her son, daughter, and son-in-law continued to work on the land that Louis Hébert's sweat and sheer determination had helped to clear.

apothecary: chemist

Louis Hébert came to the colony of Quebec in 1617. Hébert and his family cleared a small plot of land and eventually developed a very successful farm.

Chapter 14

A NEW PLAN

News of the pitiful conditions in New France reached Cardinal Richelieu. He was an important man in France because he was in charge of all the voyages to the colonies. He heard about the few permanent settlers in New France, and the small amount of land that had been cleared for farming.

Richelieu devised an impressive new plan, and with it a new fur-trading company. The Company of One Hundred Associates was given control of New France which the French government said included all of North America from Spanish Flor-ida to the Arctic. There were several people already in North America who would dispute that claim.

The Company agreed to bring settlers to New France—at least 4000 in the next fifteen years.

The Kirke Brothers

Unluckily for the new French plan, France and England were close to war, and plans were being made in England to take over New France. The men behind the scheme were the Kirke brothers, David, Louis, and Thomas.

These men did something that the Company of One Hundred Associates never dreamed would happen. They arrived on the St. Lawrence before the Company's supply ships came in the spring of 1628. They captured all of these supplies—a tidy prize indeed. They also managed to get news to Champlain at Quebec that they wanted him to leave his premises. Champlain stubbornly, but politely, told them to forget their plans. The Kirkes just as politely replied that they would be back the next spring. Without the crucial supplies for the coming winter, how could the colonists hope to survive?

True to their word, the Kirkes returned the next summer. Champlain's group at Quebec had suffered a long and miserable winter. The brothers, Louis and Thomas, anchored their ships off Quebec and demanded surrender. Champlain had no choice. He and most of the colonists were taken on the Kirkes' ships back to Europe. Madame Hébert and a few others decided to remain in New France.

In Europe Champlain discovered that he had been made to surrender after the war between France and England had officially ended. Quebec still

This picture of the capture of Quebec by the English in 1629 is obviously exaggerated. List some of the inaccurate details.

belonged to France! After a few years of haggling. Quebec was finally given back to France by England in 1632.

The Company of One Hundred Associates, with all its elaborate plans, had lost a lot of money and time. In 1632 they were able to begin again.

1. What were the "pitiful conditions" that Richelieu was told about?
2. Explain Richelieu's plan to help New France.
3. Why was Quebec given back to France?

Who Claimed What in North America (1627)?

New France had the St. Lawrence settlements (Quebec was the only one of any size), 107 people in all.

Acadia—France claimed it but had only 20 people there.

The British said it was theirs and called it Nova Scotia.

In 1629 two Scottish settlements were started:

> William Alexander and colonists took over Port Royal.
> James Stewart and about 60 colonists settled on Cape Breton.

Virginia (an English colony) was a rich tobacco producer with a population of 2000.

The Hudson River valley, about 200 people (Dutch).

New England had two small colonies, Plymouth and Salem, about 80 km apart with about 310 people.

Newfoundland had George Calvert's colony of Ferryland on the Avalon Peninsula, about 100 people.

Champlain leaving Quebec, a prisoner on Kirke's ship, 1629.

The Father of New France?

In the fall of 1635, Samuel de Champlain fell ill with a stroke at Quebec. The Jesuit priest, Father Lalement, took care of the dying man until he passed away on Christmas Day.

Champlain was buried with much ceremony, and a little chapel was built over his grave. Unfortunately this chapel later burned down, and his exact burial place is not known. It may well be somewhere beneath the streets of present-day Quebec City.

Champlain is often referred to as the "Father of New France." Considering his accomplishments, do you think he is deserving of the title?

Part 3

NEW FRANCE: THE STRUGGLE TO SURVIVE, 1632-1663

Chapter 15 | STARTING AGAIN

seigniors: landholders

censitaires: settlers

Pioneers starting their new life in Quebec had only to look around to see what their life would be like. Make a word collage of things, people, ideas, and activities that would be new to these arriving Europeans.

New France could hardly be called a colony when the ship carrying Father Le Jeune, two other priests, and forty settlers and traders dropped anchor at Quebec in the summer of 1632. The English, who had held New France for three years after the surrender of Champlain, had left Quebec in a mess. They had destroyed some of the buildings and looted others, taking windows, doors, furniture, and all of the company's furs.

The first job facing the new colonists was to rebuild. Proper shelter was needed, as was some form of defence against future English raiders or pirates. The people set to work. Within four years a fortress had been constructed at Quebec and a smaller fort had been built at Trois-Rivières. A system of streets was organized for Quebec, and the first seigniories were granted along the St. Lawrence. These would become the first farms in the colony.

Large parcels of the Canadian wilderness near Quebec were given to **seigniors** by the Company of One Hundred Associates. In return for their land, the seigniors were required to bring out settlers to farm the land. The settlers, or **censitaires**, were given land by the seigniors on condition that it be cleared and cultivated. In this way, the Company hoped to make the colony grow. Each family, whether seignior or censitaire, arrived at Quebec hoping to make a better life. They were encouraged by the Jesuits.

1. Explain why the colonists were concerned about defending New France. Against whom were they defending their colony?
2. Construct a diagram to show how the colony was intended to grow and develop.

The Jesuits

The Jesuits were important men in the colony. They were determined that New France would succeed in overcoming all of the obstacles in its path—the cold winters, the shortages of food, the isolation, and the tomahawks and guns of the raiding Iroquois. Champlain had been the chief promoter of New France for over thirty years, but he had died on Christmas Day, 1635. His place as protector and friend of the colony was taken over by the men of the Catholic religious order, called the Society of Jesus (the Jesuits).

The men of the Jesuit Order worked tirelessly at the task of spreading Christianity among the Indian tribes of the New World, encouraging the settlement of New France to help fulfil their goals. They did what they could to speed up the slow growth of the colony, but even their best efforts weren't enough to bring rapid development to the tiny settlements. The father superior at Quebec sent an annual report to France describing the Jesuits' work among the Indians and inviting immigrants to leave France for a new life in Canada. These reports were called the Jesuit *Rélations*.

French families were reluctant to take a chance on life in the New World. Pioneers faced many obstacles. First, there was the uncomfortable and dangerous Atlantic crossing. Then came the back-breaking job of clearing land and beginning to farm. Europeans were not always prepared for the cold, snowy Canadian winters.

The population of New France grew very slowly. In 1640 there were fewer than 400 settlers, and ten years later only 675. This was far short of the thousands the Company of One Hundred Associates had promised to bring, and far short of the tens of thousands of Dutch and English living in the colonies to the south of New France. The Company preferred furs to settlers. They did little to encourage settlement.

1. List three things that had kept New France from becoming a large colony.
2. Explain why the Company of One Hundred Associates had not honoured their promise to bring settlers to New France.

The Jesuit *Rélations*

The *Rélations* are a valuable source of information about life in New France. They contain first-hand accounts of conditions in the Huron and Algonquin villages. They explain how the fur trade was carried on, and they describe some of the frustrations and hardships of the Jesuit missionaries as they worked to teach the Indians about Christianity. The Jesuit fathers told the story of New France as they saw it and lived it.

Father Le Jeune writes about winter and feet:

On the 3rd of December we began to change our footgear, and to use raquettes; when I first put these great flat skates on my feet, I thought that I should fall with my nose in the snow at every step I took.[1]

What about these early Canadian clock watchers?

They (the Hurons) never cease coming to visit us from admiration since our mill and clock have been set to work. As to the clock, they all think it is some living thing, for they cannot imagine how it works of itself.[2]

Father Biard describes a problem the French priests dealt with as they tried to learn the Algonquin language from some "teachers" who were also practical jokers:

The Indian teachers often ridiculed, instead of teaching us, and sometimes palmed off on us indecent words, which we went about innocently preaching for beautiful sentences from the gospels.[3]

Father Le Jeune gives us an example of another of the missionaries' problems—making Christianity understood:

When I talk to them [the Algonquins] about the Son of God, they ask me if God is married, as he has a son. They are astonished when I tell them that God is neither a man nor a woman; they ask how is he made then.[4]

1. Draw a picture of Father Le Jeune's raquettes.
2. Why would the Indians play tricks on the Jesuit fathers?
3. What difficulties would the Jesuits have had explaining their ideas to the Indians?

The Jesuits had tried to aid the colony in many ways. Their *Rélations* did much to arouse the interest of French men and women. Canada did not seem so far away after Europeans had read the *Rélations*. Once a family had made the difficult decision to emigrate to Quebec, the fathers provided more help. They educated French boys in their college, which was established in 1636. They encouraged two orders of nuns to come to Quebec to operate a girls' school and a hospital. By 1640 there were forty-eight girls studying with the Ursulines. The Hospitalières were open for business in their new **Hôtel-Dieu** in 1639. Canada's first Indian Reserve was an attempt by the Jesuits to provide a home for the Montagnais Indians of the Quebec area. There were other developments that pleased the builders of New France.

Hôtel-Dieu: hospital

The arrival of the Ursuline nuns in New France meant that schools and hospitals would soon be in operation. After stepping off the ships pictured here, what challenges did they face in starting their schools and hospitals?

1. List four ways the Jesuits tried to promote New France.
2. Why might a family have found it hard to decide to leave France? What things might have helped them decide in favour of emigrating?

From Ville-Marie to Montreal

Montreal was begun with a prayer. The huge metropolis was started on its way to future greatness by a tiny group of deeply religious men and women. Their first night in what they called Ville-Marie was spent in tents. The fifty-five founders were led by a soldier, the Sieur de Maisonneuve; Jeanne Mance, Canada's first nurse; and Father Vimont, a Jesuit priest. These pioneers had a goal: to bring the message of Christianity to the Indians of the area, and to provide them with

Storms at sea were terrifying experiences for immigrants on their way to New France. Their safety was never assured until their feet touched Canadian soil, for the violent storms that occurred occasionally on the St. Lawrence River could send a ship to the bottom.

Ville-Marie in 1642. This artist's version shows only one building. Suggest ways the founders of Ville-Marie might have used the building. When would the most appropriate time be to build a palisade? Why?

homes, food, schools, and a hospital.

The task was a difficult one for several reasons. The location of their settlement was the most important barrier to the missionaries. Montreal, as the area was later called, was too convenient for fur traders, who realized the benefits of meeting the fleets of Indian fur canoes at this new post rather than at Quebec or Tadoussac, far down the river. Fur traders soon overtook the missionaries of Montreal in importance, and the settlement grew slowly.

The founders of Montreal intended their village to be a missionary outpost. What other role did it assume? Why?

Chapter 16 | TRADERS AND FURS

The fur trade involved the wild animals of the North American woods, the native peoples, who lived and hunted and traded in those woods, and the Europeans who wanted the animal pelts.

Why did the French, Dutch, and English want pelts, particularly beaver pelts? For hats, since beaver pelts were used to make excellent felt for hats. And fashion, after about the year 1600, said that any man in Europe who wanted to be in style had to wear a felt hat. Millions of beaver became the targets of the trappers.

The Jesuit *Rélations* of 1626 explained how the fur trade was carried on in the port of Tadoussac:

We see here not more than two ships once a year, about the beginning of the month of June. These two ships bring all the merchandise which these Gentlemen use in trading with the Indians; that is to say, the cloaks, blankets, nightcaps, hat, shirts, sheets, hatchets, iron arrowheads, bodkins, swords, picks to break the ice in Winter, knives, kettles, prunes, raisins, Indian corn, peas, crackers or sea biscuits, and tobacco. In exchange for these they carry back the hides of the moose, lynx, fox, otter, but they deal principally in beavers. I was told that one year they carried back as many as 22 000. The usual number for one year is 15 000.[1]

1. Organize the goods traded to the Indians into three lists. The headings for the lists should be: clothing, tools, food.
2. Construct a diagram to show how the fur trade was carried on in New France. Show merchant ships, traders, hunters, animals.

Change and More Change: Europeans and Indians

What did this trade do to the Indians who took part in it? It changed their way of life forever. As they began to see the benefits of using iron axes rather than stone ones, of cooking in iron kettles (large pots) instead of hollowed-out tree trunks, and of hunting with

These Indians have obviously been in contact with Europeans. Name the things that prove this and then sketch them.

iron rather than stone arrowheads, the Indians would never again return to their old ways of doing things. They wanted an easier life style, and the traders' goods seemed to promise that. All they needed to do in exchange was to hand over their pelts, especially the beaver pelts.

The Indians wanted iron goods, particularly axes and kettles. They did not realize that soon they would be spending most of their time hunting for beaver to trade for the things they wanted. They kept wanting more and more blankets, food, and guns. All of these things wore out, were lost, were used up, or were buried with the dead, for use in the next world. Replacements were needed, and all it took were beaver skins. As one Montagnais chief told a priest, "The Beaver does everything perfectly well, it makes kettles, hatchets, swords, knives, bread; and in short, it makes everything."[2]

It wasn't long before the Indians came to depend on the European trade goods, and on the beaver, who "makes everything." They forgot how to make stone arrowheads and how to use a stone axe. They soon preferred to combine European clothing with their own skin and fur styles, using blankets for cloaks and feeling proud of their French hats. They learned to enjoy the convenience and taste of European foods, losing some of the old skills of farming and obtaining their own food.

There were times when the Indians must have regretted ever seeing the Europeans and their marvellous trade goods. Times when mothers watched their children die of European diseases. Times when wives watched their husbands prepare to go to war for a few more furs. Times when children watched their fathers being carried home wounded in a fight over the white trader's brandy. But the clock could never be turned back.

Thousands of Indians died of measles, influenza, smallpox, or dysentery. These diseases spread through their villages in epidemics, affecting most of the population. They were brought by the Europeans who came in contact with the Indians. Death resulted because no Indian had developed any immunity to these "imported" diseases. The results were disastrous.

1. List the trade goods that the Indians preferred.
2. List five changes to the Indian way of life that resulted from the fur trade. Choose one that you feel was beneficial to the Indians, and explain your choice. Choose one that was not beneficial and explain why.
3. Explain why the Indians could not "turn back the clock" and return to their old way of doing things.

What did the French learn from the Indians?
— food: meat, eels, blueberries, maple syrup, corn, beans, squash, pumpkins
— birch-bark canoes
— woodcraft techniques
— sled, toboggan, snowshoes
— moccasins
— clothing (leggings, fur robes)
— games, dances
— methods of warfare
— some medicinal herbs
— tobacco for smoking

Which of these items do you think would have been most beneficial to the French? Put the items listed in order of importance to the French; then explain your first and last choices.

Fur Trading, Indian Style

The fur trade divided the participating Indians according to their different jobs in the trading cycle. The hunting tribes were generally those farthest from the centres of trade at Tadoussac, Quebec, Trois-Rivières, and Montreal. Their furs were traded not to the French, but to other Indians.

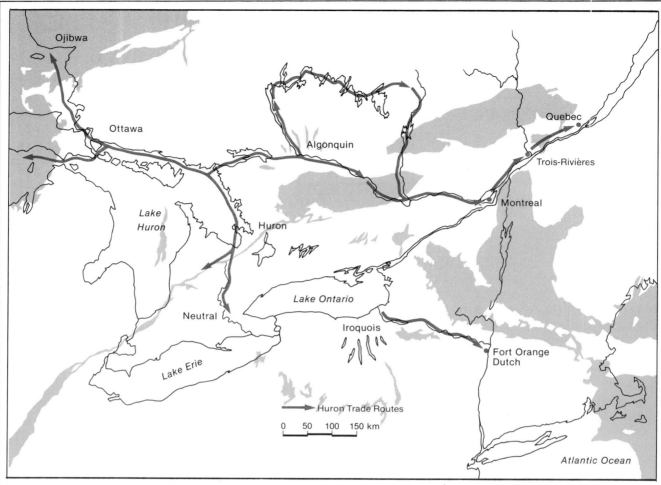

Ojibwa

Ottawa

Algonquin

Quebec

Trois-Rivières

Lake
Huron

Huron

Montreal

Neutral

Lake Ontario

Iroquois

Lake Erie

Fort Orange
Dutch

Huron Trade Routes

0   50   100   150 km

Atlantic Ocean

These had the most prestigious role—they were in the "middle" between the hunters and the Europeans, dealing with both. These Indians also had the job that brought them most often into conflict. Raids, ambushes, and wars became frequent.

Place the "middle" Indians in your fur-trade diagram (p. 86).

Hurons and Iroquois: Trouble for New France

The necessary conditions for being successful "middle" traders were met by two ancient rivals, the Hurons and the Iroquois. They had a good food supply—corn grown in their fields supplied the canoeists. They were intelligent traders, unafraid to travel hundreds of kilometres in their fragile birch-bark canoes searching for tribes that needed their trade goods. Their rivalry in the race for more beaver pelts led from small raiding parties lying in ambush to all-out war. The five Iroquois nations lived south of the Great Lakes, where good pelts were scarce. They needed the furs carried by the Huron fleets.

Marie de l'Incarnation, the Ursuline Mother Superior at Quebec, explained the situation:

Their [the Iroquois's] intention is to remain alone in all these regions, so they may have all the beasts for food and the skins to give to the Hollanders [Dutch]. It is not that they love the Hollanders, but that they need someone by whose means they can obtain what they need from Europe; and as the Hollanders are closer to them, they trade with them more easily.[3]

Seigniorial forts such as Fort Rémy at Lachine provided protection for settlers in the midst of the guerrilla warfare that raged around them. Suggest uses for the buildings and fortifications as numbered.

The Hollanders, or the Dutch, had an important fur-trading post at Fort Orange, now Albany, New York. The Iroquois were their closest trading partners.

The Iroquois aim was to paddle their fleets of canoes to Fort Orange loaded to the gunwales with furs from north of the Great Lakes. They were desperate for the furs of the Huron trading area.

Because the Hurons and French were partners, Iroquois warriors were a constant menace to the French settlers for many years. This served to keep the population of New France from increasing. Montreal was an easy target, especially after the Iroquois had destroyed their Huron enemies in the years between 1640 and 1650.

A Jesuit priest described Iroquois warfare: "They come like foxes. They attack like lions. They take flight like birds."[4] An Iroquois brave would hide for hours, waiting for a chance to end the life of a settler working in his fields or paddling along the river. Large war parties in fleets of canoes posed a serious threat to the colony's existence, forcing the settlers to take shelter in the fortified towns. It was a long **guerrilla war** that faced the people of New France.

Until peace could be achieved, New France could never grow, and the dreams of Champlain, the Jesuits, and all those who wished to build a thriving, strong colony would never be realized.

1. Why would the Hurons and Iroquois want to be "middle" traders?
2. Why did Iroquois raiders attack New France? What advantages would guerrilla warfare have for the Iroquois? What disadvantages would there be for settlers?

guerrilla war: an irregular war waged by small groups, not large armies

Adam Dollard's defence of his crumbling palisade has caught this artist's imagination. What point in the battle at the Long Sault is being illustrated? What happened next?

Dollard at the Long Sault

The Iroquois bullets thudded into the logs in front of Adam Dollard. He knew how flimsy their defences were. How much longer could they last? He and his 16 French friends and their few Algonquin and Huron allies faced an army of 800 determined Iroquois fighters.

Seven days had gone by since they had sought shelter behind the palisade of this crumbling fort. Seven days of constant gunfire, war whoops, and death. Seven days of nagging thirst, deadening fatigue, and terror.

Adam knew that no help was coming. There was no escape. The Iroquois had smashed the Canadians' canoes. He and his followers must fight to the last person, or force their Iroquois attackers to get back into their canoes and leave.

He tried to think. The noise and smoke clouded his brain. If only he had some grenades. His eyes spotted a large hand gun. Grabbing the musket, he crammed it full of powder, shoved in a fuse, and lit it. This would save the Canadian fighters, and save Montreal, too.

Adam lifted his homemade grenade to throw it over the shaky wall. Why wouldn't it go over? The grenade fell back inside the palisade.

The explosion was deafening. The battle was soon over. Many of Adam's men were killed by the grenade. The rest were quickly finished off by the expert Iroquois fighters who crashed through the smashed palisade wall.

What Had This Battle Been About?

Adam Dollard's battle at the Long Sault in 1660 is a legend in Canadian history, a heroic story of a few brave men who fought an army. Their story was first told by one of Adam's allies, who escaped and reached Montreal.

When Montrealers heard the news, they were thankful for the brave sacrifice made by Dollard and his followers. They felt that this battle had given the Iroquois something to think about before they decided to attack New France again. If 17 Canadians and 4 Indians could hold off 800 Iroquois for seven days, what might an army of them do? The Iroquois returned to their villages. One-third of the braves would never fight again. Adam Dollard had saved the colony, at least temporarily.

1. What might have happened if Adam Dollard's homemade grenade had worked? Write a different ending to the story.
2. Was Adam Dollard a hero? What is a hero?

A French artist in the 1700s portrayed this Iroquois warrior ready for battle. What weapons will the warrior use?

STE. MARIE AMONG THE HURONS

In 1635 pioneering Jesuit missionaries began their work in Huronia. They lived in the Huron villages and struggled to convert the Indians to Christianity. Their efforts met with many obstacles.

HURON WARRIOR:
Why must these **Blackrobes** continue to bother us? They speak of their God. We have our own gods.

CHRISTIAN HURON:
Their God is kind and brave. So are the Blackrobes. They care for our sick and are unafraid to face all dangers, even death. After death, they say their Heaven is a happy place.

HURON WARRIOR:
Why should we listen to these weaklings? They don't hunt or fish or fight our enemies. They have no guns. They have no wives. They aren't like real men. Our shamans are right. We should drive the Blackrobes from the longhouses. Their prayers put spells on us. They make the fish swim from our nets.

CHRISTIAN HURON:
Spells cannot bring good crops or good hunting. Ask the Blackrobes' God for help. If you accept their teaching, the French will trade their guns for our furs. Then the hunting will go well.

HURON WARRIOR:
The Blackrobes speak of their Hell. We're filled with fear when they tell of this fiery place. We know the French have sent them among us to frighten our people and kill us with their powerful magic. We have seen

Blackrobes: Jesuit priests

Huronia

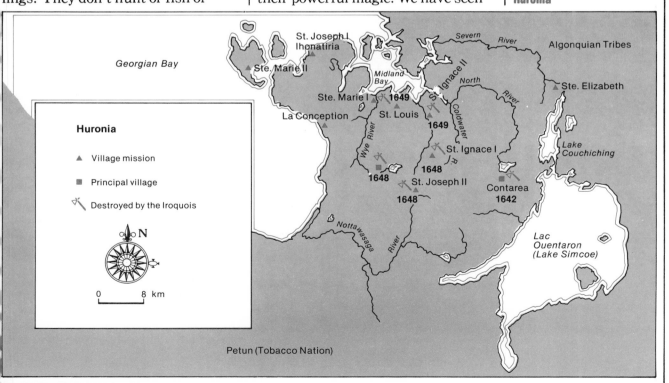

Huronia

- ▲ Village mission
- ■ Principal village
- ⚔ Destroyed by the Iroquois

N

0   8 km

Georgian Bay

St. Joseph I.
Ihonatiria
Ste. Marie II
Severn River
Algonquian Tribes
Midland Bay
St. Ignace II
North
Ste. Marie I   **1649**
La Conception
St. Louis
1649
Coldwater River
Ste. Elizabeth
St. Ignace I
1648
Wye River
1648
St. Joseph II
1648
Contarea
1642
Lake Couchiching
Nottawasaga River
Lac Ouentaron
(Lake Simcoe)

Petun (Tobacco Nation)

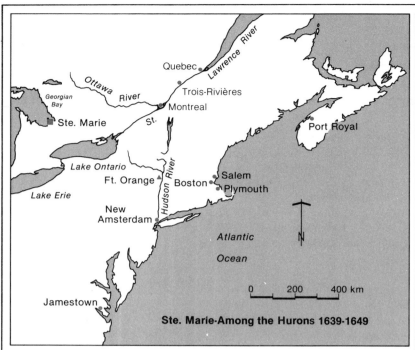

Quebec
Lawrence River
Ottawa River
Georgian Bay
Trois-Rivières
Montreal
Ste. Marie
St.
Port Royal
Lake Ontario
Ft. Orange
Hudson River
Boston
Salem
Plymouth
Lake Erie
New Amsterdam
Atlantic Ocean
N

0   200   400 km

Jamestown

Ste. Marie-Among the Hurons 1639-1649

Ste. Marie in Huronia was 1300 km from the capital of New France. The route by canoe from Quebec to Ste. Marie was long and difficult. Find and name the bodies of water used by the Huron paddlers on their trips between Huronia and Quebec.

sagamité: thick soup made with corn

Huron shamans feared the power of the Jesuits over their people. This dancing shaman performs inside a longhouse. What feelings would this mask generate among those watching?

their spells at work. Not one long-house has been spared. Their sickness has touched every family. We have all seen our children die after the chanting of the Blackrobes. We should drive them away.

1. What reasons does the Huron warrior give for not welcoming the Black-

robes and their religion? List at least five
2. What reasons might the Huron shamans have for wanting to protect their people from the Blackrobes?

There is another side to the story. The Jesuits have their version. ...

From A Jesuit's Journal
1635 The first of our brave fathers have begun to work among the Huron people, at St. Joseph mission. God chose this work for us. Our suffering reminds us that we do God's work. St Joseph is 1300 km from Quebec, deep in the Huron country.

It is difficult for the fathers to reach the Huron mission. The Indian canoe-ists treat them very roughly, forcing them to sit motionless in the canoes for hours, making them sleep on the bare rocks at night, and providing only a bit of **sagamité** for meals. The fathers know nothing of the Huron language at first. They have trouble communicating with the villagers once they arrive in Huronia.

They must live in the Huron cabins filled as they are with smoke, dogs, and hostile people. The food is strange to the fathers, and is often in short supply. The suffering seems greater when the fathers have no one with whom to share their ordeals. Their problems are worst when the Huron shamans are active, for these men always work to drive out or kill the fathers.

1639 Our mission station at Ste. Marie is nearly complete. The large chapel, the hospital, barns, the canal, the sturdy log palisades, and the houses for our sixty faithful French Christians are now a reality.

The fathers have a place to come for companionship and rest before returning to their missions. Our gardens and the cattle, chickens, and pigs we have brought by canoe from Quebec, will provide food for us and our Huron Christians.

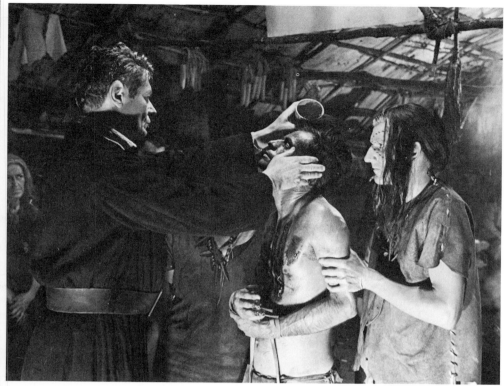

This Indian's baptism by a Jesuit priest (taken from a modern film) makes him part of a select group — the Christian Hurons. What reasons might he have had for choosing to become a Christian?

1640 The fathers have faced many trials as they work among the Hurons in their villages. Their task is always made more difficult by the shamans. But the fathers are learning to deal with the shamans. When God answers their prayers for rain or good hunting, the Indians are more ready to believe in them.

Our work progresses. We have baptized many Hurons, especially those who are dying because of the epidemics which have struck every village.

1648 We have heard the news of Father Daniel's glorious death at the hands of the Iroquois. His death came while he prayed and baptized many of the villagers at St. Joseph mission as they perished in the murderous attack. The villages were burned to the ground. Hundreds of Hurons were killed.

1649 The Iroquois raiders continue to spread death and terror among the Hurons. Over 3000 have left their villages for the shelter, food, and hospital care at Ste. Marie. We have provided a safe harbour in a sea of Iroquois warriors. Many hundreds have turned to God in this disastrous time.

The deaths of Fathers Brébeuf and Lalement have sent two more holy **martyrs** to God.

The smoke rising into the spring sky from the burning Huron villages can be seen here at Ste. Marie. More terror fills the hearts of our Hurons as survivors from the ruined villages trickle in through our gates.

1650 One winter here at Ste. Marie II on St. Joseph Island has brought us further agonies. We were all filled with sorrow as we burned our beautiful Ste. Marie I. Then we embarked with three hundred Christian Huron families to winter here. Our winter was disastrous, for food was scarce and disease struck hard. Too many have died—over half of the 8000 who first came here.

We have decided to leave this place, and travel to Quebec as best we can. We will provide there a shelter for our

martyr: someone who chooses to suffer or die for a belief

An artist's version of the martyrdom of all the Black-robes (Jesuits) killed by the Iroquois over a period of years. Describe the priests as pictured here. What qualities do they seem to have that would have impressed the Iroquois? What inaccuracies or exaggeration might be there?

remaining Hurons. Many have left the ashes of their villages, some to join their Neutral and Tobacco neighbours, others fleeing farther west or siding with the Iroquois. The land of the Hurons is empty.

1. What problems did the priests face in the first few years of their mission?
2. Why was Ste. Marie built? Why was it burnt to the ground?
3. The Huron refugees who crowded into Ste. Marie in 1649 shared much with present-day refugees. Prepare a brief report comparing a Huron refugee and a twentieth-century counterpart.
4. The Jesuit martyrs were glad to die serving their God. Find evidence in the Jesuit journal to support this statement.
5. Explain why the Jesuit fathers decided to move back to Quebec with the remaining Hurons.

Christian Hurons had their own story. ...

A Christian Huron's Tale
1645 A Christian Huron faces problems. Our people don't understand that we have put aside the old ways.

They fear that we will take away their luck in the hunt. They persecute us, beating some who have chosen the Blackrobes' ways. We must be brave and obey the teachings of the Blackrobes.
1649 The courage of the Blackrobes

Jesuit mission of Ste. Marie among the Hurons. Locate and name as many buildings and features of the mission as possible.

Canada's first canal was built at Ste. Marie to permit canoes to pass from the Wye River into the mission. Why did the builders go to the trouble of constructing this canal?

Would Ste. Marie have been well protected from an attack?

Hurons who came to Ste. Marie could stay in this guest longhouse. Fuel, food, and friendly surroundings made their stay comfortable.

The Jesuits' chapel at Ste. Marie was an important building for the missionaries. What are the men doing?

has helped us to face our attackers. Our villages are quickly disappearing. Our enemies surround and destroy us.

1650 The long journey from our fires to the white man's villages has ended here at this place the Blackrobes call the Île d'Orléans. They have given us longhouses, food, kettles, clothing, and care.

1656 We have moved our village to a new place near the French town, Quebec. Our Iroquois enemies attacked our island home, killing many of our people.

We are now nothing. Our people have been killed by the diseases of the Europeans and the tomahawks and bullets of the Iroquois. Our villages have been destroyed by fire, our people scattered like the milkweed scatters her seeds.

The Hurons who became Christians faced special problems because of what had come with the Jesuits to Huronia—disease, death, and a fur-trade war. Christian Hurons were often treated cruelly in their villages, and faced harassment from their families and neighbours. They received better treatment from the Blackrobes.

Inside the mission station at Ste. Marie was a special compound for Huron Christians. It provided a chapel, housing, and a large hospital. Here visiting Hurons could cook their own meals, sleep in a familiar long-house, and carry on as they did in their own villages. They received medical and spiritual care from the Blackrobes.

1. Why would the Hurons persecute those who had become converts to Christianity?

2. How did the Jesuits try to make visiting Hurons feel at home? Why would they do this?

From an Archeologist's Notebook

1948

—big chance to search for clues about mission at Ste. Marie—what will we uncover?
—tool house now ready—trowels, shovels, whisks, screens, stakes
—tasks: 1. survey site—divide site into three-metre squares marked by stakes
   2. remove all topsoil block by block
   3. level and clean soil in each block, looking for clues
   4. make charts, sketches, maps, photos, diagrams of materials found

1952

—many exciting finds—soil of Ste. Marie is a gold mine of information
—crews have uncovered:
   1. double-palisade wall around mission—post moulds show this
   2. two stone bastions for defence
—buildings—European compound:
   1. barn and stables—urine and manure mixed with soil prove this
   2. cook house—cellar full of bones of fish, cows, chickens; also eggshells, grape seeds show food prepared here
   3. chapel—clues were H-shaped stone structure (altar base?) also prayer beads
   4. carpenter shop—many nails, wood chips
   5. blacksmith shop—locks, keys, nails
   6. canal with locks—exciting find
—Indian compound, separated from European compound by palisade:
   1. cemetery contains graves of one European killed by a hatchet, twenty Indians
   2. Indian church, hospital, longhouse for visiting Hurons

1965

—Ste. Marie will live again—reconstruction beginning, permission and funding settled
—researchers looking in archives, libraries, documents for clues to the past—new Ste. Marie must be authentic
—we can now build an accurate reproduction

1980

—visitors go back in time on entering Ste. Marie, an authentic recreation of the original mission—history lives
—building crews followed ancient methods to create new Ste. Marie as accurately as possible
—a proud achievement

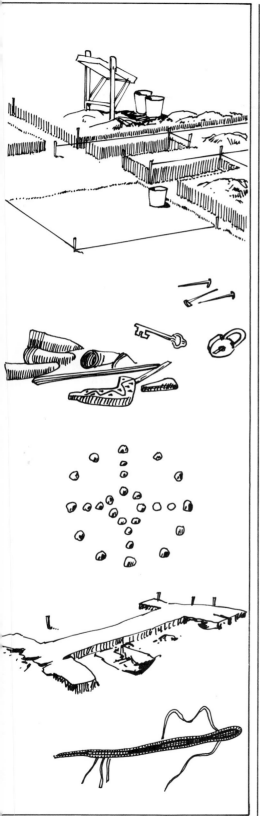

From an Archeologist's Notebook

1. List and sketch some of the clues used by the archeologists at Ste. Marie.
2. What "clues to the past" might be found in archives and libraries? Why would these be needed for the rebuilding of Ste. Marie?
3. Make a flow chart telling the story of Huronia and Ste. Marie. Begin before the arrival of Champlain. End in 1980.
4. What do you consider to be the causes of the destruction of Huronia? Could it have been prevented? How?

By 1660 the few colonists of New France wondered if their tiny settlements would ever grow. They were desperately in need of more settlers and an end to the fighting with the Iroquois. This imaginary poster shows the colonists' feelings.

We the people of
NEW FRANCE
need
HELP
Send more
COLONISTS
Send
SOLDIERS
to defend us
Make
PEACE
with the Iroquois

SAVE OUR COLONY

In 1660-61 there was a constant feeling that at any moment everyone might pack up and go back to France.[1]

Part 4

Chapter 18

LIFE IN NEW FRANCE, 1663-1713
A COLONY IN TROUBLE

New France needed help. The tiny colony of Canada on the banks of the St. Lawrence was dwarfed by its problems. There weren't enough people to fend off the attacks of the Iroquois. Food and other necessities had to be brought from France. A few storms or pirates on the Atlantic could mean severe hardship for the settlers if ships carrying supplies were sunk or captured. In Acadia the French colonists were ruled by England. It was clear that something had to change, or the story of New France would be a very short one.

The dense forests of the wilderness had been pushed back from the river's edge for a few kilometres above and below the town of Quebec. On the heights stood the largest buildings of the colony: the governor's palace and fort, the Jesuit College, the Ursuline nuns' convent, and the Hôtel-Dieu hospital. Far below, along the edge of the St. Lawrence and St. Charles rivers, were the homes and warehouses of the Lower Town.

A traveller wishing to paddle to the two other settled areas of New France, near Trois-Rivières and Montreal, had to be very cautious. Iroquois warriors lay in ambush along the river, Canada's only "highway." Montreal and Trois-Rivières were both small, lonely settlements in a sea of hardwood forests. Each village contained a few homes, a mill, and a fur warehouse, inside a small fort. And all around lay the forest.

A King's Dream

Louis XIV was a determined man. He wanted to be the ruler of the most powerful and exciting nation in the world. He felt that colonies would help him achieve the wealth and power that he wanted for France. He was more than interested in the cries for help coming from New France—he was prepared to act. Louis conferred with his hard-working minister, Jean-Baptiste Colbert. It was agreed that Canada would become a royal province of France. Thus the colony could receive all of the aid and attention needed to make it a healthy part of Louis's kingdom.

Colbert was Louis XIV's most important adviser. His plans for New France resulted in many changes and improvements in the colony.

Earthquake!

Used to attacks from the Iroquois, New France was unprepared for nature to strike a blow. In February 1663, an earthquake rocked the whole St. Lawrence valley. Mère Marie de l'Incarnation describes its effect on the convent at Quebec:

The day was calm and still when we heard a fearful rumbling as if hundreds of carts were rattling wildly over the cobbles. A horrifying sound as of rushing waters assailed our ears from under our feet, from over our heads, and all around us. In the granaries and in our rooms a sound like a shower of stones on the roofs. ... Clouds of dust swirled through the air. Doors banged open and shut. Church bells and clock chimes rang of themselves. Bell towers and houses swayed like trees in a storm and inside confusion reigned as chairs and tables toppled over, the walls cracked open and stones fell out of them, floors split, and the animals ran howling in and out of the house.

"All the woods are drunken!" cried the Indians as the forest turned into a tangled jungle of fallen trees. They fired their guns wildly in the air to frighten away the souls of the dead who they thought had caused this havoc. Landslides poured into the St. Lawrence; the rocks and clay turned it white and made it unfit to drink. An entire hill near Tadoussac sank into the water before the astonished eyes of some fishermen, to come up again as an island. *The end of the world is at hand!* flashed into everyone's mind, and a wave of religious fervour took

hold. Springs dried up, rivers ceased to flow, and streams changed their course as the tremors continued into the summer.

By September, both the shocks and the fears subsided and the atmosphere of calm returned. ...[1]

Modern experts have calculated that the earthquake that struck New France in 1663 was at least as powerful as the one that destroyed San Francisco in 1906. Since then at least thirteen severe earthquakes have occurred in the St. Lawrence valley. This makes it among the high-earthquake-risk zones of the world.

1. List five effects of the earthquake.
2. Whom did the Indians blame for the earthquake? Why?

The panic and terror on the faces of these pioneers of New France reflects their feelings about the earthquakes that struck the colony in 1663.

In 1663 Louis XIV and Colbert began the chain of events that started the growth of New France. It developed from a few scattered specks of settlement along the St. Lawrence to a thriving colony of 65 000 people who claimed nearly half of North America for France. The first chapter in this story began with the appointment of a new government for Canada.

Government in New France

The colony's government consisted of a group of men whose job it was to carry out the king's orders. He regarded the colony as part of his family, and ordered his officials to do their best to make New France a happy, industrious, peaceful place.

habitant: a French Canadian farmer

GOVERNMENT OF NEW FRANCE

King

Minister

Governor-General   Sovereign Council   Intendant

Local Governors   Governor-General

Intendant

Bishop

Councillors (up to twelve)

Make charts like this to show the governments of your community, province, country.

The ships swept up to the docks of Quebec with a flourish. It was 1665. All that summer and early autumn, ships had been arriving, filled with exciting cargo—food, building materials, and especially people. From France had come settlers, soldiers, and now these official-looking men. Men wearing gorgeous brocade coats, wide-brimmed hats, lace-trimmed shirts, and knee-high boots stepped down the gangways and onto Canadian soil. They were met by a quiet but enthusiastic crowd—curious **habitants,** children, smiling nuns, priests in long black coats, and a thin-faced man in a bishop's robe. This was Bishop Laval. All welcomed the new arrivals.

At last Canada would be safe and strong, for King Louis had sent the men to build up the colony. Who were these men?

The Governor-General

The most important official in New France was the governor-general. Most of the governors the king sent from France were military officers. There was a good reason for this: the governor's job was to defend the colony against attack and to handle the colony's relations with the Indians. Montreal, Trois-Rivières, and Acadia each had a governor who was responsible to the governor-general at Quebec. He was the king's representative, and lived in the impressive Château Saint-Louis.

The first job facing each governor was to ensure that the colony was safe. In many cases this meant that forts had to be built. It often meant leading expeditions of French soldiers and Canadian militia against the Iroquois. The governor also appeared in a very prominent role when peace talks were being held. Here is one historian's description of such a peace conference, at which Governor Frontenac met a group of Iroquois chiefs:

Frontenac's aim was to dazzle the Iroquois. Sixty solemn-faced sachems [chiefs] walked in procession between the rows of stiff-backed soldiers towards Frontenac's pavilion. Suspicion and awe mingled in their faces, for they were approaching a breathtaking sight: Frontenac, wearing a long curly wig, a plumed hat, and a gorgeous suit, was seated on a gilded chair like an emperor.[2]

1. List the governor-general's duties.
2. Why would Governor Frontenac put on such a show for the Iroquois?

Bishop Laval greets New France's first governor-general, the Marquis de Tracy at Quebec. Why would so many of the colonists wish to be present at this historic event?

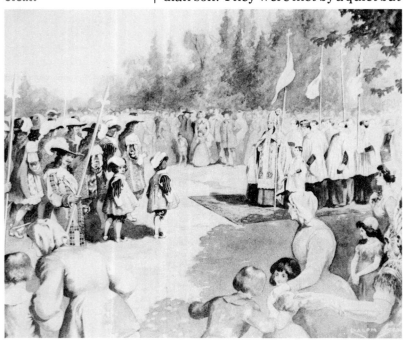

Frontenac

One of the most colourful of Canada's early governors was Louis de Buade, Count Frontenac. He arrived at Quebec in 1672 to begin the first of two terms as governor. This impressive governor was also a fighting governor. He managed to fight with just about everybody in Canada—the bishop, the intendant, the Jesuits, and the Iroquois.

Frontenac was a soldier with a high opinion of himself. He couldn't seem to co-operate with the other officials in New France and was threatened more than once by the king. He built Fort Frontenac (at Kingston) to make some money for himself by fur trading. This made him very unpopular with the fur traders of Montreal. He quarrelled with Bishop Laval about trading brandy to Indians. The king agreed with the bishop that this trade was not a good idea.

Frontenac was recalled to France in 1682 but was sent back seven years later. Conditions were bad in the colony. People were tired of the Iroquois raids. Louis knew he could depend on the count to make the Iroquois accept peace. Louis was right. New France had peace in 1701, thanks to Frontenac.

1. Why would the Montreal fur traders be angry about Frontenac's fur fort?
2. What reasons might the Iroquois have had for wanting peace with the French?

Frontenac was not intimidated by invaders from Boston. The envoy pictured here demanded the surrender of New France in 1690. Frontenac's answer? "I have no reply to make to your general other than from the mouths of my cannon and muskets."

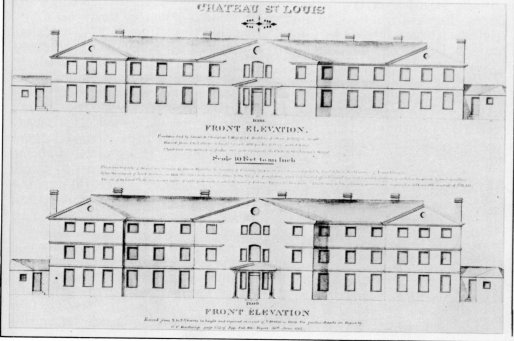

The governor-general's palace at Quebec, the Château Saint-Louis, was begun by Champlain. Other governors made improvements to this important building on the heights at Quebec.

Jean Talon's instructions from Colbert and Louis XIV included orders to visit the homes of all settlers in New France. What would he learn from such visits? How do citizens make their concerns known to governments today?

barque: riverboat with sails and oars, used for freight

Talon's plans for Canadian industry were ambitious. New France's shipyards were the construction site for barques, timber ships called "flûtes," and other large merchant ships.

The Intendant

The busiest man in New France was the intendant. The job of this official was to act as a manager of the colony. He looked after law and order, prices, financial matters, industry, trade, and justice. It was a very important job. Deputies in the three towns helped him. There were surveyors, harbour managers, and road inspectors. The intendant was expected to visit the habitants each year so that he could listen to their complaints and find ways of helping them.

The "Great Intendant," Jean Talon, arrived at Quebec in 1665. For the next three years he worked tirelessly to make New France grow. An ambitious man with a good imagination, Talon had big plans for New France. He felt that the colony needed people, especially women, so he dreamed up an unusual plan. His idea was to bring single women from France to marry the men of New France. He wouldn't let the men go hunting or trading until all of the women were engaged or married. It worked.

Talon had other ways of increasing the population. He began the first baby bonuses to reward parents who had large families. Canadians who married young were also rewarded. A sixteen-year-old bride received a gift of money from the king.

Jean Talon had other plans for New France. He wanted to build up some industries so the colony wouldn't have to depend on France for everything. He helped set up sealing and whaling businesses, and had lumber mills constructed. He had ship masts cut and sent to France. Tar and hemp were produced. An iron foundry was opened. Shipbuilding was begun, as were brewing beer and making shoes. When Talon returned to France in 1672, he could feel pleased with his achievement. He didn't know that the industries he had begun would be only partly successful.

Iroquois attacks were a constant problem in New France in the seventeenth century. Talon felt that settlers would find it easier to defend themselves if they lived in compact villages. He designed and started three "round villages." The buildings were in the centre. The fields radiated out from them like spokes on a wheel. Unfortunately, the Canadians didn't like Talon's idea or his villages. They all wanted some land along the banks of a river.

1. List the industries begun by Talon.
2. Why did Talon go to the trouble of starting industries when the goods New France needed could be obtained elsewhere?

Les Filles du Roi

Jeanne's eyes were wide with amazement. Such a beautiful river. And the town was unlike anything she'd ever seen. Her feet ached from walking up the rough path to the top of the cliff. Quebec. Who would ever have believed her if she'd said that one day she'd be in Quebec?

She felt specially chosen. After spending nearly all of her eighteen years with the nuns in an orphanage, she'd expected to become a nun herself. Then the king's letter had arrived. Any healthy women who wanted to go to Quebec could do so. She couldn't let such a chance go by. And the king's gifts were so lovely and useful—land in Canada, clothing, money, and her passage on the ship. And here she was.

A friendly nun took her small bag of clothing and led Jeanne to a little bedroom. Here she would stay till tomorrow. Then the women (ninety-two had been on her ship) would get a chance to meet the Canadian men—the men who were looking for wives. It would be very exciting. And frightening.

Jeanne wondered if she'd made a mistake in coming to New France. Marriage. And a new life in a strange, wild land.

The idea of the **"filles du roi"** was very successful. Many marriages resulted, and the settled areas grew larger as these new families began to farm the land Talon had cleared for them.

1. What incentives were used to persuade young women to go to Quebec?
2. Why might Jeanne be both excited and frightened about the future?

filles du roi: daughters of the king — women brought to marry Canadians

Jean Talon welcomes the "filles du roi" to Canada. Many young women accepted the king's challenge to pioneer in New France. The families they began were the foundation of modern Quebec.

Bishop Laval was one of New France's most prominent men. He was the religious leader of the colony from 1675 to 1688.

The Bishop

Religion had always been important in New France. The bishop of Quebec was a very influential man. He was a member of the Sovereign Council, and the religious and moral leader of the colony.

The first bishop of Quebec was François de Laval. He took an interest in everything that went on in the colony. He was particularly upset by the evil effects of alcohol, especially when it was traded to Indians. Fur traders used brandy to wangle good deals from Indians. They feared that if the brandy trade were cut off, the furs would go to the Dutch or English, whose rum the Indians also liked. Laval was appalled by the great suffering caused by alcohol in the Indian villages. However, nobody could stop the brandy trade.

Laval was also concerned about behaviour. He was a very strict man. Here's what he thought about dances: One may permit her [a young woman] a few honest and moderate dances but with people of her own sex only and in the presence of her mother, for fear that none too decent words and songs are used, and never in the presence of men and boys.[3]

Laval was bishop of Quebec from 1675 to 1688. He died at Quebec in 1701.

Notices to the people of New France about new regulations or special events were issued from the intendant's palace.

Complete this chart:

THE BRANDY TRADE·

Reasons for	Reasons against

The Sovereign Council

The Sovereign Council was made up of the "big three" in New France—governor, intendant, and bishop—and a group of councillors. Each Monday morning, the Council met at the intendant's residence in Quebec. The members sat around a polished oval table. They advised the governor and intendant, helped set rules for the colony, acted as a court, and worried about traffic problems (some people drove their horses too quickly). They were also concerned about market days and the high cost of food. Here are some of the regulations they passed:

1. What government or governments now do the jobs done by the Sovereign Council of New France? Who else is involved now who wasn't in New France?

2. Why would regulations such as these be necessary?

The Sovereign Council of New France met each week to deal with various problems. Find the bishop, secretary, and councillors in this painting.

105

Chapter 19

FUR TRADERS GO WEST

The king and Colbert thought that New France should remain a small area along the St. Lawrence River. They wanted some Canadians to be farmers, and others to work in industries and service jobs in the towns. They wanted to see carpenters, merchants, and shoemakers at work. They decided to license only a few men to trade at the fur fairs held each year in Montreal.

A fur fair was an exciting event. Huge fleets of canoes (up to 500 of them) filled with furs and Indians eager to trade arrived at Montreal each year. After the governor-general and the chiefs had made their speeches and smoked their pipes, the trading began. Feasting, dancing, singing, and gambling always accompanied the fairs. They were discontinued after more and more traders began to go out

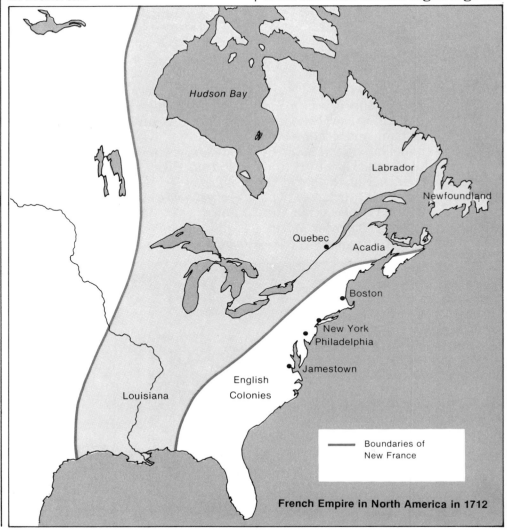

Hudson Bay

Labrador

Newfoundland

Quebec

Acadia

Boston

New York
Philadelphia

Jamestown

Louisiana

English
Colonies

——— Boundaries of
New France

French Empire in North America in 1712

The Montreal fur fairs were turbulent events. The trading couldn't begin until gifts had been exchanged between the governor and the trading chiefs. Why would the trading take place outside the palisade walls of the fort at Montreal?

to the wilderness in search of furs. The Indians soon realized that they could save themselves a lot of paddling if they waited in their villages for the Canadians to come to them for furs.

The traders who travelled all across North America, exploring the rivers and lakes, searching for adventure and furs, were called **coureurs de bois.** Anyone with a canoe, a strong back, and some trade goods was free to become a trader. These men claimed all of the interior of North America, from Hudson Bay to the Gulf of Mexico, as their territory.

The Canadian coureurs de bois met others trading in the North and West: the Iroquois and the English. Everybody wanted the same furs. Competition was fierce. Soon fur forts spread across the pays d'en haut. This was the country "beyond Quebec." New France by 1700 meant over half of North America. It was 10 000 000 km² of land, or about twenty times as big as France. It was not at all the kind of colony that Louis XIV and Colbert had intended New France to be.

Here's what Louis XIV wrote to Governor Frontenac:

It is far more worthwhile to occupy a smaller area and have it well populated than to spread out and have several feeble colonies.[1]

The coureurs de bois did not agree. They wanted to spread New France all across the map. They did not appreciate the king's efforts to control the fur trade by issuing licences. Those who were unlicensed ignored the whole procedure.

1. How did the coureurs de bois enlarge the area of New France?
2. What conflict was there between the king and the coureurs de bois?
3. Write a newspaper story about a fur fair.

coureurs de bois: woodsmen

The Demand for Furs

The demand for furs in Europe was going up. Furs such as ermine, fox, otter, and marten were used for trim on the clothing of the very rich. Beaver pelts were needed for the stylish hats worn by all who could afford them.

It was from forts such as Fort Frontenac that the coureurs de bois set out on their trading voyages. Describe the various activities that you can identify in this picture.

Coureurs de Bois: What a Way to Make a Living

Here's what Denis Riverin, Intendant Duchesneau's secretary, said about the coureurs de bois in 1705:

Coureurs de bois are always young men in the prime of life.

Some take their own merchandise, others borrow it from merchants; some are paid workers, others form partnerships.

Since all of Canada is a vast and trackless forest, it is impossible for them to travel by land; they travel by lake and river in birch-bark canoes occupied by three men.

Three men embark at Quebec or Montreal in such a canoe to go 300 [1440 km], 400 [1920 km], and sometimes 500 leagues [2400 km] to search for beaver among Indians. Their food consists of a little biscuit, peas, corn, and a few small casks of brandy. They carry as little as possible to make room for a few bundles of merchandise. If fish and game are scarce, they are forced to eat moss that grows on rocks. They make a moss broth which is black and awful, but they would rather eat it than die of starvation. If they have nothing to eat, they will resort to the moccasins....

In winter, the coureurs travelled through the frozen wilderness on

A coureur de bois. What are his clothes made of?

A group of fur traders camps for the night, their day's work over. Write the story of one of these adventurers in diary or short-story form.

snowshoes, endlessly searching for furs. Riverin wasn't too impressed by the coureurs du bois:

These coureurs de bois will frequently commit a thousand **base** actions to obtain beaver from the Indians. Then they sleep, smoke, drink brandy, gamble, and spend time with the daughters of the Indians.[2]

King Louis XIV tried to keep the coureurs de bois on the farms:[3]

FUR TRADING IN THE INDIAN VILLAGES IS FORBIDDEN. VIOLATORS WILL BE FINED. THEIR FURS WILL BE CONFISCATED.

Intendant Duchesneau reported to the king:[4]

I CAN'T STOP THE COUREURS DE BOIS FROM TRADING. THERE ARE 500 OR MORE MEN TRADING RIGHT NOW. THEY WON'T STAY AND WORK ON THEIR FARMS.

Were the coureurs de bois villains? Governor Vaudreuil had another opinion:[5]

THE COUREURS ARE USEFUL TO THE COLONY. THEY ARE EXCELLENT FIGHTERS IN WAR. THEY ARE STRONG AND USED TO THE WILDERNESS. AND THEY KEEP THE INDIANS FROM TRADING WITH THE ENGLISH.

A modern historian says this about the coureurs de bois:[6]

WHEREVER A CANOE COULD GO, THESE MEN WENT... BUT THEY CHANGED THE FACE OF THE LAND HARDLY AT ALL. THEIR CANOES LEFT NO MARKS ON THE RIVERS AND THE LAKES AS THEY PASSED.

1. What things do you like about the way of life of the coureurs de bois? What do you dislike?
2. Were the coureurs de bois heroes or villains? List the evidence for each point of view.

base: mean

Fort Michilimackinac was the starting point for the French explorers who travelled down the Mississippi River to its mouth. What factors made Michilimackinac such an important place?

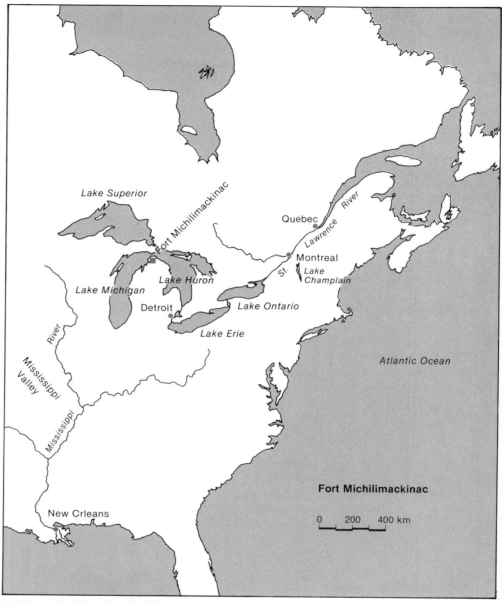

Fort Michilimackinac

0   200   400 km

Michilimackinac

The trading fort at Michilimackinac was always a very busy place in summer and fall. It was the most important post in the pays d'en haut. Situated on the strait between Lakes Huron and Michigan, it was over 1100 km west of Quebec.

Hundreds of people rushed around in a flurry of activity. There were coureurs de bois preparing to go west looking for furs, or back to Montreal with their loaded canoes. There were Indians eager to trade, soldiers from Quebec, and Indian women helping their Canadian husbands prepare for their trading trips.

Bold explorers such as Father Marquette and Louis Joliet set out from Michilimackinac. They travelled with a handful of men through country where no white man had ever been before. In 1673 Marquette and Joliet paddled south on the Mississippi River, filled with fear and wonder at the countryside they passed through.

La Salle's *Griffon*: A Great Lakes' Mystery

September 18, 1679, was a beautiful day on Green Bay. But the people on shore were worried. They watched the ship sail away toward Fort Niagara. Its hold was filled with furs. The *Griffon*'s six-man crew might be in trouble if a sudden squall hit the lake. It was the *Griffon*'s first voyage and an exciting future lay ahead. The twenty-two-metre ship had been built at Fort Niagara during the winter. It was designed to haul supplies to build a chain of forts in the Mississippi country and then return to Fort Niagara loaded with furs.

The *Griffon*'s owner, René-Robert Cavelier, Sieur de La Salle, was an adventurer. He dreamed of building a French fur-trading empire in the Mississippi country. The *Griffon* would save hundreds of kilometres of paddling. La Salle expected the *Griffon* to help make him a wealthy man.

La Salle waited impatiently for the ship's return. He expected it back before the winter snows. His coureurs de bois built a small fur fort on the Illinois River. They expected to trade there for enough furs to send the *Griffon* loaded, back again to Niagara. Soon the news came—the *Griffon* was lost. The Indians' stories were confused and full of gaps. Who knew what had happened to the ship, its crew, and its cargo of furs? La Salle named his new fur-trading post Fort **Crève-coeur**. He never saw the *Griffon* again.

Nobody ever saw the *Griffon* again—for nearly 300 years! In 1955 the keel of a very old boat, uncovered near a Georgian Bay island, was positively identified. It was the *Griffon*. La Salle's ship had been found. The story of the detective work that was involved is very exciting.

1. Why had La Salle gone to the trouble and expense of building his ship?
2. Do some detective work of your own to find out how the Griffon *was identified and what has become of its remains. A book by John MacLean called* The Fate of the Griffon *is a good place to start.*

crève-coeur: heartbreak

La Salle's crew built the Griffon during the winter of 1678-79. List the jobs being done and try to explain them. Find the priest and explain why he was there.

La Salle was a courageous explorer and an inventive fur trader, but he was not a thoughtful leader. He was shot by his men after a planned settlement far down the Mississippi failed, and La Salle had forced his crew to walk north to the Illinois country to obtain help from Canadian fur traders there.

Indians exchanged their furs for valued Hudson's Bay Company trade goods at forts such as York Factory, pictured here. Ceremonies, speeches, peace pipes, singing, and dancing preceded the actual trading. Why would the Company use red-coated soldiers to parade the trading chiefs up to the fort?

Competition for furs increased tremendously as the demand for luxury furs and beaver pelts rose in Europe. After the opening of the Hudson's Bay Company posts in 1670, conflict between the English and Canadian fur traders became constant.

The English Come to the Bay
London, 1680

A new company has been granted the right to trade for furs in North America. Fur-trading posts have been built on Hudson Bay and James Bay.

Hundreds of Indians have paddled to these forts bringing excellent furs. The Hudson's Bay Company is pleased to report that prospects look good and profits are rising as ships full of furs arrive in England.

New France Protests
Montreal, 1687

Because of the threat to the Canadian fur trade posed by the English on Hudson Bay, Governor Denonville has acted.

One hundred and five men, mostly Canadians, set out from Montreal and captured three English posts full of pelts on the shore of James Bay. The heroic Pierre Le Moyne led his men to victory over the English.

1. There was conflict between Canadian and English fur traders, and also between fur traders and settlers. Explain the conflict between fur traders and settlers.
2. List the differences between the Hudson's Bay Company's trading methods and those of the fur traders from New France.

Madeleine de Verchères: Canadian Heroine

Madeleine was just fourteen. The Iroquois attacks on the seigniory had been frequent. The fort was strong, but she had only six "troops." She was their commander-in-chief. Six troops led by a girl. Two of Madeleine's brothers, aged twelve and ten, two soldiers, an old man and a settler were her "army." The fifty Iroquois attackers were held off for a week—a week of fear, doubt, and courage. Then Madeleine gladly handed over her command to the forty soldiers who arrived to rescue the seigniory. She had saved her own life, and the lives of the men, women and children who had been sheltered inside the fort. The fur trade war had, for a week, been her war.

Pierre Le Moyne d'Iberville.

Madeleine's courageous defence of the seigniorial fort of Verchères in 1692 was an example to Iroquois and settlers alike. Who else was inside the fort but not pictured here? Explain what Madeleine's brothers are doing.

Pierre Le Moyne, Sieur d'Iberville: Canadian Hero

Pierre Le Moyne's eight brothers were all involved in building New France. Pierre was a courageous, daring soldier. He captured English forts on James Bay in several expeditions by land and sea. He led raids on the English colonies of New York, Maine, and Newfoundland. He was the leader of an expedition to Louisiana to start the town of New Orleans. His long record of service to Canada was unequalled.

What "heroism" did Madeleine de Verchères and Pierre Le Moyne display? Do many people have an opportunity to be heroic today? Explain.

Canadians in the latter part of the 1600s faced two main problems: the English who wanted their furs, and the Iroquois who harassed the settlements. Some part of New France always seemed to be at war after 1680. The two sides, French and English, were practising for the wars that would come in the middle of the eighteenth century.

Chapter 20

THIS CONTINENT IS GETTING CROWDED

The cod fisheries of the Grand Banks of Newfoundland were an important food source for Europe. The various steps involved in preparing fish for shipment are shown here. Can you identify and explain the activities of each group?

Friction All Around

The fur trade caused conflict in the area around Hudson Bay and James Bay, as Canadian and English traders battled for control. In the settled areas of New France and New England, guerrilla raiders from both sides spread terror as houses were burned and colonists were murdered.

The English Colonies

Newfoundland

Sir Humphrey Gilbert claimed Newfoundland for England in 1583, but this didn't mean for settlement, it meant for fish. The main attraction was the seemingly limitless cod fisheries. Ships from all over Europe fished

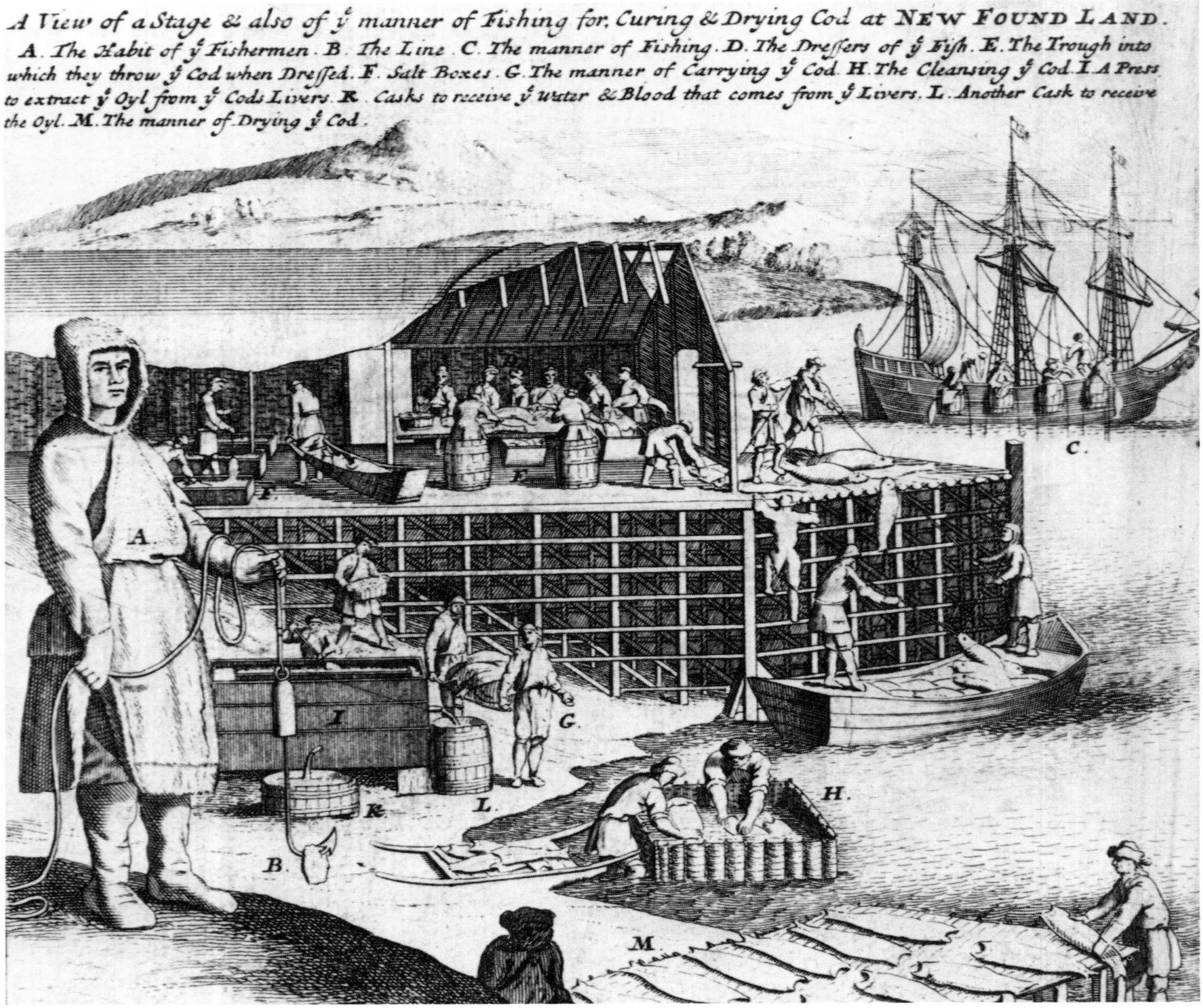

A View of a Stage & also of ÿ manner of Fishing for, Curing & Drying Cod at NEW FOUND LAND.
A. The Habit of ÿ Fishermen. B. The Line. C. The manner of Fishing. D. The Dressers of ÿ Fish. E. The Trough into which they throw ÿ Cod when Dressed. F. Salt Boxes. G. The manner of Carrying ÿ Cod. H. The Cleansing ÿ Cod. I. A Press to extract ÿ Oyl from ÿ Cods Livers. R. Casks to receive ÿ water & Blood that comes from ÿ Livers. L. Another Cask to receive the Oyl. M. The manner of Drying ÿ Cod.

"Bankers" at work off the Newfoundland coast faced many dangerous challenges, as this picture indicates. Write a diary page for one of these fishermen, describing a typical day on the Grand Banks.

there, but few respected the English territorial claims.

Settlement was discouraged. In fact, it was against the law. The shores of the rocky island were used to dry the catches of cod before they were packed in the ships to return to Europe. A few brave fishermen and their families built homes, especially around St. John's, but their homes on the island were never secure. At any time, they might be forced to leave Newfoundland.

Nova Scotia

Control of Acadia was passed back and forth many times between France and England until 1713. In that year, the mainland of Nova Scotia became English property while Cape Breton and Île Saint-Jean (Prince Edward Island) were French territory. The fortress of Halifax was begun in 1749.

Down South

The first English colony in North America was founded in 1607 at Jamestown, later called Virginia. Other colonies soon followed—Massachusetts Bay in 1620, Salem and Boston in 1628, Maryland in 1634, and Carolina in the 1660s. The Dutch colonies begun in the 1620s were captured

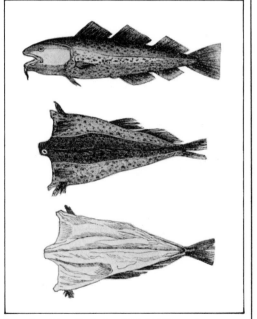

The treasure sought by European fishermen who crossed the Atlantic each year — the cod. Top: alive and well. Bottom: trimmed for salting (back and interior views).

by the English in 1664. They became New York, Pennsylvania and New Jersey. Thousands of settlers made these English colonies grow rapidly. They were prosperous farming, manufacturing, and trading centres. As the population increased, more and more settlers wanted to push westward across the Appalachian Mountains into territory claimed by English and Canadian fur traders.

Chapter 21

TOWN LIFE

When Quebeckers went to market, they often bartered for the things they wanted. Money was hard to come by. Playing cards were actually used as money! But you couldn't make your own. Each card was officially sealed and issued by the intendant.

The idea of using playing cards for money had come to Intendant Demeulle in 1685. Soldiers who relied on ships from France to bring their pay were not happy when the ships didn't arrive. The intendant's solution was "paper money": playing cards. Today Canadians are familiar with coins, paper, and "plastic" money in the form of credit cards. People in New France used their playing-card money for years. Inflation was as much a problem for them as it is for Canadians today.

Quebec, October 1682

New Governor Finds Lower Town in Ashes

As Governor La Barre walked down the ship's gangway to take up his new post, he was shocked at what lay before him. Most of the Lower Town was nothing but ashes and the blackened remains of buildings. The governor inquired about the fire.

On August 4, a fire had started in one of the warehouses. Fire-fighting equipment and methods were very poor. A bucket brigade was unable to slow the spreading fire. Fifty-five buildings, well over half of the homes and warehouses along the water's edge, were destroyed. The buildings were made of wood or had cedar shingles. This helped the fire spread rapidly. So did the habits of some Canadians who had not heeded the Council's warnings about fire prevention.

AVIS / NOTICE

to the people of

QUEBEC

The sovereign council of New France has passed the following regulations

No dumping ashes in the street

No fires outside

No carrying burning coals outside except in a covered pail

No hay outside

Chimneys must be cleaned every two months

Fire escapes are required on all large buildings

Draw a picture story to illustrate how disobeying one of these regulations could cause a serious fire.

Quebec Thirty Years Later

The streets of the Lower Town are narrow. The houses are set very close to the streets, which wind along the river banks and up towards the Heights. Houses here are made of stone. Merchants and their families live in the upper storeys of their large houses and conduct their businesses on the ground floor. Small shops and inns and large warehouses are side by side on the unpaved streets.

Market day—an exciting day to visit Lower Town. Everybody's in a hurry. The habitants have brought in their carts filled with hens, bags of flour, dried fish, cheeses, eggs, and vegetables. The careful women of Quebec walk from cart to cart, shopping for bargains. Sailors from the nearby harbour stroll through the

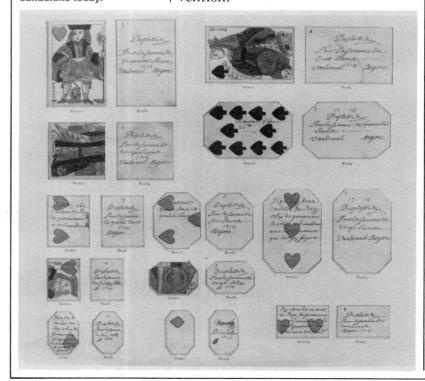

market, eager for fresh vegetables. A platoon of smartly uniformed Troupes de la Colonie marches across the market square. The Troupes are billeted with families in Quebec, since there are no barracks large enough for them. They pass in front of the famous church of Notre-Dame-des-Victoires before disappearing along a narrow street.

The soldiers then march past the homes and shops of the **artisans**. Their shops are found tucked into the side of the cliff. Here are the shoemakers, innkeepers, carpenters, stone masons, women to make a jacket, and men to build a corner cabinet. The streets here have interesting names: la Rue Sous-le-Fort, le Sault-au-Matelot, la Côte de la Montagne.

Things are different in the Upper Town. The skyline is dominated by the large stone buildings. Here is the governor's beautiful Château Saint-Louis, with its balcony facing the river. The bishop's seminary is a fine building surrounded by gardens.

Peter Kalm, a Swedish traveller, describes the Jesuit buildings in 1750:

The building the Jesuits live in is magnificent. It is built of stone and is three storeys high. Three hundred families would find enough room to live in it. There is a long corridor with rooms and apartments for the fathers. They also have a library and apothecary shop [drug store]. On the outside is their college, which is surrounded on two sides with great orchards and gardens. They eat in a large dining hall. In this spacious building you do not see a single woman.[1]

Part way down the hill is the Hôtel-Dieu hospital. Busy sisters in their white gowns care for the sick and wounded. There are many large churches in the Upper Town, all made of beautifully cut stone.

The rich and important people of New France live and work in the Upper Town. The governor, bishop, some councillors, military officers, and colonial officials are Upper Town

dwellers. Their homes are larger and more impressive than those below the cliff with their tile roofs, dormer windows, and graceful entrances. The ladies of the Upper Town dress in the most fashionable styles. Their beautiful clothing is made of lace, silks, and velvet imported from France. Their husbands dress elegantly in lace-trimmed clothes also made of fine fabrics from France. They carry swords and, of course, wear stylish beaver hats.

Market day in Quebec's Lower Town was a busy time. Locate buyers, sellers, sightseers in this artist's version.

A view of eighteenth century Quebec, from the south shore of the St. Lawrence River.

artisans: skilled workers

The Jesuit College at Quebec as it appeared in 1750. Compare this picture with Peter Kalm's description.

The Street of the Récollets in Quebec. How would a quick glance at the picture tell you the artist was in Upper Town?

Another view of life in Upper Town, Quebec. Compare this picture with the Street of the Récollets drawing. Look at: human activity, buildings, and transportation. Note similarities and differences.

1. Make a chart comparing and contrasting Upper Town and Lower Town.
2. Why were there Troupes de la Colonie in Quebec?

The most exciting time of year, and the best entertainment, was in the spring. Ships arriving from France after the long winter freeze-up brought everybody down to the harbour. They cheered, gossiped, and stared.

During the summer, Canadians went for trips on the river, rode in their carriages, raced their horses, and went on picnics. Winter was no time to sit around inside. The weather may have been so cold that words froze in the air and couldn't be heard till spring, but Canadians were used to it. They loved to travel on the frozen river in horse-drawn sleighs or on skates. Horse races on the river were exciting. And Carnival was fun for everybody.

Draw a sketch to illustrate some of the winter activities of early Canadians.

Trois-Rivières

Trois-Rivières was founded by Champlain in 1634. It grew slowly. By 1720 only about 800 people lived on the winding streets inside the palisade walls. Travellers between Quebec and Montreal usually stopped to rest at Trois-Rivières. The town had a governor and a small military force. The Récollet fathers had built a beautiful church. Nearby was a school and hospital run by the Ursuline nuns.

The people of Trois-Rivières were fur traders and merchants, canoe makers and ironworkers. The canoes made there were paddled all over North America. The Saint-Maurice ironworks, a few kilometres from town, produced pots, stoves, cannonballs and a few cannons.

Canada's first "company town" was at the Saint-Maurice forges. A traveller describes this pioneer industrial community:

The establishment is sizeable. It consists of two forges, a trip hammer and a number of buildings used as lodgings for all those connected with it.

It is now being managed on behalf of

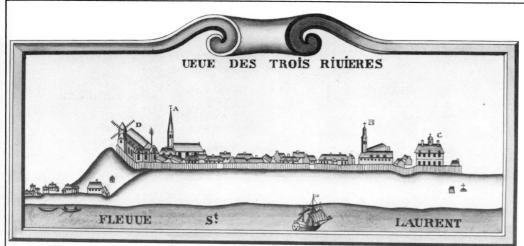

UEUE DES TROIS RIUIÈRES

FLEUUE St LAURENT

This sketch of Trois-Rivières was made around 1700. Name the groups that built and used the largest structures in the town. What similarities are there between Trois-Rivières and Quebec?

the King.

The main employees are a manager, a cashier, a shop assistant, a merchant having the right of supplying food and merchandise, and a chaplain. ...

There were problems at the forges:

Because of their scarcity, workers are generally paid very high wages. Some are paid wages according to the time of the year, but all receive housing, heating and transport at the expense of the King. Besides these resident workers, there are others who have to be lured from the villages or from the garrison in Trois-Rivières when the work load becomes heavy. The villagers refuse to come here on grounds that they must farm their land. Sometimes the work drags on and the King suffers great losses.[2]

1. What evidence is there that there was a "company town" at the Saint-Maurice forges?
2. List three problems in the operation of the forges. Why do you think the king kept the forges working?
3. Suggest reasons for the slow growth of Trois-Rivières.

Montreal

Speed Limits to Be Enforced (1749)

The intendant's latest ordinance, read today on the market square by the sheriff, warned all Montrealers that speed limits would be enforced. Reckless cart or carriage drivers, and teamsters with heavy wagons were reminded to drive their horses at a walk. The town's narrow streets and

Busy Notre-Dame Street, Montreal, as it looked in 1786. Cobblestones kept the mud down and thus pleased users of the street.

Unpaved streets on steep hills made life difficult for the teams of horses that provided transportation in the towns of New France.

What's it like inside those big impressive buildings? Here's a look at a cosy room inside the Château de Ramezay in Montreal.

busy walk ways were never meant for speeding horses. Many streets are unpaved, and potholes can injure animals driven too quickly.

Defences Necessary

The town had always needed protection from attack. During the long years of the Iroquois wars, everyone in the area was forced inside the wooden palisade that surrounded the town. Later, the threat of attack was from the New Englanders or the English. A thick stone wall was begun in 1716. High on Mount Royal, overlooking the town, was Fort Bellemont. Montreal's defences were maintained by a large number of troops and officers, commanded by the governor of the district.

A Centre for Trade

Montreal's location on the river made it an ideal spot for a fur-trade centre. Brigades of Indians brought their loads to the fur fairs held each spring for many years. After the coureurs de bois began to paddle to the West to trade, the fur fairs gradually disappeared. The furs still found their way to the warehouses on the Rue Notre-Dame. And the coureurs assembled their canoe-loads of goods at Montreal before paddling off to trade.

Explorers also used Montreal's shops to supply their expeditions before heading off into an unknown wilderness. All set out from the busy wharfs which ran along the river bank. Three main streets were parallel to the river—Saint-Paul, Notre-Dame and Saint-James.

1. *What was the main function of Montreal? Why?*
2. *In which of the towns of New France would you have chosen to live? Explain why.*

COUNTRY LIFE

Chapter 22

Patterns of Settlement

Our canoe glides swiftly through the water. Waving oarsmen on the barque ahead of us point toward the town of Quebec, high on the cliffs. We quickly pass the slow barque. Ahead are two large rafts. These **cajeux** are big enough to transport heavy loads of furs and wheat. They save a voyageur's back and cut down on the paddling.

The forest here is many **leagues** [many kilometres] from the river bank. The settlers have cleared their land and ploughed their fields. They are now ready for the seeding. The fields are long and narrow. Each one runs back from the river and ends in the tangled forest. The houses seem very close together, as if they were part of a long village street. But the river is the street.

Let's stop paddling and stay here to rest and visit with Joseph Paquin and his family. Joseph will tell us about his farm.

Joseph obtained his land from his seignior, M. Asselin. M. Asselin was given a large grant of land by the king. In return for this seigniory, M. Asselin had to promise to permit settlers to obtain a portion of this land from him. Then the settlers could clear the land and farm it. Those who failed to do this

cajeux: large freight raft

league: unit of distance about four kilometres

Some St. Lawrence settlements in 1709. The seigniorial pattern is clearly visible here: long, thin farms that front on the rivers. Talon's "round villages" are in the top central part of the map.

lost their portion of land. It went back to the seignior. Seigniors who didn't grant land lost their seigniory to the king. The seignior and censitaire each had a bargain to live up to. The seigniorial system was designed to encourage settlement in New France.

Seigniorial Rights and Duties

Who had the most burdensome duties, the seignior or the censitaire? Why would anyone want to be a seignior?

Seigniorial Rights and Duties

THE SEIGNIOR	THE CENSITAIRE
Duties	**Duties**
— swear loyalty to the king	— live on his land and farm it
— grant land for settlement	— pay rent and work three days
— build and operate a mill	a year for the seignior
— provide local courts to	— help build roads and bridges
settle disputes	for the king
— help pay for local church	
— help build roads and bridges	
Rights and Privileges	**Rights**
— special honours in church	— land to farm
— free pew in church in a prominent place	— use of the mill and seignior's court
— rent and work from censitaires	

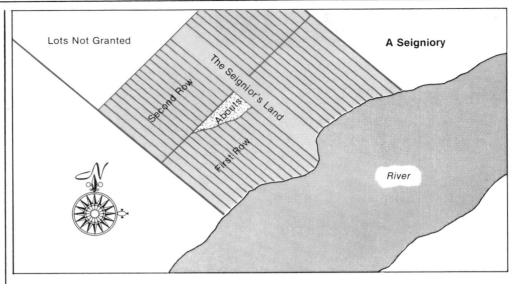

Lots Not Granted

A Seigniory

Second Row

The Seignior's Land

Abouts

First Row

N

River

chemin du roi: king's road

the Mai: May 1st celebration and rent paying

The St. Lawrence River was crossed in winter on roads built on the ice. This nineteenth-century photograph (hauling hay to market in Montreal) gives a good view of the river's function as the main highway of New France, no matter what the season. Which would be easier, transporting goods by wagon? By barque? By cajeu?

Joseph Paquin is pleased to tell us about the seigniory. He explains why the farms are long and narrow, and always at right angles to the river.

The river is our road. In summer we use canoes and barques. In winter the ice carries our sleds and toboggans. Everybody wants a piece of land on the river bank. The system has been like this since the first seigniories were granted.

For many years, we had no road at all, only a path. Now the **chemin du roi** runs past our farm. Each habitant must look after the road in front of his land. That means that my boys and I spend a few days each spring, patching the holes in the road. In winter, we must mark the roadway with stakes and keep the snowbanks flattened.

Life on the Seigniory

Here comes Louise Paquin, aged eight. She's in a big hurry to speak to her father.

"Papa, come quick! The **Mai** is ruined!"

We all jump up. What can Louise mean?

Louise explains, "The Mai is tomorrow. The mice have made a mess of the sack of wheat for M. Asselin. We'll never clean it up in time. We must pay M. Asselin the cens tomorrow." The little girl is near tears. May 1 is a very big day. She doesn't want a few mice to spoil her fun.

We all walk up the river bank toward the house. Like most of the habitant houses in Canada, the thick walls are made of stone and clay, and are whitewashed. The steep roof has a wide overhang. The small windows are made of greased paper, which lets in some light. On the end of the house is a massive stone chimney. Returning from the thatch-roofed stable are Michel, fourteen, and Jacques, ten. They have finished milking the two cows and feeding the chickens and pigs.

122

We all step into Marie-Louise's warm kitchen. By the huge fireplace sits twelve-year-old Annette, stirring the kettle that hangs by the fire. The smell is delicious. The long pine table in the centre of the room is already set with fresh bread, a large bowl of milk, and wooden plates. Annette smiles as baby Noel whoops at Jeanne, four. His cradle is in the corner. Annette puts on a mitt to carry a steaming dish to the table. It's time for supper—**tourtière** of rabbit and pork, and fish soup with bread. In a few weeks, we'll be eating tasty peas and lettuce from the garden.

"Come on children, join our guests in thanking God for this fine meal." Joseph bows his head to pray.

"What about the Mai, Papa? Can we go?" Louise is still worried.

"Don't fret. We'll be there, along with everybody on our seigniory. Finish your supper. After that, an evening prayer and then to bed."

The furniture in the large room was all made by Joseph. The table, chairs, beds, and cupboard are made of solid, beautiful pine. The warm colour of the wood makes the room seem cozy. A few small rugs lie on the floor. Marie-Louise has pieced them together from scraps of cloth. The sleeping loft is reached by a short ladder. Here the children go to their beds, covered with blankets and quilts made by their mother.

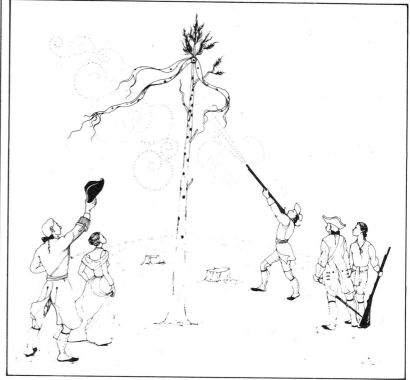

May 1 is a beautiful day. Everybody rushes to finish chores. Faces are clean and smiling, clothes are fresh. We go to the manor house to celebrate the Mai as usual, and pay the annual cens. Marie-Louise has cleaned the grain for the seignior. There is little boat traffic, for all over Canada, people are going to the Mai.

We walk past the seignior's mill, built by M. Asselin so that the habitants could grind their wheat, corn, and

Censitaires and their seignior took turns shooting at the Maypole until it was black. Then everybody joined the seignior's family for a feast.

tourtière: a pie filled with meat

Canadians needed sturdy, well-insulated houses for their families. The habitants built homes to last. Stone walls over a metre thick wouldn't soon crumble. Chimneys and fireplaces were massive so that a fire big enough to heat the whole house could be built. Shutters helped keep out the winter winds.

oats into flour and meal. Everybody on the seigniory uses M. Asselin's mill.

And here is M. Asselin's beautiful stone house. It is much larger than Joseph and Marie-Louise's house. The roof is covered with slate tiles, not cedar shingles. And there are lots of windows with real glass.

Friends wave and shout. The Maypole is ready. A tall spruce tree has been stripped of all but a few top branches. The Maypole is now planted in the front yard of the manor. The **curé** blesses the Maypole and now the seignior steps outside his house. Shouts of "Vive le roi" and "Vive le seignior" are heard. Taking his musket, M. Asselin fires at the pole. Then he hands the gun to his wife. Her shot makes the pole even blacker.

Everyone takes a turn, covering the pole with black smoke.

Now it's time for the feast. M. Asselin invites everyone to crowd into the manor for meats, tourtières, tarts, brandy, and expensive wine from France. By noon, all have eaten and sung and talked enough.

We must return to the Paquin's house to begin the hard work of planting this year's crops. If the weather is good all summer, with plenty of sun and rain, the fall harvest will be good. The Paquins will put away enough food to pay their seignior the rent and have lots to eat next winter. Their icehouse will be full of pork, bacon, chickens, geese, fish, and eels frozen for the long winter. In the root cellar will be garden vegetables. Jams and dried fruit will also be stored to add variety to Marie-Louise's menus. Like many habitants, the Paquins barter for a few treats of imported spices, salt, and sugar. With plenty of firewood, the Paquins will be comfortable in their snug house by the river.

1. Draw a sketch to illustrate part of the "Mai" story.
2. Write a newspaper account of May 1 in New France.
3. Why do you think the "Mai" was celebrated as it was?
4. List the ways the Paquins stored their food.
5. The Paquins did many things for themselves that Canadians today have done for them by others. Give some examples.

cure: parish priest

The exterior walls of this windmill built in about 1700 were of thick stone. Thus the mill was a sturdy fort as well as a necessity for local farmers. What features made this mill a good fort?

What Did the Habitants Grow?

FIELD CROPS	GARDEN CROPS	
wheat	peas	pumpkins
oats	asparagus	celery
barley	lentils	carrots
corn	cabbages	cucumbers
hay	onions	melons
flax		

A Woman's Work ....

Marie-Louise is a very busy woman in every season. She's the mother of six children and a farmer's wife. That means plenty of work in the house, barn, and fields.

Marie-Louise — A Busy Woman

— helps prepare fields for planting, plants crops, helps with harvest
— plants, tends, harvests garden
— helps prepare food for storage
— prepares all meals—no restaurants!
— helps look after farm animals
— makes most of family's clothing
— makes family's blankets, towels, rugs, curtains
— looks after house, husband, and children; teaches skills to children

Explain why you would or would not like to trade places with Marie-Louise for a year.

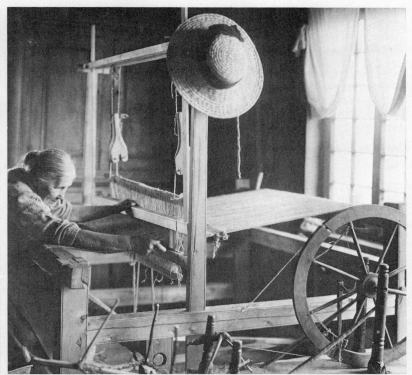

The women of New France had many skills and talents. This weaver is making homespun cloth on a hand loom.

Bread was an important item in the habitant diet. Outdoor ovens were preferred because of their larger capacity. They could bake a week's supply of loaves much more quickly and efficiently than a kitchen oven.

Marie-Louise doesn't work all the time. She, like all of her neighbours, is a Roman Catholic. She enjoys attending Mass with her family and resting on the frequent holy days of the year.

At their parish church the Paquins meet their friends and neighbours, worship God, and often hear important announcements from the governor or intendant. The church and curé's house were built by the habit- ants and their seignior. Everybody contributes to pay the curé and keep the building repaired. The curé is an important man in the community. He keeps track of births and deaths, per- forms services like weddings and fun- erals, and sometimes even teaches the children to read and write. Weddings are lots of fun, with plenty of food, wine, beer, dancing, and noise as friends and family celebrate. A big

Farmers without oxen were at a disadvantage in New France. Oxen were good workers without big appetites, and they were able to withstand Canadian winters. Describe the construction methods and materials used to build this barn.

capitaine de milice: militia captain

Food production increased when farmers used animals to help prepare their fields for planting. Agricultural implements made the habitant's work easier and more efficient than more primitive hand tools.

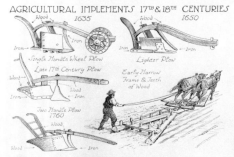

AGRICULTURAL IMPLEMENTS 17TH & 18TH CENTURIES

The parish church, such as this one of Sainte-Anne-de-Beaupré built in 1660, was an important centre of community life in New France.

event for all Canadians is the feast of Saint-Jean-Batiste on June 23-24. Huge bonfires, dances, and special prayers mark this important holy day.

Some people go to church to worship, but others go to meet people, gossip, and show off their clothes and horses.

Joseph Paquin stays after Mass to meet Jacques Trudel, the **capitaine de milice**. Jacques has been chosen to lead the local militia. Sometimes he brings messages from the Sovereign Council. When the governor wants a police force or support for the army, the militia is ready to follow the capitaine wherever guns are needed. Every man in the colony between the ages of sixteen and sixty-one is automatically in the militia.

1. Why was a militia necessary in New France?
2. Does your community have a militia? Investigate.

AVIS/NOTICE FROM THE
BISHOP
of
✝ QUEBEC ✝

NO ONE MAY LEAVE THE CHURCH DURING MASS WITHOUT GOOD REASON

NO ONE MAY TALK OR SHUFFLE THEIR FEET DURING PRAYERS

NO SMOKING AT THE CHURCH DOORS

NO HORSE RACING NEAR THE CHURCH

NO WEARING OF REVEALING GOWNS TO CHURCH IN SUMMER

NO CHEATING ON THE TITHE (PAYMENT TO THE CURÉ)

1. List the jobs done for their community by the Paquin's church or curé. Who or what does them in your community?
2. What do the rules from the bishop tell us about the way some Canadians behaved in church?

THE CHURCH IN NEW FRANCE

The church had always been a part of life in New France. From the earliest days of the colony, religion had been one of the reasons the colony had existed, grown, and developed. Missionaries had gone into the wilderness to teach, preach, and explore. These men were men of religious orders or brotherhoods: Jesuits, Sulpicians or Récollets. They were the first to serve the spiritual needs of New France. As the colony's population grew after 1663, other priests (curés) worked in each parish, supervised by the bishop of Quebec.

The missionaries had always been concerned with converting and helping the Indians. The first Indian reserve was set up at Sillery, near Quebec. Indians came to live there, attend school, and farm the land. Others came to escape from the Iroquois or the evils of alcohol, taking shelter in the reserve.

Brave religious women, who were members of Roman Catholic holy orders, came to Canada to work as pioneers in the schools and hospitals of the colony. These nuns faced as many hardships as the wives of the habitants, especially when the colony was only a few scattered settlements in a wilderness of snow. The sisters worked long and hard at difficult tasks, serving God by caring for the Canadians. Courage and service were their gift to New France.

Many large seigniories had been granted to such religious orders as the Jesuits, Sulpicians, Ursulines, and Récollets. The Roman Catholic Church was an important landowner in New France, holding eleven percent of seigniorial land in 1663 and about twenty-five percent in 1760. Much of that was made up of valuable river lots. The Jesuits, in particular, were active in promoting settlement on their land. Many censitaires preferred having religious seigniors; their seigniories were well-managed and settlers were encouraged.

Education

Annette Paquin was anxious to talk about something she found very exciting: school. It was a new experience for

In 1697 a group of Ursuline nuns arrived at Trois-Rivières to open a convent and set up a school for girls in that village.

The Ursulines, who arrived at Quebec in 1639, spent three years in a hut before moving into their first large convent. It was destroyed by fire in 1650 but was replaced by this handsome stone structure. What reasons might the Ursulines have had for building such a large convent when the population of New France was less than 3000 in 1650?

the Paquin family. Two teachers from the Sisters of the Congregation had recently begun a school for the seigniory. Now the children had a chance to study in a class taught by the sisters, rather than with their mother at home. Annette explains:

"I like to study with the sisters at our seignior's house. We're learning to read and write. Lots of new words. There are two sisters who come to teach us every week."

Annette was sitting by the river bank on a warm June afternoon. Beside her lay some needlework. Marie Asselin, who was thirteen, was Annette's closest friend. Marie had never been to the sisters' classes. Her parents had sent her to Quebec. Marie lived with the Ursuline nuns at their school. She was home for a visit.

Marie was impatient to describe her school.

"I love to study with the Grey Nuns. It's fun to live in Quebec. There's so much to learn.

"We live in fine rooms—almost as cozy as home. The food is good and the sisters are kind to us. We are taught religion, Latin, French, writing, a little science. My favourites are drawing and needlework. The sisters are always reminding us to watch our manners. Sometimes we forget to be polite.

"There are only girls in our school. No boys at all.

"Sometimes I get lonely and wish I could be back here. But I love to go to school in Quebec. I hope Papa will let me return to the convent when the harvest is finished."

Annette gazed across the water. She dreamed for a moment of going to Quebec, a wonderful town she'd never seen. But she knew that her mother needed her here. There was too much work to be done on the farm, especially for the oldest girl. Annette would have to be content with her studies at the manor house with the Sisters of the Congregation.

The Sisters and Their Schools

Marguerite Bourgeoys arrived in New France in 1653 eager to teach children to read and write. She began her career in a "stone stable" in Montreal—not a very impressive schoolhouse. Other schools soon followed, managed by Marguerite's group of teachers, the Sisters of the Congregation. The sisters operated a nursery school and kindergarten. Later they opened **petites écoles** to teach reading, writing, and mathematics to the children of Montreal and district. Other sisters went out to the isolated parts of the colony to teach the habitant children. Classes consisted of boys and girls of all ages. It was one of these "schools" that Annette attended.

What About the Boys?

Boys in Canada could choose from several schools. They could remain on their own seigniory to study with the Sisters of the Congregation, who taught them to read and write. There were petites écoles in the towns and in many parishes. Here boys were taught many subjects by the Récollet or Sulpician fathers—grammar, mathematics, French, and music. If they did well, they could go to the Jesuit College at Quebec. It was not a place for boys who weren't interested in learning. Students were taught religion, grammar, philosophy, and mathematics. There was another choice for serious students: the bishop's seminary.

petites écoles: small schools

Marguerite Bourgeoys, founder of the Sisters of the Congregation of Notre-Dame.

Young men planning to become priests went there. A trade school was an alternative for some. There they could learn reading, writing, and a trade.

1. What did Marie like about her school at Quebec?
2. Compare the education of Annette with your own. Note similarities and differences.
3. Which school would you prefer to have attended? Marie's, Annette's, or your own?
4. Historians have found that women in New France were more literate (able to read and write) than men. Why might this be?

There were two kinds of hospitals of Canada: the Hôtel-Dieu and the general hospital. Both were places for the sick, wounded, and elderly, but the general hospitals had extra jobs to do. They provided medical care and a permanent home for the elderly who had no family to care for them. They were also a refuge for orphans, cripples, and retarded persons. All of these people received help from the Grey Nuns who served those who needed constant care.

Where do those whose needs were served by the general hospitals of New France go for help in your community?

Epidemics

In Canada, there were many epidemics, which caused the deaths of thousands of people.
1685: **typhus**
1687: **smallpox**—500 deaths
1700: **influenza**

1702: smallpox—2000 deaths
1710 and *1718:* fevers
1734: smallpox
1743-1746: typhus
1750: typhus
1755: smallpox
1756 and *1759:* typhus

typhus, smallpox, influenza: serious infectious diseases

Health Care

Wanted: courageous pioneers willing to work long hours in difficult surroundings for no pay.

This job is especially difficult during frequent epidemics. Then applicants must be on duty twenty-four hours a day, seven days a week, until the disease no longer threatens to wipe out the population.

Candidates for this job must also care for the wounded, especially the king's soldiers. Accident victims, the elderly, and the dying must be looked after.

Applicants must have sufficient knowledge of routine cures and methods of treatment to assist in administering medicinal herbs, bleeding, and purging. They may also be required to assist surgeons performing amputations or other operations.

White uniforms are provided, as are comfortable living quarters in a large stone building in the Upper Town. Residents are provided with clean bedrooms, large workrooms, dining room,

chapel. The place of work is next door. Iron stoves are provided for winter.

Only those interested in the service of God and his people in New France should answer this call.

Interested women and girls may apply in person to the Hôtel-Dieu, Quebec.

Les Soeurs Hospitalières,
Hôtel-Dieu, Quebec.

What type of woman would answer such a "want ad"? What benefits could she expect from the job? What difficulties would she face? What tasks did a nurse perform?

Montreal's Hôtel-Dieu as it looked in the seventeenth century. Nursing sisters were never short of work in the hospitals of New France.

129

Chapter 24

THERE'S MORE TO NEW FRANCE THAN CANADA!

Louisiana

Louisiana was the large territory in the centre of North America on either side of the Mississippi River. The area had been explored and claimed for France by Father Marquette, Louis Joliet, and the Sieur de La Salle. A few fur-trading forts were built in the territory.

Acadia: The Orphan of New France

The government of France sometimes seemed to have forgotten about the colony of Acadia. Quebec was always sure that when help was needed, France would send it—soldiers, or teachers, or carpenters, or food, or money. The Acadians could never count on aid from France. In fact, their isolated little colony around

Port Royal was to be under English control for many years. The two countries seemed to use the Acadians as chips in their global poker games. Sometimes Acadia was won, then just as easily lost, by the French government, as France and Britain battled for control of North America.

How did the Acadians handle this situation? Generally, they tried to ignore it. They went about their lives, expecting little from France. They felt angry when raiders from New England brought ships to their shores seeking revenge for attacks made by Canadians. They were pleased to be independent, hard-working farmers and fishermen. When they weren't defending themselves against New England pirates, they were trading their grain, fish and furs for brandy, molasses, cooking pots, and cloth

The town of New Orleans was begun by two Canadians. Pierre Le Moyne d'Iberville, and his brother Jean Baptiste Le Moyne, Sieur de Bienville. Bienville was governor of Louisiana from 1732 to 1743.

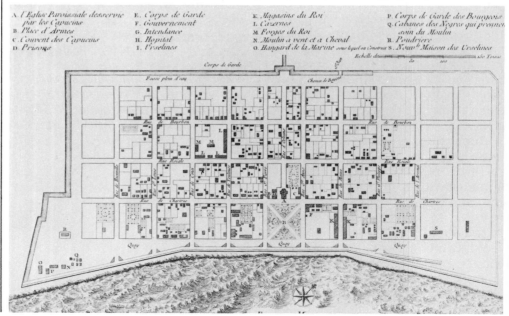

brought by the New England ships.

Their harvests were good because their crops were grown on the fertile flats behind dykes. The Acadians had settled along the Bay of Fundy. Great flat lands were uncovered when the bay's high tides fell. These lands were good for farming, but had to be protected from the tides. The Acadians built strong dykes to keep the sea off the flats. Then they planted their crops of wheat, oats, and flax.

The Acadians had the usual pioneer farm animals—cattle and pigs, plus sheep. They also had apple and pear orchards.

Their snug houses kept out the winter's chill and provided homes for the large numbers of children born to Acadian families. Ten was not considered too many children for one family! Acadian women had all of the skills for pioneering. Long hours of making clothing, blankets, rugs, candles, preparing food, and caring for children were routine. When they needed a prayer, they relied on a Récollet father.

The Acadians wanted to be left to farm their land and live in peace. The

"poker game" between France and England made this impossible.

Acadia Changes Hands
Here's how the poker players dealt with Acadia:

1603-1613: French
1628-1635: English pirates
1635-1654: French
1654-1667: English
1667-1690: French
1690-1697: English
1697-1710: French
1710-1760: English

An artist's romantic view of the Bay of Fundy near Port Royal, later named Annapolis Royal by the British.

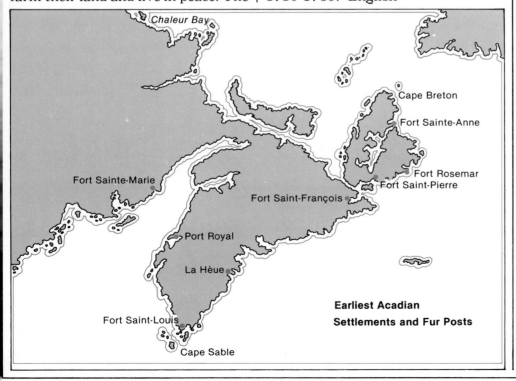

Earliest Acadian
Settlements and Fur Posts

Earliest Acadian settlements and fur posts.

Part 5

THE FINAL YEARS, 1713-1774

Chapter 25

THIRTY YEARS OF PEACE

By 1712 both Britain and France were growing tired of war. They had been fighting to gain control of the North American fur trade. The fighting ended with the signing of the Treaty of Utrecht in 1713.

The terms of the treaty weren't as bad for the French as it first appeared.

As long as the English kept to their trading posts on Hudson Bay and didn't venture too far inland, they wouldn't be a serious threat to New France. The French were allowed to use part of the north shore of Newfoundland to carry on their fishing operations on the Grand Banks. The

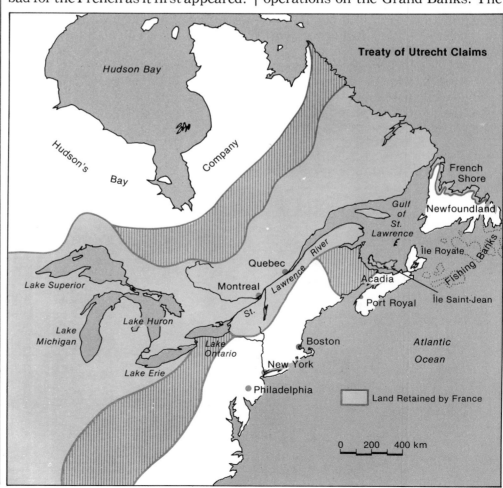

Treaty of Utrecht Claims

Hudson Bay

Hudson's Bay Company

French Shore

Gulf of St. Lawrence

Newfoundland

Île Royale

Fishing Banks

Lake Superior

Quebec

St. Lawrence River

Montreal

Acadia

Port Royal

Île Saint-Jean

Lake Michigan

Lake Huron

St. Lawrence

Lake Ontario

Boston

Atlantic Ocean

Lake Erie

New York

Philadelphia

Land Retained by France

0   200   400 km

fisheries were not only important for the fish. This was an excellent training ground for sailors of the French navy. In Acadia, the French were allowed to keep Île Saint Jean (Prince Edward Island) and Île Royale (Cape Breton Island).

One of the terms of the peace treaty did cause concern for New France. A clause said that the area of North America south of the Great Lakes and west of the Appalachian Mountains was open to fur traders of both France and Britain. This left the way open for traders based in the English colonies on the Atlantic coast to move inland. With their cheaper trade goods and cheaper rum, it wouldn't be long before they would win the Indians over to their side. The French weren't about to stand idly by and watch their influence west of the Appalachians dwindle.

Building Forts

In 1720, the French received permission from the Iroquois to build a fort and trading post on Lake Ontario. The fort was named Niagara. Not to be outdone, the English pressured the Iroquois into allowing them to build a fort on the south shore of Lake Ontario in 1724. Fort Chouaguen (Oswego) posed a serious threat to the interests of New France in the Great Lakes trading area. French officials were forced to offer trade goods at much reduced prices, and many gifts were given to the local Indians.

Niagara was rebuilt later as a gigantic stone fortress, and work was begun on a series of forts down the Lake Champlain waterway. This was one of the main routes for an invasion force from the English colonies on the Atlantic. A series of French forts spread along the shores of Lake Champlain might discourage any invaders.

In order to soften the impact of the English trading posts on Hudson Bay, the French encouraged the opening of trading posts in the West. The Indians there might prefer to go to these inland posts for trade goods, especially blankets, which the Indians valued highly. Every spring, canoes would travel the long and often treacherous route from Montreal to the western trading posts. They would bear the trade goods that were exchanged for furs. The returning canoes would carry the valuable cargo of furs to Montreal.

New France began to grow quite rapidly. The population had increased from a flimsy 19000 to a respectable 50000 by the year 1744. The fur trade was still the backbone of the economy, but other industries were established.

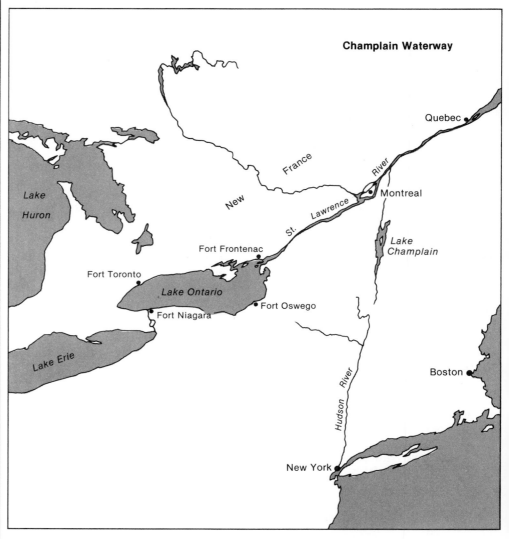

By 1730 New France was exporting lumber, flour, tobacco, fish, whale oil, beef, and peas to France and the West Indies.

1. Indicate on an outline map the areas of North America claimed by the English and the French after 1713.
2. Which term of the peace treaty of 1713 did officials of New France worry about? Explain.

Louisbourg Established

Plans were made by New France to build a naval base on Île Royale (Cape Breton Island) to protect the French fishing fleets on the Grand Banks and to keep control of the Gulf of St. Lawrence. The St. Lawrence River was the lifeline from New France to France. If the French couldn't control the St. Lawrence and its entrance, they might run dangerously low on supplies. The route had to be kept open.

In 1720 work began on a fortress at Île Royale to be called Louisbourg. Much money and effort went into this fort. From the very beginning there was trouble at Louisbourg. The workers used sea sand for the mortar in the walls, and this made the stonework very weak. Even after the great fort was finished, there was unrest.

La Vérendrye: The Search for the Western Sea

The rich fur-trade merchants in Montreal were mainly responsible for the opening and upkeep of the western trading posts. These posts were intended to draw some of the furs away from the English posts on Hudson Bay.

The man in charge of the Lake Nipigon post in 1729 was Pierre La Vérendrye. With Pierre were his wife, two daughters, and four sons.

La Vérendrye schemed to push westward to the "Western Sea" he had heard so much about. Of course, he would need consent from the proper authorities in New France, so he wrote to the governor to tell him of his plans. Governor Beauharnois in turn had to seek permission from his superiors in France. The answer was not encouraging for La Vérendrye. He was allowed to look for the Western Sea at his own expense. He was given the right to trade with the Indians during his travels.

Pierre had little money to pay for his dream. He had to strike a bargain with the Montreal merchants. They would supply him with trade goods and provisions in return for some western furs.

La Vérendrye's party set out from Montreal in 1731 and began to build a

chain of fur-trading posts in the West.

Pierre La Vérendrye and his sons explored an enormous territory that no European had ever seen before. It's not certain how far they travelled but they probably saw the Rocky Mountains.

La Vérendrye's contributions weren't always appreciated by the French authorities. He was often accused of being more interested in making his fortune from the fur trade than in exploring.

La Vérendrye was far from becoming a rich man. In 1743, very much in debt, he was recalled to Montreal to answer to merchants' complaints. His rights of exploration were taken away. On December 5, 1749, Pierre La Vérendrye died in Montreal.

The La Vérendrye brothers explored territory in the West that no other European had seen. According to their accounts, they were in sight of the western mountains on New Year's day in 1743.

There was low morale among the troops posted there. After all, who wanted to be stuck in this cold and barren place where the food was awful and there wasn't enough room for everyone to sleep comfortably? The food supply for Louisbourg was also a cause for concern. It was difficult to encourage Acadian farmers to come to Île Royale to farm the rocky land.

Why was the fortress at Louisbourg built?

Louisbourg II

Did you see those two guys at the gate? What a sloppy-looking pair! Scuffed shoes, ruffled hair, and filthy uniforms. And they sure looked bored. Maybe they have reason to be. Look at the rooms where they sleep. This whole place looks very uncomfortable. 1744? No, it's 1980, and the "scruffy" pair at the gate are employed for the summer by Parks Canada to re-create the way the soldiers actually looked in 1744.

In 1960 the rebuilding of the great fortress of Louisbourg began. The same plans, and indeed, the same foundations were used. Everything is authentic—the untidy soldiers, the cold stone walls, even the smell of fish

from a nearby processing plant. Every year thousands of tourists visit this fascinating "living museum."

The End of Thirty Years of Peace

In the spring of 1743, the British Royal Navy attacked ships of the French navy. In the spring of 1744, France declared war on Britain.

In North America, the merchants in the English colonies were reluctant to go to war against Canada. However, New England did have reason to fight the Canadians. Their privateering ships from Louisbourg had captured many New England ships that fished on the Grand Banks. These New Englanders would have been happy to see Louisbourg done away with.

The Canadians struck first. They captured one of the English forts in Acadia and attacked the naval base at Annapolis Royal.

In March of 1745, an invasion force of some 4000 New England militia and four British ships of war prepared for an attack on Louisbourg.

This invasion force couldn't have chosen a better time. Morale at Louisbourg was low, so low in fact that there had been an unsuccessful mutiny a few months before. The great fortress contained only 455 soldiers and 800 sailors and fishermen. Provisions were very low.

After a seige which lasted almost seven weeks, Louisbourg surrendered.

There was some talk of an attack on Quebec, but Britain couldn't spare the personnel and materials. Britain was too busy with the fighting in Europe.

The French were also unable to send troops to North America in 1745, so any thoughts of retaking Louisbourg would have to be postponed.

The loss of Louisbourg upset the rest of Canada. The signal fires down the St. Lawrence to Quebec were readied. Quebec fortifications were improved. The raids on the frontier English settlements began again.

By 1748 New France's resources were running low. The costs of maintaining the frontier raids and supplying the Indians were enormous. Officials in France ordered the raids to stop. New France was to remain on the defensive.

The war in Europe had become a stalemate by then. Peace was declared in 1748. To everyone's surprise, the great fortress of Louisbourg was handed back to New France. The exact location of the borders between the French and the English claims in North America was still in dispute.

1. Why do you suppose Louisbourg was given back to the French?
2. What reason did New Englanders have for a war against Canada?

Louisbourg in 1731.

CLASH IN THE OHIO COUNTRY

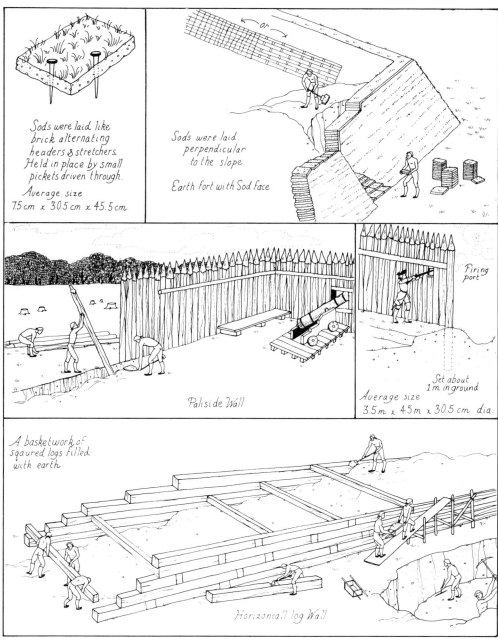

Sods were laid like brick alternating headers & stretchers. Held in place by small pickets driven through.
Average size
7.5 cm x 30.5 cm x 45.5 cm.

Sods were laid perpendicular to the slope

Earth fort with Sod face

Paliside Wall

Firing port

Set about 1 m in ground
Average size
3.5 m x 4.5 m x 30.5 cm dia.

A basketwork of squared logs filled with earth.

Horizontal log Wall

Construction of a fort.

By 1750 the English colonies on the Atlantic coast had blossomed to well over a million people. Good land at a reasonable price was becoming hard to find. Settlement had to expand, and the only possible direction was over the Appalachian Mountains to the west. Fur traders from the English colonies had been venturing into the territory westward over the mountains for about twenty-five years. In fact, they had control over the fur trading in the area of the Ohio River valley. The Indians there showed a preference for cheaper English trade goods.

The Indians were nervous about these people moving into their hunting grounds, but they didn't do much to discourage them. After all, they did want the useful English trade goods.

It was becoming obvious to the French that they would have to drive the English out of the Ohio country. In 1752 the new governor, Duquesne, made some elaborate plans to build a series of forts in the Ohio country. In this way, the French would be able to drive the English out by force. At the same time, they could keep the Indians happy with trade goods.

Two thousand workers were to build a series of forts in the area.

The work was back breaking. By that fall, 400 had died, including the leader himself. Many of the rest were too ill to continue. The mission hadn't been totally successful, but it did cause the English to leave the Ohio country.

George Washington's Stand

The English colonies were concerned enough in 1753 to send a formal protest. George Washington, along with a few soldiers, carried the letter to the French in the Ohio country.

The letter was politely received, but Washington was sent back to Virginia with a message from the French, "We have no intention of leaving this area which you must agree is part of New France."

Governor Duquesne of New France sent troops to reinforce the area. A group of 500 French workers built Fort Duquesne on the Ohio River.

The Indians in the region now joined the French side. They wanted to be on the side of the winners. It was clear that the French had the advantage in soldiers in the area.

In 1754 Washington returned with troops. The French received a warning from the Indians that Washington's expedition was approaching. The French sent a small band of men to tell Washington to leave the territory. The two parties met. The details of what happened are unclear. In any case, the French advance party was killed except for one man who escaped to tell the story at Fort Duquesne.

This clash had taken place in time of peace. The French reacted quickly. A force of 500 men was sent out to intercept Washington's force. They were to drive them out of the Ohio country.

Meanwhile Washington and his men built a rough log wall which they named Fort Necessity. The French attacked. The battle lasted only a short time. Washington surrendered. He and his men were ordered to march back over the mountains.

With the English army retreating over the mountains, the French were then in control of the Ohio country. The Indian nations in the area at the time all supported the French.

It was one thing to win the support of the Indians, but it was quite another thing to keep their loyalty. The Indians had become used to the English trade goods. The French would have to do at least as well if they hoped to count on Indian support.

It proved to be quite a task meeting these demands. About 400 voyageurs had to be kept working all summer carrying supplies and trade goods to the forts on the Ohio. There was also the matter of feeding about 500 soldiers who were on duty in the forts in the area. All of this was a great drain on the resources of New France.

1. Why did the French fur traders want to keep the English colonists out of the Ohio country?
2. Why did the English colonists want the French fur traders to stay away?
3. Why were the Indians in the area concerned?

In Acadia

When the British hoisted their flag over Acadia in 1713, the Treaty of Utrecht may have given them control of the land, but the people there weren't British. The countryside was covered with farms that were run by people who were descendents of French settlers. After many attempts to establish a permanent settlement at Port Royal from 1604 onward, some French families put down their roots in the area around Port Royal. These families grew and the farms spread until 1713 when there were some 2000 people.

Now that the British were in control again, the name Nova Scotia was used instead of Acadia, and Port Royal was renamed Annapolis Royal.

The British didn't want to get rid of the Acadians. After all, what good was empty farm land when few people from England wanted to move there? It was decided that the Acadians could stay if they promised loyalty to Britain. This meant taking the oath of allegiance. The Acadians stalled. Taking the oath might mean fighting against their fellow French in a future war. No one really pressed the issue, and the question of loyalty was left unsettled.

Once the great fortress of Louisbourg was begun in 1720, the French wanted the Acadians to move and start farms on nearby Île Saint-Jean (Prince Edward Island) and Île Royale (Cape Breton Island), which France still owned. Farmers were badly needed in those areas to grow food for the men at Louisbourg. The idea met with little success. The Acadians preferred to stay where they were.

Britain decided that it was time to build a naval base and fortress in Acadia. In 1749 some 2000 English settlers arrived on the east coast of Nova Scotia to establish the settlement of Halifax. Fortifications were the first consideration of the builders, shown here studying their plans.

Chapter 27

INCREASING FRICTION

The news of Washington's defeat in the Ohio country wasn't long in reaching Britain. It certainly looked as though the English colonists were unable to handle the situation themselves. Help would have to come from Britain.

France and Britain were not officially at war, but there was conflict between the two countries in North America. Both France and Britain claimed that they were only defending territory that belonged to them. The trouble was that both countries claimed the Ohio Valley.

Help from England came in the form of two regiments of soldiers, and General James Braddock who led them. His orders were to push the French out of the Ohio country, put up some forts to protect the region, then attack French forts all along the "border" from the Ohio country to Acadia. The British hoped to teach the Canadians a lesson.

No sooner had General Braddock arrived in the English colonies than his troubles began. He had difficulty obtaining supplies for his army. Many of the merchants in the colonies were trading with the French across the border. They saw little reason to give these valuable supplies to Braddock's army. The general also had trouble recruiting new soldiers in the colonies.

In spite of all his problems, Braddock's plans took shape.

Braddock decided to lead an attack on Fort Duquesne. His army of some 2000 began their long trek in May of 1755. The way to the Ohio country was long and rugged. The troops had to build a wagon road through the thick forests and over the swamps. The heavy siege artillery had to be dragged over the mountains. The soldiers and workers had to be fed along the way. A herd of cattle, a long wagon train of supplies, and several camp helpers followed the advance of the soldiers.

Early in July, Braddock's troops were close to Fort Duquesne when a party of about 850 French and Indians from the fort met Braddock's much larger force not far from the fort. The French and Indians fled into the hills on both sides of the British troops.

The British were not prepared for this kind of bush fighting. They had been trained for the open-field style of warfare used in Europe. Their densely packed bright red lines were an easy target.

Battle between Braddock's forces and the French near Fort Duquesne in 1755.

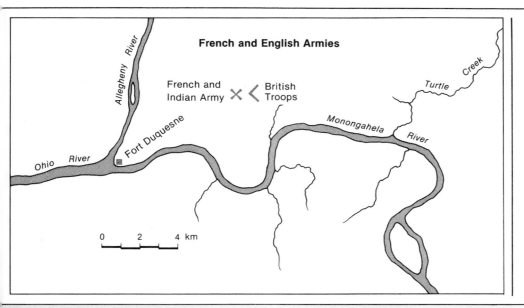

French and English Armies

French and
Indian Army ✕ ❮ British
Troops

Allegheny River

Fort Duquesne

Ohio River

Monongahela River

Turtle Creek

0 2 4 km

The Acadians Lose Their Homeland

The question of Acadian loyalty to Britain had remained unsettled since 1713. The Acadians wanted nothing to do with the quarrelling between the French and the British. They only wanted to live peacefully on their farms.

In the summer of 1755, Governor Shirley's New England militia had captured the French fort, Beauséjour, on the Acadian border. Inside the fort, they found hundreds of Acadians who were helping the French in the fight.

The Acadians had been persuaded to help the French by threats, but even so, the situation was serious. Governor Lawrence of Nova Scotia decided that it was time that the Acadians took the oath of allegiance. When the Acadian leaders refused, the results were disastrous.

The New England soldiers rounded up every Acadian they could find in the countryside. The soldiers had instructions to burn all the Acadian farm buildings.

Ships were brought from the English colonies. These ships were used to carry over 6000 Acadians to the English colonies. They watched from the ships as a lifetime of work went up in smoke.

Once in the English colonies, the Acadians were left to fend for themselves. Some found their way west to Louisiana, where today their descendents are known as "Cajuns." Some eventually found their way back to Acadia. Some reached France, and others stayed in the English colonies to begin a new life.

Much has been written about the why and the how of this unfortunate event. Whatever the real story is, this was certainly recorded as one of the saddest and most tragic events in our history.

How else might Governor Lawrence have handled the question of Acadian loyalty?

Expulsion of the Acadians from Grand-Pré, N.S. The Acadians were escorted from their homes by soldiers and put on ships bound for the English colonies.

In less than three hours, the battle was over. Many of the British soldiers had been killed. The rest fled in panic over the mountains. Behind them on the blood-soaked ground they left their horses and supplies. They also left their dead general, Braddock.

To add to all this, the French found Braddock's detailed plans for other attacks on New France. The French were able to defend themselves against most of these attacks because of the information found in Braddock's abandoned luggage.

1. Why did General Braddock have trouble supplying his army in the English colonies?
2. Why did Braddock lose the battle in the Ohio country?

At War Again

On May 17, 1756, England officially declared war on France. The final struggle for North America was about to take place.

The French sent a general to take over military operations in New France. His name was Montcalm. General Montcalm proved himself right away by capturing the important British fort of Oswego on Lake Ontario.

In spite of being the underdog, Montcalm and his troops enjoyed more victories in 1757. Another vital English fort on the Lake Champlain invasion route was destroyed. Maybe North America would belong to New France after all!

The Tide of War Turns

A series of "border" clashes in North America had become a full-scale war between France and Britain by 1756. The situation was grave. Plans had to be made, and soldiers and ships had to be strategically placed for the deadly game.

Britain sent a large, well-trained force to wage war in North America. The plan was to attack and conquer New France on several fronts. The most important of these fronts was

Embarkation of the Acadians.

142

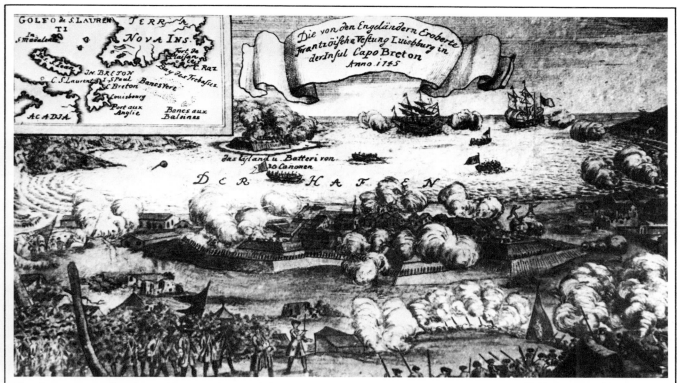

the fortress at Quebec, the very heart of New France.

The French had few troops to spare to send to North America. Their only hope was to try to hold off the British until peace came in Europe. Then French victories in Europe could perhaps be traded for losses in New France. The French minister in charge of the war operations explained the plan in a letter to Montcalm and Governor Vaudreuil:

The principal object is to conserve at least a sufficient portion of the colony, and to maintain yourselves in it, so that the whole may be recovered when the peace treaty is signed. In short, you should try and maintain yourselves as best you can in the coming campaign, and await the negotiations which may preserve Canada or operations to rescue it.[1]

The French navy was weak. Britain's strong navy was able to exert control over the Atlantic Ocean route to North America. Even if France had troops to spare, they might not make it past this British naval blockade.

In spite of this blockade, a few French ships did manage to get through to Louisbourg in 1758.

The British plan included taking Louisbourg and Quebec in the summer of 1758. The siege of Louisbourg was late getting started. Then it took seven weeks of bombardment to convince the French to give up. By that time, it was too late to attack Quebec. That battle would have to be put off until next year.

The British also received the stunning news that General Abercromby's force had been defeated at Carillon (Ticonderoga) by the French general, Montcalm, and his badly outnumbered group. This was a glorious victory for the French, but it was to be their last one in this war for North America.

The other British offensives that year were successful. Colonel Bradstreet easily took Fort Frontenac on Lake Ontario, and later in the year Fort Duquesne was blown to pieces by the French as the British commander, Forbes, was approaching the fort. New France's grip on North America was becoming extremely shaky.

Wolfe (on the left) at the siege of Louisbourg. James Wolfe was promoted to commander to lead the British attack on Quebec the following year.

Chapter 28

SETTLING THE ISSUE

Cast of Characters

Montcalm
— in 1756 was sent to Canada as a major-general
— in 1758 was promoted to commander of French forces in North America.

Vaudreuil
— was governor of New France
— was very corrupt: he and a few others did all they could to profit from their positions.

French army and navy
—about 13000 men ready to defend Quebec
— only about 2000 were European-trained soldiers
— the rest were Canadian soldiers and men and boys of New France and Indian allies
— these troops were no match for the British soldiers when it came to open European-style warfare
— the French navy was very small, but the French didn't think that the British could possibly navigate the tricky St. Lawrence without heavy losses.

Wolfe
— was a hero as one of the brigadiers at the siege of Louisbourg
— was promoted over other senior officers to command the British attack against Quebec
— was only thirty-two years old at the time.

Murray, Monckton and Townshend
— served as Wolfe's officers in the siege of Quebec.

Saunders
— was in command of the huge fleet that carried the British troops and supplies to Quebec
— his great skill brought British ships to Quebec without a loss.

British army and navy
— 8500 expert soldiers
— over 13000 sailors and nearly 200 ships formed an awesome navy.

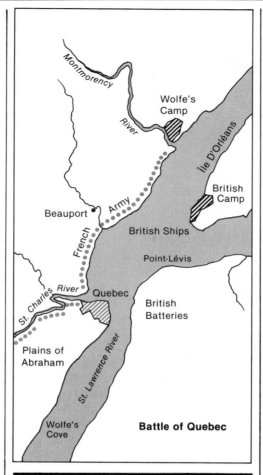

Battle of Quebec

Map labels: Montmorency River, Wolfe's Camp, Île D'Orléans, British Camp, Beauport, French Army, British Ships, Point-Lévis, St. Charles River, Quebec, British Batteries, Plains of Abraham, St. Lawrence River, Wolfe's Cove

Strengths and Weaknesses

By the spring of 1759, the vast territory that New France had once claimed as her own had shrunk considerably. The great fortress, Louisbourg, had fallen the year before. The crucial St. Lawrence supply route from France to Quebec was now in British control. British flags were raised over many forts that had been built by the French.

The heart of New France, the city and fortress of Quebec, was still in French hands. The city prepared for the attack that was sure to come in the summer of 1759.

The resources of Quebec were indeed slim. Crop failures in the last few years made the supply of food very short. The troops got used to eating horse meat, but only after a lot of grumbling.

To add to these problems, Governor Vaudreuil and General Montcalm quarrelled over policies that seriously affected the defence of Quebec. And then there was the Intendant Bigot, busily devising schemes to increase his personal wealth by cheating the government at every turn. Many of the supplies intended for the soldiers in New France never reached the soldiers.

On the positive side, Quebec was in a favourable position for defending itself against the British invaders. Champlain had chosen wisely when he picked the site for this settlement:

All of the shore for kilometres to the east of Quebec was a steep cliff. It would be difficult if not impossible to land troops here without being slaughtered.

The river here was very narrow—this gave the Quebec fortress some control over ships passing underneath her guns. The currents here were very strong and tricky. The British would have great difficulty navigating upstream past Quebec.

The St. Charles River and another line of steep cliffs protected Quebec in the north.

To the east of the town, wide mud flats made landing of troops very tricky, except at high tide. The only real landing site on the entire north shore was at Beauport, just east of the St. Charles River.

Consider the strengths and weaknesses of both the British and the French. In your opinion, which side had the better chance of victory? Explain your answer.

British Strategy

On June 26, 1759, the first British troopships arrived at Quebec. They anchored off Île d'Orléans to await the others. When the entire fleet had arrived, Wolfe and his engineer went ashore at Île d'Orléans. Wolfe looked up the river towards Quebec. He was no doubt impressed with the magnificent fortress with its high protective cliffs.

Late on the night of June 28, the British received their welcome from the French. It was a very impolite welcome in the form of fire ships that were floated towards the anchored British fleet. Only quick action saved the British from disaster. They towed the burning ships out of harm's way.

On June 29, the British took possession of the west point of Île d'Orléans, then crossed the channel to take Point-Lévis from a small band of French defenders. The French had blundered in not putting up better defences at Point-Lévis. From that point of high ground, the British could bombard Quebec.

On the evening of July 12, a small group of daring townspeople from Quebec made their way across the river to attack the British on Point-Lévis. They intended to drive the red-coats off the point. Just as they were within striking distance, something went terribly wrong with the plan of attack. In confusion they fired at dark figures among the trees. The figures turned out to be their own men. The Quebec force fled in disorganized panic. The terrible pounding of the British guns began that very night. It shook the town for the rest of the summer, flattening houses, stores, and churches.

The British commander, Wolfe, had several options for the attack on Quebec but couldn't decide which one to take. The French had kept Wolfe off balance. He had originally planned to land upriver past Quebec. Montcalm sent a force of soldiers to march back and forth along the shore west of Quebec, following the movements of the British ships. This prevented any landing on that shore.

Plans were made and cancelled. Another group of fire ships were launched by the French on the night of July 27. Again they missed their target.

The British had nothing to gain by a stalemate. They couldn't hope to stay anchored in the St. Lawrence River indefinitely. Wolfe would have to force Montcalm into an open battle and soon. But how?

Wolfe kept the exact location of the landing place a secret to the last moment. His officers were not on very good terms with him, and this did little to improve their loyalty.

Only a great deal of skill and luck prevented the British from losing any ships as a result of the deadly fire ships that the French used. French boats were set on fire and floated towards the anchored British fleet.

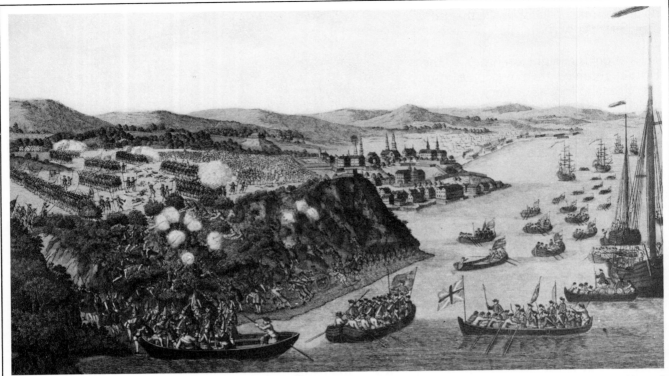

The British troops landing at Anse-au-Foulon near Quebec. The artist has shown a series of events that took place on that day. Describe the events in this picture as they occurred.

Wolfe Finally Strikes

On July 31, the British launched an assault. Wolfe planned to attack the French gun placements on the Beauport shore east of the city. Here he hoped to land his troops and force Montcalm out into the open for a battle. The plan was complicated. The tricky shoals and the tide had to be overcome.

From the very beginning, the campaign went sour. The British ships were caught on unseen shoals far from the shore. When the tide went out the British soldiers waded in waist-high water and sloshed across the mud flats towards the French defences. The muddy slopes were a slippery mess. As the British grenadiers tried to claw their way up the bank, the French picked them off with careful aim.

Suddenly it began to rain—a torrential downpour. With powder soaked on both sides, the shooting ceased and bayonets were readied. Another assault on the greasy slope began. Once again the frustrated redcoats slipped back. Wolfe ordered his men to retreat before the slaughter was complete. What a disaster for the British!

The Final Days

Time was running out for the British. The Canadian winter was one element that the British were not prepared to fight. Wolfe's brigadiers were getting impatient. They pressured their commander for a plan of attack. Wolfe's health was failing.

The French waited patiently, hoping that winter would arrive before the redcoats took action. During most of the month of August, the British had to be content with raids on the Canadian farms and villages in the countryside.

Near the end of August, Wolfe gave in to his officers and agreed to their plan. They would land their troops west of Quebec and force Montcalm into open battle. The problem still remained: where could they land safely? Montcalm's troops were still patrolling the shore above Quebec.

Wolfe scouted the north shoreline for days, then decided on a spot and a plan:

The main part of the British fleet would land at a spot called Anse-au-Foulon, just west of Quebec. There was a steep and narrow path leading up to the Heights. While this was going on, a fake attack would take place at Beauport. Wolfe kept the landing spot secret from his brigadiers until the last moment.

In the darkness of the early hours of September 13, the British plan was well on its way. Several small boat-loads of redcoated soldiers drifted down the river on the outgoing tide. When the darkened outline of their boats was spotted by a French sentry on the shore, an alert British officer saved the day by replying in French. They were mistaken for French supply ships sneaking down the river.

Montcalm's Stand

At about four o'clock in the morning, the first of the British troops climbed the slippery path to the heights. The sentries were surprised and easily overtaken. So far, so good.

By nine in the morning, almost 5000 British soldiers were assembled on the Plains of Abraham, west of Quebec. It was a daring move that had succeeded, mostly because of good luck, but it had worked!

Montcalm's response to the news was one of complete disbelief:

God only knows Monsieur, how to perform the impossible and there is no need to believe that the enemy has wings which would enable him, all in the same night, to cross the river, disembark, and scale the cliffs; more particularly since for the last manoeuvre he would need ladders.[1]

Montcalm eventually realized the truth and decided that it would be best to try to fling the British back down the steep cliffs before it was too late.

General Montcalm led his 4500 troops into battle at ten o'clock. They

were no match for the well-trained British. Within the half-hour the remnants of the French troops were forced to retreat to the walls of Quebec. Their general, Montcalm was wounded. He died the next day. General Wolfe died on the bloodied battlefield.

Four days later the once-magnificent Quebec, the heart of New France was forced to surrender.

The Battle of the Plains of Abraham, September 13, 1759. The British, in a daring move, lured the French into an open battle. The British won easily.

Montcalm was wounded in battle. He died a short time later. The British leader, Wolfe, also died during the fighting.

The British bombardment of the city of Quebec took an awesome toll on the buildings. These two pictures show some of the damage that was done.

The Winter at Quebec

The Quebec that the British soldiers entered on September 18, 1759 was a sorry sight. The constant bombardment from Point-Lévis that summer had taken its toll. Hardly a building was left undamaged.

The countryside was also in a battered condition. The British had burned over 1400 farms and manor houses during the raids that summer.

The harsh Canadian winter was approaching and the victorious troops were ill-prepared. The 7000 men who were stationed at Quebec repaired the torn buildings as best they could. They also repaired and strengthened the town's defences and tried to save some of the crops. The food shortage was serious.

The conquered Canadians were treated well by the soldiers. In fact it was the soldiers rather than the conquered who seemed to suffer the most. The Ursuline nuns knitted woolen knee-bands for the soldiers who were wearing kilts.

A young British soldier named James Miller wrote:

A severe winter now commenced while we were totally unprepared for such a climate, neither fuel, forage or indeed anything to make life tolerable. The troops were crowded into vacant houses, as well as possible; numbers fell sick, and the scurvy made a dreadful havoc among us.

In short, the fatigues of the winter were so great, that the living almost envied the dead. Liquors were extremely scarce, and when the men could procure them they generally drank to excess; it was no uncommon thing in the morning to find several men frozen to death from that cause.

By the end of that winter, over a thousand of the garrison were dead and two thousand "totally unfit for any service."[2]

THE END OF NEW FRANCE

Quebec had fallen but the bulk of the surviving French and Canadian soldiers had managed to retreat to Montreal. They had hopes of retaking their beloved city. The new French commander, Lévis, learned that the Union Jack had been raised over the fallen fortress of Quebec on September 18.

Later that fall, the British fleet returned to England. Brigadier Murray was left with the British army to winter at Quebec. They spent a cold and miserable winter with inadequate supplies and clothing.

Lévis managed to send a French ship to France to ask for reinforcements to attack Quebec in the spring.

Early in the spring of 1760, Lévis moved his 7000 troops to attack Quebec. Another battle took place outside the fortress walls. This time the French were victorious. Murray's force retreated within the walls of Quebec. The fate of Quebec now depended on the results of a waiting game. Whose ships would first appear on the St. Lawrence River?

Unfortunately for the French, British ships began to anchor off Quebec on May 19. Lévis and his men once again retreated to Montreal.

Later that summer, a massive force of some 15 000 British soldiers marched on Montreal. Many of the Canadians threw off their uniforms and returned to their farms in the countryside. The situation was hopeless.

On September 8, 1760, Governor Vaudreuil surrendered. New France was no more.

Explain what might have taken place if the French supply ships had arrived at Quebec ahead of the British supply ships.

In the spring of 1760, the French attempted to recapture Quebec. A battle took place outside the city walls, and the British were forced to retreat to the safety of the Quebec fortress.

This picture shows the surrender of Montreal to the British on September 8, 1760.

Chapter 30

AFTER THE CONQUEST

Jean-Pierre was having trouble concentrating on his farm work. What future was in store for Jean-Pierre and his family? Things were comfortable enough for the time being. The British army had become the government of Canada. Jean-Pierre had been surprised at how well the conquered Canadians had been treated. As a matter of fact, things were much better now than they had been while the corrupt Intendant Bigot had been in charge. British soldiers paid for all their goods and services in coin instead of the worthless paper money that Bigot had used. Jean-Pierre and his people were allowed to practise Roman Catholicism and to continue with all of their own customs. The British army even kept the old laws of New France and carried on all business in French. Governor James Murray and his officials were very kind to the Canadians.

But things were bound to change and they did. Peace between Britain and France was finally declared in 1763. New France officially became the property of Britain. What would happen now?

1763: Making Canada English

British officials decided in 1763 to shrink the boundaries of what was then New France and to call the new colony Quebec. British civil law was proclaimed. This meant that the Canadians were expected to adjust to English language and laws.

This Royal Proclamation of 1763 was doomed to failure. The French-speaking population of Quebec continued to grow, and only a few wealthy English-speaking merchants moved in to the newest English colony. Governor Murray had been instructed to form a governing assembly that excluded all Roman Catholics. This would have meant that all the power went to the English-speaking minority. Murray thought this unwise and unfair. He disliked the English merchants. He thought they were too anxious to take advantage of the conquered Canadians. He delayed the formation of an assembly despite many loud complaints from the English minority. The protests were so loud, in fact, that Governor Murray was recalled to Britain to answer the

This picture shows some of the rebuilding that took place in Quebec after the conquest. Why would the British army want to repair the damage that had been done?

merchants' accusations. A new governor, Guy Carleton, arrived at Quebec.

Governor Carleton treated the situation in much the same way as Murray had. Soon the merchants were complaining again. Carleton realized that the proclamation of 1763 would never work. Another way of governing Quebec had to be found.

The Royal Proclamation of 1763 was intended to make Quebec into a colony like the other British colonies in North America. What made this difficult? What might Canada be like today if that plan had succeeded?

The Quebec Act: Britain Tries Again

After years of debate about how Quebec should be treated, the British government agreed on a new plan. The Quebec Act of 1774 allowed Canadians to keep their French language, Roman Catholic religion, and customs. The boundaries of Quebec were expanded again to include almost all of what had been New France. The English colonists on the east coast of North America were very upset about this. They badly wanted the Ohio Valley for their own use, but the Quebec Act had put an end to that idea.

Would this plan have any more success than the proclamation of 1763?

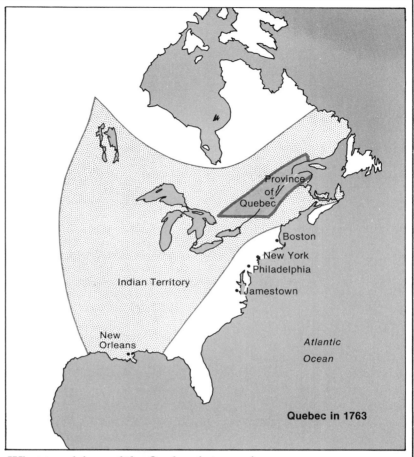

Quebec in 1763

What provisions of the Quebec Act would please the Canadians? What provisions displeased the English colonists? What "use" would they have for the Ohio Valley? What use would Quebec have for the Ohio country?

According to the terms of the Royal Proclamation of 1763, the new (and smaller) colony of Quebec was created. What territory was France allowed to keep in North America?

Pontiac

In the years after the conquest of New France, British merchants had gradually taken over the trading posts in the Great Lakes' fur-trading area. Indians who had been used to trading with the Canadians and receiving good prices for their furs were faced with a change. Now that the fur trade had been taken over by the English, competition was reduced and the prices paid to the Indians were much lower.

What made the situation worse was the fact that English traders and settlers began to move into the area to stay. Settlers cleared land for farms.

They considered the Indians a nuisance to be eliminated.

The chief of the Ottawa Indians, Pontiac, decided that unless his people acted, they would eventually be wiped out. He led an Indian rebellion in 1763 against the British. Indians took over many of the fur-trading forts around the Great Lakes. The bloody fighting continued for most of the summer. But the Indians were doomed, and so was their old way of life. The British army was able to subdue them.

What conflict was there between settlers on the one hand and Indians and fur traders on the other?

153

Unit Three
THE AMERICAN REVOLUTION AND THE LOYALISTS

Part 1

Chapter 31

BRITAIN'S THIRTEEN COLONIES

By the end of the Seven Years' War in 1763, the thirteen English colonies on the Atlantic coast of North America had grown with remarkable speed. Small groups of immigrants from Britain had established settlements in North America as early as 1607. The population of these thirteen colonies had grown to about 1 500 000. This was larger than the population of

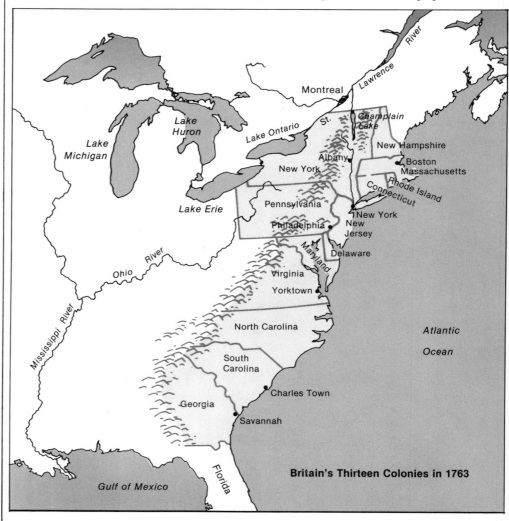

Britain's Thirteen Colonies in 1763

many European countries.

The colonies were far from united. Communication among the colonies was poor. There were very few roads between the colonies, and many of those that existed were little better than footpaths. Most colonists weren't interested in what was happening in the other colonies. Their main concern was with the flow of goods and information to and from Britain. The colonists of Virginia thought of themselves as Virginians; but all the inhabitants along the coast had one common bond. They were British subjects.

Most of the colonies had long since passed the stage of struggling for survival. They were thriving economically. Manufacturing was well developed; in Philadelphia alone there were bustling shipyards, flour mills, tanneries, lumber mills, and brickworks. The New England colonies were important shipbuilding and fishing centres. Prosperous farms provided surplus food for sale in the towns of the colonies and for trade to the West Indies.

The colonies were becoming more self-confident and self-reliant as they developed and prospered.

The colonies had their own style of government. Citizens were elected by the colonial voters to serve on **legislative assemblies**. Many towns also had their own elected councils. The governor was appointed by Britain.

The population of the colonies had been increasing steadily for many years. Some settlers who thought that it was getting too crowded near ·the coast moved westward over the mountains to clear new farm land.

New Laws

In 1763 and 1764, the British government passed laws which caused many American colonists to feel that Britain was trying to exert unfair control over the colonies' affairs. Imagine the feelings of Thomas Allen and James Elliott, two typical colonists, as you read about them.

Thomas Allen was red-faced with anger. The news had caught him

legislative assemblies: elected groups who made the laws

Britain's Thirteen Colonies

COLONY		DATE	REASON FOR SETTLEMENT
Virginia		1607	Trade and profit
Massachusetts:	Plymouth	1620	Religious freedom
	Boston	1630	
New York*		1626	Trade and profit
New Hampshire		1630	Religious freedom
Maryland		1634	Religious freedom
Connecticut		1636	Religious freedom
Rhode Island		1636	Religious freedom
Delaware†		1638	Trade and profit
North Carolina		1653	Trade and profit
New Jersey		1664	Trade and profit
South Carolina		1670	Trade and profit
Pennsylvania		1682	Religious freedom and trade and profit
Georgia		1733	Trade and profit

*New York was originally named New Netherland by Dutch colonists.
†Delaware was originally a Swedish colony.

157

totally by surprise. Thomas's anger deepened as his mind recalled the agony of the trip with his family over the rough terrain of the Appalachian Mountain pass. Virginia seemed so far away now. The family had endured so much, like the back-breaking work of clearing their new homestead on the banks of the Ohio River. All that hard work and sacrifice for nothing!

The British government had just sent word of their "Royal Proclamation" of 1763. The lands west of the mountains were now reserved for the Indians. No settlers were allowed. Thomas was bitter.

In Boston James Elliott was equally angry.

The lights in Boston harbour twinkled in the distance. Twelve-year-old Jennifer Elliott shifted nervously from one foot to another. Her father, James, was silently cursing himself for letting Jennifer talk him into taking her on this trip. He knew what would happen if the British authorities caught his ship, *The Arrow*, and its crew smuggling molasses. Elliott would be in serious trouble. The British customs officials were cracking down on this illegal trade.

The smuggling had been going on for several years without much resistance from the British customs officers in the thirteen colonies. In 1733 Britain had imposed a tax on molasses from West Indian islands that were not British colonies. Not much of that tax was ever collected. But now conditions had changed.

The new "Sugar Act" of 1764 gave the customs officers much more power, and along with that, orders to enforce the new law strictly. It was designed to stop the smuggling of molasses into the colonies. British officials were intent on collecting the tax on molasses which the smugglers had so far avoided.

James Elliott thought it was unfair for the British government to have so much control over the trade in the American colonies. Many of Elliott's fellow colonists agreed.

1. *What reasons would some colonists have for smuggling?*
2. *Suppose that Thomas Allen decided to stay in the Ohio Valley. What do you suppose the outcome might have been?*
3. *Why did the British authorities want to restrict trading carried on by the American colonies? Do you think this policy was justified? Give reasons for your answer.*

New York in the late 1700s was one of the most prosperous towns in the thirteen colonies.

This popular cartoon was meant to persuade colonists from all of the thirteen colonies to unite their efforts against unwanted British taxation.

True stories? No, but there were certainly men and families in very similar circumstances in 1763 and 1764. Many of the colonists in America were as upset and bitter as Thomas Allen and James Elliott. Settlers were no longer allowed on any land west of the Appalachian Mountains. The settlers wondered why Britain had fought for so long to drive the French out of the Ohio Valley only to reserve it for the Indians.

Many of the colonial merchants resented the British laws that didn't allow the colonies to trade with anyone except Britain, or colonies that Britain owned.

Some colonists resented having taxes imposed on them by a government as far away as Britain. The colonists were used to having their own laws and their own elected governments. They felt it was unfair to be taxed without a vote in the British Parliament.

Conflicting Views: Can They Be Resolved?

Following the Seven Years' War, the relationship between Britain and her American colonies changed. There was disagreement over several issues. The chart summarizes some of the viewpoints:

1. For what purpose had Britain passed the Sugar Act of 1764? How else might the British have collected money from the colonies?

2. Outline in your own words the opposing viewpoints of the British government and the American colonists.

British Views

1. The colonies belong to Britain. You exist for our benefit. Britain supports and defends you. Our Parliament passes laws concerning you; you must do something in return. You must sell your raw materials to us and buy our manufactured goods. Don't trade with anyone else or you'll have to pay a heavy tax.

2. We have to deal with the Indian unrest. If we don't proclaim the lands west of the Appalachian Mountains as Indian territory (for the time being) we may soon have another costly war on our hands.

3. We have a huge debt to pay because of the heavy costs of the Seven Years' War. We think that you should help pay for this, since British armies fought to protect you from the French.

4. We need to station a British army in the colonies. You need to be defended. You should also help pay for this. Taxpayers in Britain have enough of a burden. You should share in the costs.

Colonists' Views

1. We can manufacture many of our own goods. Some of our colonists will trade illegally to avoid your rules and taxes. We want to trade at the best prices and not be restricted by British regulations.

2. Why did we fight in the Seven Years' War to drive the French out of the Ohio Valley? It belongs to us. Why are you reserving it for the Indians? We want to settle west of the Appalachian Mountains.

3. Why should we pay for a war between Britain and France? You pay for the war.

4. We don't need an army. The threat of a French attack is gone. What threatens us now?

Chapter 32

ON THE WAY TO WAR

Britain Passes New Acts

The Sugar Act of 1764 not only aroused the resentment of many of the American colonists, but the plan was also a failure. British customs officials collected barely enough money to pay for their own salaries and the costs involved in catching the smugglers. The British government would have to think of a better way to raise money to help pay for the British soldiers stationed in the colonies.

In 1765 the British Parliament passed the Stamp Act. This law required that all newspapers, pamphlets, and legal documents bear stamps that were to be purchased from the British government. Some American colonists were upset and angry.

The Quartering Act which was passed soon after made matters even worse. This law stated that the colonists would have to supply food and housing for the British army in America.

Demonstrations against the Stamp Act took place in many of the colonies. Posters were distributed, speeches were made, and stamps were burned in public. Many of the agents in charge of selling the stamps were harassed and forced to resign. Some colonists agreed to **boycott** British goods.

Colonists who urged the citizens to show open defiance of the Stamp Act became known as the Sons of Liberty. They communicated with one another from colony to colony and did their best to keep **antagonism** high. In August of 1765, there was rioting in the streets of Boston. The British Parliament decided to **repeal** the Stamp Act in March, 1766.

The Boston "Massacre"

Although there was bitter opposi-

boycott: refuse to buy or sell goods

antagonism: hostility, angry opposition

repeal: cancel

The men who were assigned by Britain to collect the stamp tax had a dangerous job. Sometimes angry groups of colonists physically attacked the collectors. This picture shows one such tax collector running for his life.

tion to Britain's attempt to tax the American colonists, it wasn't long before another tax law was passed by the British Parliament. The Townshend Revenue Acts passed in 1767 imposed a tax on all tea, lead, paint, and paper brought to the colonies from Britain.

The reaction of many of the American colonists was hostile. A widespread boycott of British goods began. Merchants who dared to continue importing British goods were often treated with violence. British soldiers in the colonies were made to feel very unwelcome.

More British troops arrived in Boston in October of 1768 to help control the situation. The conflict between soldiers and colonists grew daily.

The friction finally led to a violent clash in Boston on March 5, 1770. The exact details of what happened are not known for certain, but this seems to be what happened:

A group of colonists heckled a British soldier on guard duty. Eight of his fellow soldiers came to his aid with muskets loaded and bayonets readied. Stones were thrown by at least one member of the group of colonists. The crowd became increasingly angry and noisy, and the soldiers became more nervous. When one of the soldiers was reportedly struck by a club, the frightened soldiers opened fire on the crowd. Five colonists died. The governor arrested the soldiers and put them on trial. Two of the soldiers were found guilty of manslaughter. They were branded on the thumb as a "token punishment."

Meanwhile in Britain, many merchants were feeling the pressure of the American boycott. They appealed to their government to change the law. In 1770 the British Parliament decided that it would be best to repeal the Revenue Act.

For the next three years, tension between Britain and the American colonies was reduced. Some of the more **radical** colonists continued with their speeches, meetings, and posters.

These men didn't want to forget the disagreements between Britain and the colonies.

1. What effect would a boycott of British goods likely have?
2. Do you think the course of events would have been different had Britain not sent reinforcement troops to America? Explain your answer.

Paul Revere's picture of the 1770 "Boston Massacre" was used as an effective piece of propaganda by the rebellious colonists. How does the picture exaggerate or distort the details of the event?

Tax collectors weren't the only ones to suffer from the colonists' anger. Those who dared to support British taxation policies were often punished by a public "tarring and feathering."

radical: extreme in opinions and actions

The "Boston Tea Party" angered British officials. They were determined to punish the Boston colonists who were responsible.

The Boston Tea Party

Despite the relatively peaceful relations between Britain and the American colonies after the "Boston Massacre," writers like Samuel Adams continued their **propaganda**. Many of their fellow colonists were tired of the demonstrations, speeches, and meetings. Interest slackened. Samuel Adams didn't really have a crucial issue to stir up the people.

In 1773 the British Parliament passed a law that gave Samuel Adams the issue that he needed. This law gave the East India Company the right to sell its tea at a very low price in the American colonies. Adams and others were quick to point out to the colonists that this was another example of the British government trying to force them to pay an unwanted and unfair tax. The anger of many colonists was aroused again. Several colonial ports refused to allow the unloading of this tea.

Shiploads of the East India tea arrived in Boston harbour and a confrontation developed. A group of angry citizens demanded that the ships leave without unloading their cargo of tea, but the governor refused their demand. On the night of December 16, a group of colonists disguised as Indians boarded the ships. All of the tea was dumped into the harbour. British officials were enraged when they received news of this "Boston Tea Party." The American rebels had gone too far this time in defying the laws of Britain.

1. Why do you suppose the colonists disguised themselves as Indians?
2. If you were a British official who had just received news of the "tea party," what action would you have taken, and why?

The Intolerable Acts

The British Parliament decided in 1774 that it was time to put an end to the defiance shown by the Sons of Liberty. A number of acts were passed which were designed to punish the "Massachusetts radicals," and especially the city of Boston. The port of Boston was closed. Town meetings were forbidden. The Massachusetts Assembly lost much of its power. More British soldiers were sent to Boston, and unused buildings were taken over to house the troops. The American colonists dubbed these British laws the "Intolerable Acts."

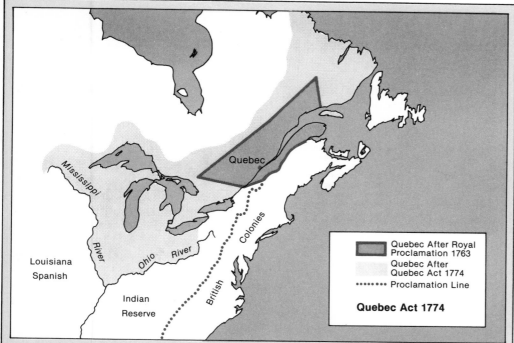

Quebec After Royal Proclamation 1763
Quebec After Quebec Act 1774
•••••• Proclamation Line

Quebec Act 1774

The Quebec Act of 1774

In the midst of all the hostility created by the "Intolerable Acts" of 1774, the British Parliament angered the Americans once more with the passage of the Quebec Act. The Act was designed to please the conquered French Canadians of the British province of Quebec. In attempting to win the support of the French Canadians, the British deepened their conflict with the American colonies. Any one of the Sons of Liberty would have been quick to point out the following:

1. The lands west of the Appalachians rightfully belonged to the American colonies, not the French Canadian fur traders or the Indians.
2. The Protestant American colonists resented the fact that Britain allowed the Quebec colonists to keep their Roman Catholic religion.
3. The Quebec government was to be appointed by British officials. The American colonists thought that Quebec should have an elected assembly, as the other colonies did.

The First Congress

A meeting of representatives of all thirteen colonies took place in Philadelphia in September of 1774. This meeting became known as the First Continental Congress. Some of the delegates to the Congress felt that strong united action against Britain was necessary. Others hesitated to oppose British law. After much debate, the delegates decided to boycott all British trade goods and to form committees of colonists to enforce the boycott. Sons of Liberty secretly began to store gunpowder and ammunition in readiness. Local fighting militias made up of "minutemen" were organized. They were to be ready to fight on a moment's notice.

1. The "Boston rebels" deserved the treatment that they got from Britain following the "tea party." Do you strongly agree, agree, disagree, or strongly disagree? Explain your choice.
2. What role were the "minutemen" expected to fulfill?
3. Outline the reasons for American opposition to the Quebec Act.

163

Chapter 33 | REBELS AND REDCOATS

The American Revolution: Facts and Figures

BRITAIN	COLONIES
1775	
NAVY	
• 270 warships	• 8 small ships
• 16 000 men	
ARMY	
• 7000 in colonies	• 6000 troops
• ample weapons stored in colonies	• unknown number of short-term volunteers
	• 2 gun factories imported gunpowder
POPULATION	
• 8 000 000	• 2 500 000
1783	
TROOPS	
• 50 000 British	• 6000-28 000 in Washington's army
• 8200 Loyalists	• thousands of others served short terms
MILITARY EXPENSES	
• $712 000 000	• $550 000 000 in U.S. money, $12 000 000 in foreign loans

Minutemen were ready to fight for their cause at any time. This farmer ploughs his field and waits for the call to arms.

Some American colonists prepared for war by making weapons.

The Sons of Liberty spent the winter of 1774–1775 preparing for the possibility of a violent clash with the British. Some radical colonists continued to hide gunpowder and ammunition.

In April of 1775, Governor Gage of Massachusetts ordered British troops to the small village of Concord to seize the secret supplies of gunpowder and ammunition. The movements of the redcoats were being closely watched by the rebels. When it became obvious on the night of April 18, that the British soldiers were headed towards Concord, Paul Revere began his famous ride. He set out to warn the keepers of the secret supplies at Concord, and also to warn the rebel leaders, John Hancock and Samuel Adams, who were hiding in nearby Lexington. Lexington was on the road to Concord, the destination of the British troops.

On the morning of April 19, 1775, about 700 redcoated British soldiers and a small group of about 80 minutemen faced each other just outside the town of Lexington. No one knows who fired the first shot. When the skirmish had ended, 8 American minutemen were dead, and 10 others were wounded. The British troops then continued their march towards Concord, thirteen kilometres away.

At Concord's North Bridge, the red-

Paul Revere's ride to warn of the British soldiers' march to Lexington and Concord was stopped before he got to Lexington. He was caught by a small group of British soldiers along the road. Another rider managed to escape to carry the warning.

There was an exchange of gunfire on the early morning of April 19, 1775. Eight minutemen lost their lives. The British soldiers marched on to Concord to seize the hidden ammunition.

coats came face to face with another determined group of American minutemen. In the battle that followed, soldiers were killed on both sides. The British were forced to retreat to the safety of Boston. Their twenty-six kilometre march back to Boston was a nightmare. Hundreds of American snipers fired at the marching British soldiers. Rebel riflemen fired from behind buildings, stone fences, and trees, as details of British soldiers tried in vain to protect the marching column.

Seventy-three British soldiers were killed and about 200 wounded. The minutemen counted 49 dead and 46 wounded. The weary British troops did not reach the safety of Boston until after sunset.

How might Governor Gage have found out about the hidden gunpowder and ammunition at Concord? Do you think Gage might have been wiser not to send soldiers to seize the ammunition? Explain your answer.

The Struggle for the Fourteenth Colony

American colonists all along the Atlantic coast readied themselves for the fighting that was sure to follow the violent clashes at Lexington and Concord.

But what about the British colonies of Quebec and Nova Scotia? Where did their loyalties lie? This question had been considered by the Sons of Liberty even before the skirmish at Concord. The Continental Congress of 1774 had sent a "letter" to the inhabitants of Quebec inviting them to send representatives to the next Continental Congress in Philadelphia. There were also strong hints that the American army would invade and "destroy" Canada if it wished to.

The Quebec colonists were given much advice on both sides of the question that winter. There were people in the colony who actively supported the Sons of Liberty, but the majority of the citizens chose to remain "neutral," not letting either side win their total support. The situation was much the same in Nova Scotia.

In the spring of 1775, the New England rebel militia decided to begin operations against Canada. On May 10, Fort Ticonderoga, on Lake Champlain, was taken by surprise, and the next day the fort at Crown Point was also captured by the Americans. These two forts guarded the invasion route between the thirteen colonies and Quebec. The way was clear to invade Montreal and then Quebec, the British stronghold on the St. Lawrence River.

Invasion of Canada

On June 27, 1775, the Continental Congress finally authorized an inva-

One of the Forty-Nine: Isaac Davis

The fighting at Lexington and Concord brought death to both American and British soldiers. Families of many of the American minutemen were given the terrible news that day. Here is the account given by the wife of a slain minuteman.

Isaac Davis was my husband. He was then thirty years of age. We had four children; the youngest about fifteen months old. They were all unwell when he left me, in the morning; some of them with the canker-rash.

The alarm was given early in the morning, and my husband lost no time in making ready to go to Concord with his company. My husband said but little that morning. He seemed serious and thoughtful; but never seemed to hesitate. He only said "Take good care of the children," and was soon out of sight.

In the afternoon he was brought home a corpse. He was placed in my bedroom till the funeral.[1]

What attitude do you suppose Mrs. Davis and the other widows would have toward the "rebel cause"?

sion of Canada.

Late that summer about 1200 American soldiers travelled up the Champlain waterway and into the heart of Canada. They easily captured Montreal, after Quebec's governor, Sir Guy Carleton, abandoned his plans to defend the town. He had received very little support from the citizens. Carleton narrowly escaped American capture and fled down the St. Lawrence River to Quebec.

Carleton travelled by bateau, disguised as a Canadian farmer. He was forced to hide in the bottom of the boat as it passed near a group of Montgomery's men camped on the river bank. For a few tense moments, Carleton must have held his breath. If he were captured, the colony would have had no governor, and the American plan to take Quebec would have had a good chance of success. Carleton reached Quebec safely, and began preparations to defend the town from the American attackers.

General Montgomery's troops and the force led by Benedict Arnold converged on the city of Quebec and, on December 3, began the siege of the fortress.

Governor Carleton was prepared to wait out the siege. The Americans had no artillery to bombard the town, their supplies were dwindling fast, and the troops were stricken with a smallpox epidemic. The only slim hope for the American invaders was a surprise assault on the fortress. On New Year's Eve, General Montgomery decided that the blizzard conditions provided a likely opportunity.

The American assault was a complete disaster. News of the impending attack was carried to Carleton by American deserters. General Montgomery was killed, along with at least 100 of his comrades. Hundreds of Americans were taken prisoner. Despite the dreadful setback, Arnold, and what remained of his troops, continued their siege of Quebec. Arnold pleaded for reinforcements and supplies. Some American reinforcements arrived in April, but on May 6 the sails of the British fleet were seen on the St. Lawrence. Arnold's struggles had been for nothing.

Arnold and his men didn't care to do battle with the British reinforcements. A hasty and disorderly retreat began, with Governor Carleton's troops driving the scattered Americans south. The American rebels' hopes of making Quebec their "fourteenth colony" were shattered.

General Montgomery's New Year's Eve attack on Quebec was short-lived. Montgomery was mortally wounded in the first minutes of the attack, and his men quickly retreated. Quebec's defenders had done their job well.

General Arnold Marches to Quebec

The American invasion of Quebec was to be a two-pronged attack. General Montgomery's troops travelled up the well-known Champlain waterway to the St. Lawrence River. Benedict Arnold led his forces on a different route, farther east. The troops directed by Arnold were the victims of a miscalculation based on faulty geographical knowledge. Arnold guessed that his army could easily travel the 280 km from Augusta, Maine, to Quebec by following the Kennebec and Chaudière rivers. He estimated it would take two weeks to reach Quebec. The actual distance was 560 km; the trip took forty-six days; the journey was a nightmare.

Heavy rains constantly soaked the men and supplies. The rivers were shallow and full of obstructions. The trails were strewn with underbrush, and the portages were back breaking. General Arnold wrote of his discouragement on October 24:

> The excessive rain and bad weather have **retarded** our march. The march has been attended with an amazing deal of fatigue, which the officers and men have borne with cheerfulness. I have been much deceived in every account of our route, which is longer and has been attended with a thousand difficulties I never **apprehended**.[2]

Later on the long trek, the troops' doctor wrote of further problems:

> Our greatest luxuries now consisted in a little water, stiffened with flour, in imitation of shoemaker's paste. In company was a poor dog who became prey for the **sustenance** of the assassinators. This poor animal was instantly devoured, without leaving any **vestige** of the sacrifice. Nor did the shaving soap, leather of their shoes, cartridge boxes, etc., share any better fate.[3]

The appalling conditions persuaded many of Arnold's soldiers to turn back, often with more than their share of the scarce provisions. Arnold's weary force, reduced to 600 men from the original 1000, reached the Quebec fortress in November. Had the men only known it, the worst was yet to come.

1. *List the problems Arnold's men faced before their arrival at Quebec. What further difficulties might they expect?*
2. *What were the men forced to eat during their trek?*
3. *Write a letter home to your family describing your troubles as you accompany Arnold to Quebec.*

apprehended: anticipated

sustenance: food

vestige: trace

retarded: slowed

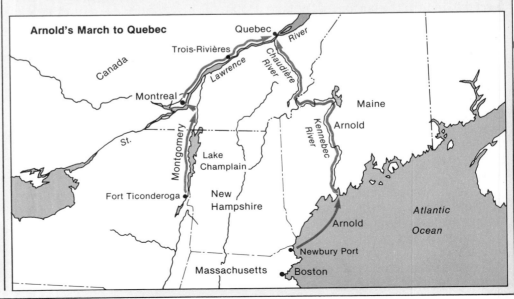

Arnold's March to Quebec

Canada · Quebec · Trois-Rivières · Montreal · St. Lawrence · Chaudière River · Kennebec River · Maine · Arnold · Lake Champlain · Fort Ticonderoga · New Hampshire · Montgomery · Atlantic Ocean · Arnold · Newbury Port · Massachusetts · Boston

Arnold's force of 1000 men endured severe hardships on their trip to Quebec. Only 600 men arrived at Quebec.

THE WAR FOR INDEPENDENCE

Even in 1776, after many lives had been lost on both sides, many American colonists hoped that negotiating would end the dispute peacefully. Those dim hopes were dashed by the signing of the Declaration of Independence on July 4, 1776. The Continental Congress decided that complete independence from Britain was the only wise choice. All that summer, the Declaration was read publicly in towns in the thirteen colonies. The issue was clearly going to be settled by war.

The fighting which had begun with skirmishes between small groups of American rebels and British soldiers became a full-scale war. Thousands of men and tonnes of weaponry were moved around. The British war machinery held a tremendous advantage both in personnel and in supplies. However, the Americans prevented the British from gaining complete control of the tremendous expanse of territory that made up the thirteen colonies. The British still held a decided edge in manpower and battle victories when the British general, Cornwallis, surrendered to the Americans at Yorktown, Virginia, in 1781.

British taxpayers were complaining about the costs of the war, and wondering whether it was really worth it. Perhaps American independence was preferable to this war. Peace negotiations were begun in 1782.

A year later, a peace treaty was signed. The American colonies were independent. A new nation was born—the United States of America.

The revolutionary war was over for these British troops. They left New York in 1783 and sailed to Halifax. The last remnants of the British army in the United States were gone.

Part 2

Chapter 35

THE UNITED EMPIRE LOYALISTS

HOW TO MAKE A LOYALIST

Walter Bates was sixteen years old when he found out what the Revolution in America meant. He was at his Connecticut home when he was accused by some rebels of concealing information about his brother and some soldiers who were known to be loyal to the British side. Here is what happened to him:

I was taken to the Guard House and threatened with death if I did not confess. At 10 o'clock at night, I was taken out by an armed mob, conveyed through the field gate to Back Creek, then having been stripped, my body was exposed to the mosquitoes, my hands and feet being confined to a tree.

I told them that I knew nothing. The Guard then came to me and said they were ordered to give me 100 **stripes,** and if that did not kill me I would be sentenced to be hanged. Twenty stripes was then executed with severity, after which they sent me again to the Guard House, where I was insulted and abused by all.

The next day the committee proposed to extort a confession from me by confining me to a log in the saw mill and let the saw cut me in two.[1]

Walter was discharged after three days of this kind of treatment but had to remain hidden in the forest near his Connecticut home. He had revealed no information to the rebels.

What had caused some colonists to treat their fellows so harshly? And why did some colonists choose to put up with such treatment rather than join the rebel side?

stripes: lashes with a whip as punishment

Tarring and feathering was a harsh treatment forced upon some Loyalists. Here a mob applies tar and taunts a Loyalist. Locate the basket of feathers. Why would such a punishment be used?

To the rebellious colonists, anyone who seemed to support the British side in the revolution was an enemy, and possibly a spy. After the Declaration of Independence, all American citizens were required to pledge their loyalty to the Congress. Anyone caught helping the British or speaking harshly of the rebels was accused of being a traitor. Property was confiscated and families were driven from their homes. People in this tense atmosphere acted rashly and were often cruel to the "Tories" or "Loyalists." The Loyalists were the people who had remained loyal to Britain. They opposed the Revolution and the independence of the thirteen colonies. Walter Bates and his family were among the estimated 500 000 Loyalists in the colonies.

Reasons for Loyalty

The reasons for preferring to remain loyal to Britain varied. People who had worked as officials of the British government (customs officers, judges, etc.), and Church of England clergy had no choice. They were literally driven out of their homes. Others had joined the British army to fight the rebels and would never be permitted to return to their homes. Many colonists preferred the British form of government. Some were loyal because they feared the mob violence of some revolutionaries, or because of their religious beliefs (people who were **Mennonites** and **Quakers** opposed all war). When the British government offered free land in other North American colonies to Loyalists, many decided to take a chance on life in a new place. They wanted the land as much as they wanted to live under the British **Crown**.

Whatever their reasons, nearly one-third of the population of the thirteen colonies was loyal to Britain. As the British forces suffered defeats in the war and retreated, thousands of people sought safety behind British lines. Many fled to New York City, a British stronghold. Carrying what they could, Loyalist families said farewell to their homes and became refugees. As they later boarded British ships to leave America, many must have been saddened and angered at what the Revolution had done to them.

Loyalists carried as many of their possessions and tools as possible in their flight from the United States to Canada.

Mennonites and Quakers: members of two Christian religious groups

Crown: British government

Annapolis Royal, Nova Scotia, received some of the 30 000 Loyalists who left the United States to come to Nova Scotia in the 1780s.

Loyalists Leave the United States

About 100 000 Loyalists emigrated from the United States during the revolutionary period (1775-1784). There were people from every colony and every walk of life—wealthy merchants, owners of large estates, small farmers, craftsmen. Eighteen thousand went to the British West Indies (the Bahamas); 45 000 travelled to what is now Canada. The remainder went to England. Here is an eyewitness account of the **evacuation** of the British and their Loyalist followers from Charleston, South Carolina, in 1782.

There were old grey-headed men and women, husbands and wives with large families of little children, women with infants, poor widows, taking leave of their friends. Here, you saw people leaving their estates, houses, stores, ships and hurrying on board the transports with what little household goods they had been able to save. In every street were to be seen men, women, and children wringing their hands, lamenting.

No sooner had the evacuation taken place than the rebels entered the town. The Loyalists [who had stayed behind] were seized, hove [thrown] into dungeons and prisons. Some were tied up and whipped, others were tarred and feathered. All were turned out of their houses and obliged to sleep in the streets and fields.[2]

After the peace of 1783, similar scenes took place throughout the new American nation. Those Loyalists who had tried to remain neutral were forced to decide in favour of leaving their homes.

1. List five reasons a colonist might have had for remaining loyal to Britain.
2. What point of view does the author of the Charleston evacuation story take, loyal or rebel? Give proof for your answer.
3. Which Loyalists fared better, those who left Charleston with the British, or those who remained behind? In which group would you rather have been? Explain your reasons.
4. What is a "rebel"? What is a "patriot"? How could the same person be called both a rebel and a patriot?

evacuation: withdrawal from a place

ON TO NOVA SCOTIA

Sarah Frost was tired, but she had no time to rest. She knew that her husband's actions in leading a Loyalist raid against a group of rebels in Connecticut meant bad news for the family. She gathered a few treasured belongings and hurried her children into the cart. Their ship would be sailing from the port of New York any day now. The Frosts prepared to begin a new life in Nova Scotia. Sarah's diary was not neglected. ...

Monday, June 9, 1783. Our women with their children all came on board [the ship *Two Sisters*] today and there is great confusion in the cabin. We bear it pretty well through the day, but as it grows towards night one child cries in one place and one in another. I think sometimes I shall be crazy.

Monday, June 16. Off at last! We have 13 ships.

Tuesday, June 24. Our captain told me we should be in the Bay of Fundy before morning. It is about one day's sail to St. John River. Oh, how I long to see that place, though a strange land.

Saturday, June 28. Our ship has anchored in St. John River. Our people went on shore and brought on board gooseberries and grass and pea vines with the blossoms on them. They say this is to be our city [in this wilderness].

Sunday, June 29. I have been ashore. It is, I think, the roughest land I ever saw. We are all ordered to land tomorrow, and not a shelter to go under.[1]

1. What hardships might Sarah Frost have faced by Sunday, June 29, 1783?
2. What future hardships and challenges await her? Write another diary page.

Sarah Frost and her family were among a group of 20 000 Loyalists who fled to Nova Scotia. Another 600 went to Prince Edward Island. Most were from the middle colonies (New York, New Jersey, and Pennsylvania). The British government decided to send most of the unexpectedly large number of newcomers to unsettled areas of Nova Scotia. These areas were at Port Roseway (renamed Shelburne) and along the valley of the St. John River.

This painting shows the landing of 180 Scots at Pictou harbour, Nova Scotia, in 1773. During the eleven-week voyage on the ocean, 18 people died. Suggest why the piper would play a tune so soon after landing.

Shelburne: An Instant Town

The fleet of ships lay at anchor as the soft May breeze stirred the ships' ropes. The crowds on board had finally removed the last of their belongings, and the small boats had carried them ashore. Shelburne was a long way from New York.

The rocky Nova Scotia shoreline revealed an excellent harbour. The Loyalist leaders had chosen their town site carefully. They planned to make a success of their town. Five days after their arrival, the Loyalists were busily chopping down trees on Shelburne's "main street."

Surveyors were marking off lots for the settlers. Chief Surveyor Benjamin Marston complained about his job in his diary:

Thursday, June 19 [1783]. Yesterday and today engaged in surveying the shore and laying out 50 acre [20 ha] lots for private parties. 'Tis a hard service, and though I make a good wage, 'tis all earned. The heat in the woods and the black flies are almost insupportable.

Wednesday, July 2. Today at town fixing the lines of some streets and measuring off some house lots. A vessel arrived from New York by which we learned six months' more provisions are promised for the settlers here.

Saturday, July 12. The people yesterday drew for their 50 acre [20 ha] lots. Several vessels arrived from New England with lumber, bricks and provisions.[2]

Commissary Edward Binkley supervised the distribution of these provisions. Salt pork and flour, the food provided by the British government, were rationed to the settlers. A boring diet it must have been, but welcome, until the Loyalists could organize their lives and obtain other food from the sea, forest, and farm. Binkley's three large warehouses were popular buildings in the first years of the town's life. In January of 1784, over 5900 Loyalists relied on the commissary for food. They also used Binkley's building materials.

Shelburne's streets were wide and straight, just right for such a large town. By the end of 1784, 12 000 people lived in the "instant town." Large graceful homes lined some of the new streets. Wharves and warehouses were busy. Wealthy businessmen and professional people had brought their families and their dreams to the new town. Farms were begun in the neighbourhood. Ships were built in the town. Fishing boats brought their cod to the harbour. Shelburne's future looked promising.

Something went wrong. Within fifty years Shelburne was nearly a ghost town. Other ports were busier. There were no thriving agricultural or lumbering communities surrounding Shelburne to provide the town with trade goods. The port lost business, the shipyards ran short of contracts to fill, the merchants moved to Halifax or other towns, and the tradespeople followed them. There were not enough jobs to keep people there, so thousands left. Here's a portrait of Shelburne in 1830:

The present population of Shelburne is not more than 500. The ruined state of the place—streets overrun with grass; tall houses with broken windows, the floors fallen in, doors ajar or broken off their hinges, ceiling broken, and walls covered with green moss; a picture of desolation.[3]

Make a time line for the years 1783-1830. On it mark major events in the life of the town of Shelburne.

commissary: person in charge of food and other supplies

This Loyalist house was built in the summer of 1783 in Shelburne, Nova Scotia. The house has been restored and is now a museum. Shelburne was Canada's largest town in 1783. More than 10 000 Loyalists arrived in the tiny fishing village, once called Port Roseway.

174

Black Loyalists

A number of Loyalist soldiers called the Black Pioneers were among the groups that migrated to Nova Scotia. These and other black Loyalists arrived at Shelburne in 1783. Most had been slaves in the thirteen colonies. The British army had promised them their freedom. The end of the war brought fearful times for these blacks. Former slaves were hunted by their masters. The British commander at New York, Sir Guy Carleton, decided to permit 3000 black Loyalists to leave the city for new homes in Nova Scotia. Altogether, as many as 14 000 blacks left the United States during the revolutionary period. The Shelburne group faced many challenges.

Birch Town

A village called Birch Town, several kilometres from Shelburne, was the black Loyalists' reward. Birch Town was a miserable place filled with struggling people. The lots granted to the people were small and heavily wooded. Farming them was nearly impossible. Jobs in Shelburne were available, but competition for them became fierce as time passed and more Loyalists seeking work arrived in the area.

Screams rang out in the darkness of the summer night. The rioters were coming closer! Flames tore through the wooden houses. By morning twenty black families were homeless. Rioting soldiers had taken out their anger and frustration on Birch Town. As disbanded troops of the king's regiments, these English and Scots soldiers had been promised grants of good land but had been forced to wait. They descended on Birch Town and filled the air with fear. Life in their new homeland was proving difficult for the black Loyalists.

Thomas Peters, a sergeant in the Black Pioneers, described their problems in a petition to the British government requesting help for his people. Although promised grants of land as Loyalists, the blacks did not receive their land. The petition said:

Though a further proportion of 20 acres [8 ha] for each private man [one-fifth of the allowance of land due them] was actually laid out and located for them, it was afterwards taken from them and they have never yet obtained other lands. They remain destitute and helpless. There are besides about 100 families of black refugees or more at New Brunswick in a like unprovided and destitute condition, for though some of them have had a part of their allowance of land, it is so far distant from their 1 acre [.5 ha] town lots being 16 or 18 miles [26 or 29 km] back as to be entirely useless.[4]

Peters suggested that the government help the black Loyalists obtain the land promised them. He also explained that some blacks wished to leave Nova Scotia. A group of 1100 pioneers was organized and sailed to Sierra Leone, West Africa. However, this colonizing venture was not very successful. The colonists faced serious problems: poor farm land, an unfamiliar and unpleasant tropical environment, and hostility from native inhabitants of the area. Many left the Sierra Leone colony.

For those who remained in Birch Town, conditions worsened as the town of Shelburne began to decline. Jobs were scarce and so was food.

This woodcutter in Shelburne, Nova Scotia, was one of the many blacks who left the United States in the 1780s.

commodious: roomy

Growth of the Atlantic Colonies

The Loyalists who settled in the Atlantic colonies faced the challenge of all pioneers—building a new life in the wilderness. Farming was not easy for inexperienced Loyalists from the city. Many were granted stony or infertile land. People who had been merchants or tradespeople in the thirteen colonies could not easily make the change to successful farming. They eventually left the Atlantic region to resettle in the United States or other parts of Canada.

Those who remained saw the creation of a new province called New Brunswick in August, 1784. The Loyalist founders of the province became government officials, farmers, merchants, ship builders, sailors, and lumbermen. Ships from Atlantic ports carried goods (legal and smuggled) to the West Indies and the United States. Busy towns were established to serve the growing population. Prosperous farms in Nova Scotia provided beef, dairy products, and potatoes for markets in the Atlantic colonies and the United States. New Brunswickers felt good about their colony. In 1791, a Loyalist described conditions:

Our province goes on slowly but sure. The inhabitants gradually extend their cultivation and we begin to feel the benefits of our exertions. We have good markets in the towns and the farmers live comfortably.[5]

A traveller to the young town of Saint John in the same year wrote:

The town is well planned. It consists of about 500 houses, all of timber, well painted. They have a neat appearance, and some of them even elegant; generally consisting of two stories. The shops, stores, and wharves are numerous and **commodious**. They have two churches, also of wood.[6]

A Loyalist pioneer in Prince Edward Island had successfully adapted to his new home. In 1803 a visitor described his trip to see pioneer farmer Joe Laird:

He lent me a horse and agreed to show me the way to Charlottetown. He began here quite bare eight years ago. He has now 50 acres [20 hectares] cleared, much hay, a good stock of sheep and cattle, an orchard, a comfortable house, and plenty of everything.[7]

List the activities going on in this sketch of the inside of a house in Rustico, Prince Edward Island.

Pioneering, New Brunswick Style

What did it take to build up a farm in the woods? Suppose that a Loyalist family came upon this poster:

Pioneers to New Brunswick did not have a chance to read the kind of advice given here, but they would have understood the ideas it presents.

1. What has the author of this advice to pioneers left out? Suggest some additional aids to a Loyalist pioneer.
2. Draw a picture story to illustrate the steps a Loyalist family had to follow in building up a farm.
3. What advantages did New Brunswick offer?
4. Draw a sketch to illustrate one of the dangers the author warns the pioneers about.

Fredericton, the capital of New Brunswick, in winter.

A New Brunswick farmer relied on sleds (bottom) and sleighs (top) for winter transportation. What might he haul on the sled?

177

Chapter 37 | MOVING TO QUEBEC

The migration began in 1778. Thousands of soldiers and Indians of the Six Nations, who had fought against the American rebels began to flee the United States. The escaping soldiers had belonged to the "provincial" regiments, which had been made up of soldiers from the colonies. Realizing that their cause was lost, they sought refuge in Quebec, the huge British colony north of the Great Lakes and the St. Lawrence River. They travelled through the wilderness of New York State to the Niagara region or Sorel, east of Montreal. Creaking oxcarts carried the soldiers' families to a new life, for wives and children of Loyalist troops were also forced to leave their homes.

Others came too, for the United States was no longer a place they could call home. There were different categories of Loyalists. Some had been organized while in New York and sent from there in groups. Others had been in the British army or were in provincial regiments. A third group had left the thirteen colonies on their own during the revolutionary war.

The Reverend John Stuart explains why he fled:

My house has been frequently broken open by rebel mobs; my property **plundered**; my farm and the produce of it was formally taken from me. I set out on my journey [to Canada] with my wife and three small children and after suffering much fatigue and

plundered: stolen

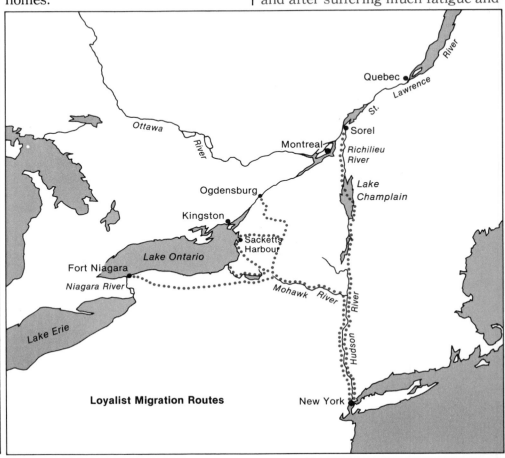

Loyalist Migration Routes

difficulty we arrived safe in Canada [after 3 weeks].

I cannot omit to mention that my Church was plundered by the rebels. It was afterwards used as a tavern, a barrel of rum placed on the reading desk. The next season it was used as a stable. It now serves as a fort to protect a set of great villains.[1]

1. Was Stuart a Tory or a "patriot"?
2. What did the rebels consider him to be?
3. How did they treat him?
4. In which category of Loyalist is the Stuart family?

The refugees gathered at Sorel on the south shore of the St. Lawrence River. They lived in barracks and tents. By December, 1783, there were 3000 people in the camp east of Montreal. The British government had a problem. What was to be done with all these Loyalists? Governor Sir Frederick Haldimand acted quickly. Food,

Providing for the Loyalists

The Loyalists who waited at Sorel in the winter of 1783-84 listed the things they hoped Governor Haldimand could obtain for them. Their first priority was food and shelter. To help them look after these needs, they asked for axes, ploughs, spades, hoes, saws, hammers, horses, cows, sheep, and seed. Haldimand did his best to provide as many of these things as he could. The Loyalists received:

— shelter in the Sorel camp
— free land
— food for two years
— clothing or fabric to make clothing
— some tools
— seed to grow potatoes, corn, wheat, flax, peas
— transportation

Clothing for the Loyalists, issued at Sorel, May 24, 1784.

Coats	70
Waistcoats	70
Breeches	pairs 70
Hats	70
Metres of linen	420
Woollen cloth	103
Blankets	127
Short leggings	70
Stockings	pairs 127
Shoe soles	pairs 127

Land for the Loyalists:

To every head of family	60 ha
To each family member	20 ha
To each single man	20 ha
To each field officer	600 ha

The grants were increased in 1788.

1. List the Loyalists' needs in 1784. How many of these were met by the British government?
2. What would the Loyalists do with their 420 m of linen? Their 127 pairs of shoe soles?
3. The British government felt obliged to care for the Loyalists. Explain why you do or do not think that Britain should have provided such things as free land, food, and tools for the Loyalists.
4. What might have happened to the Loyalists if Britain had not been generous? Suggest three possibilities.
5. What reasons might there have been for giving officers in the army such large grants of land?

Loyalists camped at Johnstown on the St. Lawrence River in June of 1784. The crowded camp at Sorel behind them, they prepared to begin a new life. Identify some of the activities of the people in this picture.

clothing, and shelter were provided immediately. In the spring, Haldimand sent Surveyor General Samuel Holland up the St. Lawrence River to begin looking for sites on which the Loyalists could be settled. Holland located some good spots—along the St. Lawrence River west of Montreal, near Cataraqui (now Kingston), along Lake Ontario, and in the Niagara region. The Loyalists would receive grants of free land, but first it had to be purchased from its original users, the Mississauga Indians. This was done. In the spring of 1784, the surveyors got out their chains and began to mark off townships and lot sites. They had to hurry. The settlers wanted their land.

Drawing Lots

It was June, 1784. The bateaux had moved through the rapids cautiously. The men, women, and children were weary but excited. Soon they would be out of the boats. Their new land was just ahead. Then their journey would end. No more sleeping in the barracks at Sorel, no more crowded camp conditions. But weren't they starting on a new set of problems? The forest was dense and their tools were inadequate for the job of clearing their land. They had no oxen or horses to help prepare the land for planting the seed provided by Governor Haldimand. The government's food and clothing rations would last the winter, but what about shelter? Tough times lay ahead. The bateaux drew up to the shore. Now they would find out where their lots and their dreams were to be.

In the surveyor's hat lay the ballots. Each ballot was numbered according to the lot numbers on the surveyor's map. Each family drew out a ballot, studied the lot numbers on the map, and received a "location ticket," or certificate, for the chosen lot. Most families received more than one lot. All wanted a lot on the river. It would be their highway, for there were few paths through the thick forest. Other lots, to complete each family's grant, were located on the concessions farther back from the river. After the lot was located, each family set to work—the back-breaking work of all pioneers in the wilderness. Many of the Loyalists had pioneered before. They had been farmers in New York and Pennsylvania. They knew what needed to be done.

A Bateau

A bateau, as described by a traveller in Canada in 1793:

A bateau is a particular kind of boat used upon the large rivers and lakes in Canada. The bottom of it is perfectly flat, and each end is built very sharp, and exactly alike. The sides are about 3 feet [one metre] high and, for the convenience of the rowers, four or five benches are laid across. It is a very heavy, awkward sort of vessel, either for rowing or for sailing, but it is preferred to a boat with a keel for two reasons; first, because it draws less water, at the same time that it carries a larger burden; and secondly, because it is much safer on lakes or wide rivers, where storms are frequent.[2]

1. Give three reasons why the bateau was used on Canadian lakes and rivers.
2. Sketch a bateau.

Thomas Davies's painting of farms, just below Quebec, in 1789. Is this a good location for these farms? Explain your answer.

FACING THE WILDERNESS

What challenges confronted the Loyalists who had come to Quebec? How well did they respond to these challenges? Catherine White was a little girl when her family moved to the Bay of Quinte to pioneer. Here is how she remembered their life there.

Mother used to help to chop down the trees, and attended the household duties. We were very useful to her, attended the cattle, churned the butter, making cheese, dressing the flax, spinning, making our own cloth and stockings. We had no neighbours but an old Englishman who lived at some distance off, who was an occasional visitor. Before our crops came around, having brought the seed with us, supplied by the government, we had rations from the military posts; also, when these were nearly **exhausted**, father collected our butter, cheese, and spinning, taking them in a bateau to Kingston, where he traded them off for salt, tea and flour.

The Bay of Quinte was covered with ducks, of which we could obtain any quantity from the Indians. As to fish, they could be had by fishing with a scoop. I have often speared large salmon with a pitchfork. Now and then provisions were very scant, but there being plenty of bullfrogs, we **fared sumptuously**. This was the time of the famine, I think, in 1788; we were obliged to dig up our potatoes, after planting them, to eat.

We never thought of these **privations** but were always happy and cheerful. We left everything to our faithful Governor.

Of an evening, my father would

fared sumptuously: ate well

privations: hardships

exhausted: used up

Many Loyalists journeyed from Sorel to the Bay of Quinte region. A group of families is shown landing on the Bay of Quinte shore. What might their feelings have been at that time?

make shoes of deerskins for the children and mother made homespun dresses.

We had no doctors, no lawyers, no stated clergy. We had prayers at home. An old woman in the next clearing was the chief physician in the surrounding country as it gradually settled.[1]

1. Catherine White had happy memories of her family's pioneer days. What evidence is there that she took a rosy view of the past, that her family's "good times" were remembered, while the bad times were overlooked?
2. What qualities did Catherine say were needed in order for a pioneer to succeed?
3. List the chores done by the White children.
4. List the food Catherine remembers.
5. Find evidence that the White family was self-sufficient with regard to their food supply.
6. Find evidence that they received help from others in supplying their food.

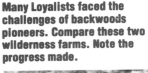
Many Loyalists faced the challenges of backwoods pioneers. Compare these two wilderness farms. Note the progress made.

The Early Years

Not all Loyalist families were as happy and successful at pioneering as Catherine White's had been. During the hungry years of 1788-1789, food was scarce throughout Canada. People ate what they had and then went hungry. Starvation faced many. Families made stew of their dogs, the roots of plants, or the bark of trees. They existed for months on oatmeal porridge or thin soup made by boiling bones over and over again in water. What had caused such terrible conditions? The government had decided that food rations were no longer needed. Then nature was cruel to the pioneers. Crops failed in a bad drought. A snowy, cold winter followed. Rivers froze so hard and so thick that fishing was impossible. Even wildlife was scarce. Hunters returned to their families empty handed.

There were other problems for the

Loyalists, too. Many large grants of land were not occupied. This left some families very isolated because of the distances between their clearings. There were few mills available in which grain could be ground into flour. Transportation meant river transportation since there were no roads and few cart tracks through the forest. These things would change, and improvements would come, as more settlers arrived. One of the Loyalists' biggest complaints concerned the system of land ownership. Land in Quebec was held by the king and granted to the Loyalists as under the seigniorial system, although no rents or other obligations were paid. People preferred to have the British system, called freehold tenure, which meant that they owned the land themselves. The Loyalists petitioned the British government for change. They wanted to be landowners. The government agreed.

The Two Canadas

The government in Britain faced a problem: what should be done about the colony of Quebec? In the western part of the colony, there were thousands of English-speaking settlers who wanted the British system of holding land. They also wanted an assembly where their elected representatives could meet. In the older part of Quebec were thousands of French-speaking people. Between the two groups were long distances, different values, and different needs. The government in Britain knew that change was necessary. Quebec was not the same colony it had been in

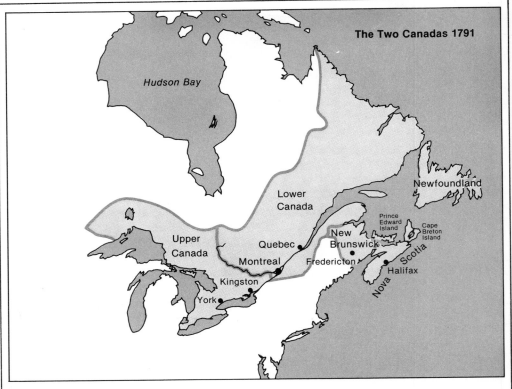

The Two Canadas 1791

1774, when the Quebec Act seemed satisfactory.

The British government had three choices: it could please the Loyalists, please the French Canadians, or please them both. It tried to do the last by dividing Quebec so that the needs of both the Loyalists and the French Canadians could be met in separate provinces.

In 1791 the British Parliament passed an Act of Constitution to deal with Quebec. The provinces of Upper and Lower Canada were created by dividing the old colony at the Ottawa River. Each had an elected assembly to raise taxes and pass necessary laws. Each also had an appointed council to assist the governors of the provinces, and the governor-general at Quebec. Canada was now made up of two provinces, thanks to the large numbers of Loyalists.

The Upper Canadian Loyalists faced many hardships, but that was to be expected for they were refugees and pioneers. In fact, they may have fared better than Loyalists elsewhere in the country. They were in a new country but were able to go to their former homes to visit. They were experienced farmers, treated well by the British government with its gifts of land, tools, food, and seed. Grants of land were increased twice so that Loyalists could receive additional amounts (eighty-one hectares to each head of family). In 1789, to honour their service to Britain, Governor Dorchester decided to register each Loyalist on a "Loyalist List." The sons and daughters of people on the list were rewarded with more free land. If their land was fertile and they worked hard, they could expect success.

1. *What did the Loyalists not like about being part of the colony of Quebec?*
2. *The British government decided to satisfy the Loyalists by the Act of Constitution. What reasons were there for changing the old colony of Quebec?*
3. *What extra rewards did the Loyalists receive from the British government?*

The Loyal Indians

Mohawk Chief Joseph Brant had led many members of the Six Nations Iroquois* tribes during the revolutionary war. They had fought on the British side against the rebels. Brant felt that the Iroquois tribes were threatened with loss of their lands, or a worse fate, if the Americans won, for then thousands of settlers would pour into the Indian country. By 1778 he feared that his followers were on the losing side. Of the Six Nations, only the Oneidas had sided with the revolutionary armies. The other tribes had followed Brant. Slowly they moved northward, away from the victorious American armies.

Governor Haldimand realized his government's responsibility to care for the Loyalist Indian allies. He made arrangements for land to be purchased by treaty from the Mississauga tribe for settlement by Brant, the Mohawks, and other Six Nations tribes. They received a large grant of land: 9.6 km of land on either side of the Grand River from its source to its mouth. A second group of Mohawks settled on a grant near the Bay of Quinte.

The British government was obliged to help the Mohawks. Do you agree or disagree? Explain your reasons.

*Tribes of the Six Nations Iroquois: Mohawk, Seneca, Oneida, Cayuga, Onondaga, and Tuscarora.

Mohawk Chief Joseph Brant (Thayendanegea, as his people called him) led the Six Nations against the French in the Seven Years' War and against the Americans in the revolutionary war. Which of Thayendanegea's personal qualities are suggested in this portrait?

Loyal Mohawk Indians travelled to their new lands near the Bay of Quinte after fleeing from the United States. What tasks lay ahead for this group of Mohawks?

Chapter 39

UPPER CANADA— THE NEW PROVINCE

The first lieutenant-governor of the new province of Upper Canada was very excited about his job. Colonel John G. Simcoe was impatient to get on with it. He had served Britain during the revolutionary war and had been appointed governor of Upper Canada. Now he was at Quebec waiting for the ice to leave the river. He had impressive plans for Upper Canada—settlers, roads, canals, towns. It would be a haven for those who loved the British way of doing things, and a strong, thriving colony.

Governor Simcoe's first priority was people, for without more settlers, the other parts of his plan would be nothing but a dream. He had spent the revolutionary war in America and felt that there were many people still in the United States who would happily live in a British colony, people who were loyal to Britain. He counted on these Americans to help populate his new province.

Simcoe's answer came quickly.

> ## AN INVITATION TO ALL:
>
> *Friendly Americans please note:*
>
>
>
> *Upper Canada offers you*
> *Free land—lots of it*
> *Few or no taxes*
> *Good water transportation*
> *Good farming*
> *No hostile Indians*

Thousands of families gathered their belongings and travelled north from the United States to Upper Canada. They soon outnumbered the original Loyalists. These newcomers wanted one thing: land.

John Graves Simcoe, the first lieutenant-governor of Upper Canada, salutes a guard of honour at his headquarters at Newark (Niagara-on-the-Lake). What would be one advantage of having Simcoe as the lieutenant-governor of Upper Canada?

Peter Martin was among them. Here is his story:

Trail of the Conestoga

I was nine when we moved to Canada. We had suffered enough! Our neighbours in Pennsylvania had treated us cruelly and unfairly, just because we did not hate King George. Father and Uncle Michael grew tired of the arguing. They heard about good land in Canada.

My brother Jacob and I helped load our Conestoga wagon. It was moving day. We piled clothes, tools, pots, dishes, and food into the big wagon. We were on our way!

The Conestoga wagon was a good way to travel. If only it wasn't so slow! Our journey was 800 km through the wilderness. There were no roads, no bridges, only a path to follow. The path wound through dense bush, past swamps, across streams and ponds. We could travel only a few kilometres a day, when the going was good. It would be seven weeks before we'd reach our destination.

We won't forget the day Jacob chased the butterfly. He was walking behind the wagon when a large butterfly playfully flew near his face. As he ran to catch it, his foot became caught in a groundhog hole. His loud scream rang out in the quiet forest. Jacob was carried to the wagon to lie down on a blanket. His ankle was very swollen. My mother wrapped it tightly in a piece of clean linen. Jacob had to ride all the rest of the way to Canada.

Each night when we camped, Jacob was carefully lifted out of the wagon and placed near the fire. The rest of us had work to do looking after the horses and cattle, and preparing supper. Mother cooked some fish or a rabbit. If we'd found a berry patch that day, we feasted on raspberries for dessert. Then we'd say a prayer before falling asleep. At night my little sister, Rebecca, sometimes cried. She wanted to go back home. My mother was glad there was a doll to help comfort

An early log cabin in Upper Canada.

Rebecca who was afraid of the strange noises in the dark forest. Each morning we were off early. As the weeks passed, we neared our destination.

At last—the Niagara River! Everybody cheered. Canada was just across the river. We watched father and Uncle Michael turn our wagon into a boat. After removing the wheels, they carefully caulked the seams of the wagon. Then it was waterproof. We all sat inside our new boat as the men paddled us across the wide river. Then the horses were ridden into the stream, herding our swimming cattle. At last we were all safely in Canada.

1. What reasons does Peter give for his father's decision to move from Pennsylvania to Canada?
2. What evidence is there that the Martins were well equipped for their long journey? For their new life in Canada?
3. What would be involved in looking after the horses and cows at night? Why was this necessary?
4. Peter's family's journey was a hardship and an adventure. Which family members would have found it an adventure? Why? Which family members would have found it a hardship? Why?

Mennonites

In many ways, Peter's story is like that of many others who came from the United States to Upper Canada. But the Martins were different. They were Mennonites. Their religious beliefs included **pacifism** and allegiance first to God, not to any human government. They had lived in separate communities, mainly in Pennsylvania, speaking Low German (called Pennsylvania Dutch) and sharing a distinctive way of life. They felt less at home in the new republic than they had in the former British colony, and many decided to leave the United States. Their chosen area of settlement in Canada was near the Grand River. Here they set to work building up prosperous farms in the area later called Waterloo. In succeeding years, other Mennonites arrived to farm, build roads, and create a thriving community.

1. List the Mennonites' reasons for settling in Canada.
2. Research the Mennonites' beliefs: their way of life today; the location of Mennonite settlements. Write a brief report on your findings.

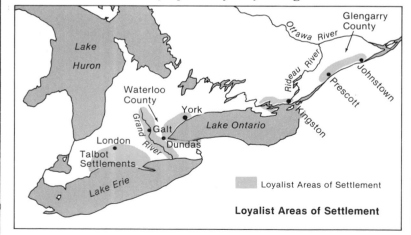

Loyalist Areas of Settlement

The Talbot Settlement

Many newcomers travelled to the north shore of Lake Erie to find a lot on the extensive lands of Colonel Thomas Talbot. Their experiences were sometimes out of the ordinary. Talbot was lord and master of his lands and imposed special rules on the pioneers there. The rules were designed to make the settlers' lives easier and to help the settlement grow and develop. Settlers who wished to pioneer on Talbot's lands had to do it his way, following his rules. Here are some of them:
— Each settler must clear half the road in front of his lot.
— Each settler must clear four hectares of land on his lot.
— Each settler must build a house.
— After five years on his land, the settler will receive a certificate of ownership for his lot.

Talbot first came to Upper Canada as secretary to Lieutenant-Governor Simcoe. He visited the western part of the province, along the north shore of Lake Erie, in the 1790s. Talbot loved the area. After spending a few years in Britain, he arranged to return to Upper Canada to run a land company. He received a large grant of land in return for promising to bring settlers to the area.

In 1803 the Talbot settlement was begun. The colonel chose a suitable site as his home base. He named it Port Talbot. The first two years of the new operation were spent building roads, a sawmill, and a grist mill for the settlement. Then Talbot waited as a slow trickle of families appeared, looking for a grant of land. Sometimes they went away empty handed.

If Colonel Talbot decided he liked the people applying for land, he treated them fairly. If he disliked something about the applicants, he was rude and nasty. He insisted on strictly supervising his settlement of thousands of hectares along the north shore of Lake Erie. Those who did not wish to follow

Talbot's system had to look elsewhere for land.

Talbot's Success

One day a Highland Scot came to Talbot's house to apply for a grant. When he and the colonel could not reach an agreement, the Highlander picked Talbot up, carried him outside, and held him down until a better deal was arranged. That episode led the colonel to install a famous window in his house. Through it, land grants were arranged between Talbot and prospective settlers. Those who did not impress Talbot were sent away with a slam of the window. The others soon found that Colonel Talbot was a man who would work with them to find and build prosperous farms.

Talbot was a **crotchety** man who often treated people rudely, but his settlement was among the best in all of early Upper Canada. Because of his insistence that settlers help with the building of roads, his territory had the only decent road in all of Upper Canada—and the longest. By the 1830s, the Talbot Road stretched nearly 500 km. Talbot's rules also helped ensure successful farms. By 1837 there were 50 000 people living on Talbot's grant, and they had settled nearly 200 000 ha of land. Talbot could feel proud of his remarkable achievement. He died at age 83 in 1853.

1. Which of Colonel Talbot's "rules" might discourage a pioneer family? Which would encourage the pioneers?
2. Make up a list of other rules that would help to promote settlement on Talbot's lands.
3. Write an obituary (death notice) for Colonel Thomas Talbot.
4. Explain why you would or would not like to meet Colonel Thomas Talbot.

Governor Simcoe's Policies

Thousands of people hiked or rode to Upper Canada in search of land to

farm. They came from the United States or the Atlantic colonies to pioneer. They approved of Governor Simcoe's policies, especially the one granting free land. Travel was somewhat easier after Simcoe had two roads (Dundas Street, west from Burlington Bay; and Yonge Street, north from York) built by the troops of the Queen's Rangers. The "roads" were cleared tracks through the wilderness, connecting the partly settled areas with areas where settlement was expected in the future. They were cleared to make it easier for pioneers to move to new locations. Simcoe brought other changes to Upper Canada: the court system, the beginnings of a militia (all men aged sixteen to sixty were to enrol), the laying out of the town site of York, and the gradual abolition of slavery in Upper Canada.

crotchety: grumpy

The town of York was Upper Canada's capital — a village in the wilderness, in artist Elizabeth Hale's painting of 1804.

THE WAR OF 1812

There was a time when Canadians and Americans went to war—against each other. It was a time when our borders were defended by forts and red-uniformed British troops along with militiamen from the farms and towns; when our border was crossed by American armies intent on invading and capturing our country; when British and American warships faced each other on the Great Lakes, their cannon pounding.

Causes of the War

The United States declared war on Britain in 1812. There were several issues which had been simmering between the two countries for many years. Britain and France had been at war in Europe since 1793. The armies of Napoleon faced those of England; the ships of the Royal Navy patrolled the seas. British naval supremacy was unquestioned. The United States, a young country, had remained neutral. Because of this, American merchant ships felt they could trade freely. This was unacceptable to France and Britain neither of whom wanted any ships trading with their enemy. Both tried to punish the United States by forbidding trade with the other.

There were other areas of conflict between the United States and Britain. In order to maintain her huge navy, Britain needed trained sailors. The British navy was authorized to stop and search merchant ships on the high seas. British captains were looking for runaway sailors. It was easy to see why they ran away. Conditions on British warships were appalling, the pay was bad, and the food was worse. Many sailors deserted. American merchant captains were upset when sailors were removed from their crews by British captains who claimed the men were rightfully theirs. American pride was hurt when ships were searched.

American fears were raised, too, about activities in the American northwest.* Here Indian tribes had

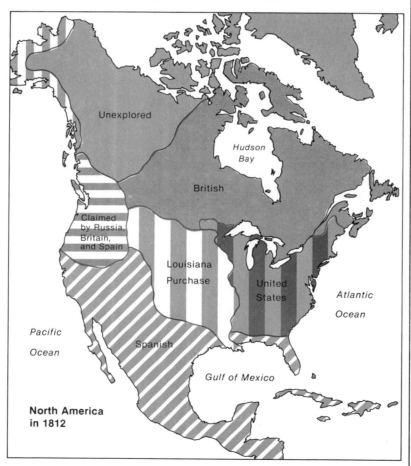

Pacific Ocean

Unexplored

Hudson Bay

British

Claimed by Russia, Britain, and Spain

Louisiana Purchase

United States

Atlantic Ocean

Spanish

Gulf of Mexico

North America in 1812

*This area now includes the states of Illinois, Indiana, Michigan, Ohio, and Wisconsin.

banded together under the powerful Chief Tecumseh and his brother, the Prophet, to defend their lands against the masses of settlers who were steadily moving west. The United States government felt that the British Indian Department was encouraging the Indians to attack frontier settlements.

The American Congress voted for war in June of 1812. The target: Canada. It was a good place to start trying to hurt Britain, for it was thinly populated and weakly defended. Many Americans felt that victory would be easy.

What about the English side of the story? To Britain, the enemy was Napoleon. The British felt that no measures were too severe to defeat the French armies. If that meant taking sailors off American ships, or disrupting American trade, or sending British warships to cruise off the coasts of the United States, that was a necessary part of war, a war which must be won.

The War of 1812 officially began in June. News travelled very slowly in those days, so many of the people directly involved were unprepared. Others hoped to stay out of the war. Most Upper Canadians had emigrated from the United States and were not eager to fight against the Americans. Many Americans were not anxious to fight either. The vote in the United States Senate in favour of war had been very close (nineteen for, thirteen against). The New England states opposed the war, other states provided only lukewarm support. Defences in both countries were weak, military equipment was in short supply, and good planning, especially in the United States, was scarce.

1. List America's reasons for declaring war on Britain.
2. Defend the British right to search ships and prohibit American trade with France.
3. What reasons might some states have for not supporting the war? What actions could individuals who opposed the war take?

The War in Lower Canada

Montreal in 1812 was a busy city of 30 000 people. About one in ten Lower Canadians lived there. The city was not easily defended. Americans had, after all, captured Montreal in 1775 and could do so again. If this happened,

Montreal was difficult to defend. All British supplies for the war effort in Upper Canada passed through the port of Montreal. It seemed an obvious target for American attackers.

all of Canada would be threatened. The St. Lawrence River was the main communication lifeline between the armies in Upper Canada and their supply base in England. A successful American attack on the St. Lawrence would mean the end of Upper Canada's participation in the war. Strangely, the American military leadership failed to hit Canadians where the blows would be most effective, at

Montreal. An American army did attempt to invade Lower Canada in October, 1813. A Canadian force called the Voltigeurs travelled from Montreal to face the Americans at Chateauguay. The Canadians' battle-hardened colonel was Charles Michel de Salaberry. Born in Lower Canada, de Salaberry had served with the British armies in Europe. His experience served him well. In a short fight, the French Canadian troops successfully defended Lower Canada from the American attackers, who retreated to New York State. The Americans had failed to capture Montreal, and the St. Lawrence waterway remained open, permitting the passage of supplies and soldiers to the main centre of the war, Upper Canada.

1. Why was the St. Lawrence River such an important target for the Americans? What reasons might there be for their failure to attack and capture Montreal?
2. What difference was there in the attitude and actions of the French population of Lower Canada when Americans attacked in 1775? In 1813?

United States general, William Hull, surrenders in shame to General Brock at Fort Detroit, in the first important event of the war.

The battle of Queenston Heights, October 13, 1812.

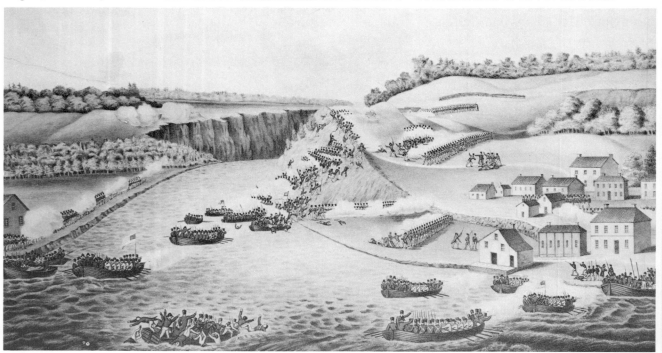

The War in Upper Canada

Most of the action in the War of 1812 took place in Upper Canada. The war began favourably for Upper Canada. General Isaac Brock's daring offensives led to the capture of Fort Michilimackinac, Fort Dearborn (Chicago), and Fort Detroit. Queenston Heights, in the Niagara region, was successfully defended by a force of British regular troops, Indian allies, and Canadian militia. General Brock was killed at Queenston. The loss of General Brock was serious, for he was an imaginative military leader. His death meant uncertainty about the future for the Upper Canadians. Their defences were vulnerable, and their success in 1812 had largely been the result of the efforts of two men, Brock and his ally Tecumseh, and the bungling of the American leaders.

Major-General Sir Isaac Brock

General Brock saw trouble ahead for Upper Canada unless somebody did something very bold. He decided to act himself, a reasonable decision, since Brock was the military and civilian leader of Upper Canada at the opening of the War of 1812. He feared that Upper Canadians were not behind the British in this war against the Americans. He hoped to give them a reason to side with Britain and defend their province.

Brock's first move was to order an attack on the American forts Michilimackinac and Dearborn (Chicago). A small force of British troops and Canadian voyageurs had no difficulty in capturing these fur posts.

In August of 1812, Brock acted again. He surprised the Americans at Fort Detroit and easily captured the shaken General Hull. Brock's quick attack and his unexpected early victory helped many Upper Canadians decide to join his cause. Then came Brock's army's defence of Canada at Queenston. After an exciting late-night gallop on his grey horse, and a courageous charge up the hill against the Americans, Brock was killed. His daring and bravery inspired the redcoats to push the Americans back across the Niagara River. Brock's loyal troops sadly buried their great leader at Fort George as the respectful Americans fired a salute from across the river. Brock's example was enough to inspire many to pick up guns in defence of Upper Canada. An account of his death in the York *Gazette* of October 17, 1812, reminded readers to "remember Brock in the day of battle."

General Brock's death at Queenston Heights was a severe blow to Upper Canada.

Brock was born on the island of Guernsey in 1769 and joined the British army when he was fifteen. He fought in Europe before arriving in Canada in 1802. Just before the war broke out, he was named president of the Council of Upper Canada. That meant that General Brock was the province's leader. He proved it by his actions.

1. What did Brock do to inspire some doubting Canadians to support the British? Why would the doubters then want to join the British effort?
2. Write an obituary for General Brock.
3. Why is there a monument to General Brock at Queenston? Do you think that such monuments are worth having? Should Canadians be encouraged to visit them?

Tecumseh

Tecumseh was a Shawnee chief who is regarded as one of the greatest of North American Indian leaders. He was born in what is now Ohio in 1768. His early life was marked by two incidents, the death of his father, and the burning of his village. Both were the responsibility of white people.

Tecumseh came to fear the increasing movement of white settlers on to Indian lands as settlers came across the Appalachian Mountains. He organized a confederacy of Indian tribes to stop white settlement. He preferred to do this by peaceful means but was prepared to lead the tribes in war.

When the War of 1812 began, Tecumseh joined the British side. He gathered a large Indian army in western Upper Canada and took part in several skirmishes on the Detroit frontier. His plan for the capture of Fort Detroit was used successfully by General Brock. Tecumseh's last fight was against an American force at the Battle of the Thames on October 15, 1813. It was an American victory and a serious loss to the British, for Tecumseh was killed.

Find out more about the life and death of Tecumseh. Write your findings in a brief report.

For two years, the armies of both sides took turns winning and losing. Naval supremacy was also divided. The Americans maintained control of Lake Erie while the British took charge of Lake Ontario, only to trade Lake Ontario back to the American naval forces several times. Neither side seemed able to maintain decisive control.

Shredded sails, smashed spars, useless rigging, and mangled bodies accompanied the sounds of the Battle of Lake Erie on September 10, 1813. Write the diary page of one of the crew (from either the British or American side) who survived to describe this battle.

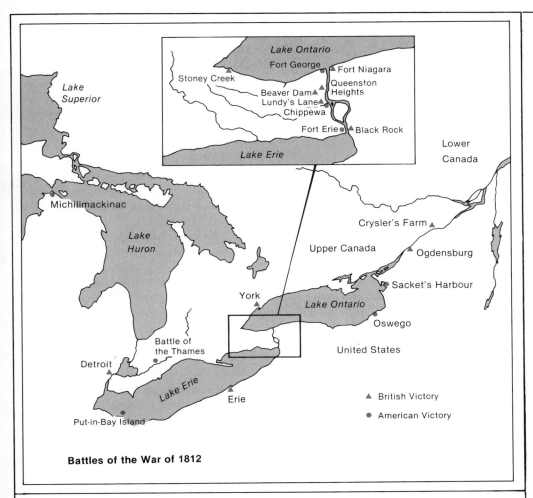

Battles of the War of 1812

Some Important Events in Upper Canada

1812
JUNE
- U.S. declares war

JULY
- U.S. invades from Detroit
- British and Canadians capture Fort Michilimackinac

AUGUST
- British and Indians capture Fort Detroit

OCTOBER
- Battle of Queenston Heights—British victory

1813
APRIL
- U.S. navy captures York (Toronto)

JUNE
- British and Indians beat Americans at Beaver Dam

OCTOBER
- U.S. victory, Battle of the Thames
- Death of Tecumseh

NOVEMBER
- British–Canadian victory at Crysler's Farm
- American offensive against Montreal is turned back

1814
JULY
- U.S. victory at Chippewa
- Large battle at Lundy's Lane—no clear winner
- British victory at Oswego

The war was also fought on water, particularly on the waters of Lakes Erie and Ontario

1813
LAKE ERIE
- Put-in-Bay is U.S. victory, Americans control the lake

Lake Ontario and St. Lawrence River
- U.S. raids on Gananoque, Brockville
- Canadian raids knock out guns at Ogdensburg
- U.S. defends Sackets Harbour
- Shipbuilding war for lake supremacy

Laura Secord delivers her famous message to Colonel Fitzgibbon. The planned American attack on Beaver Dam must be defeated. Write a conversation between Secord and Fitzgibbon.

Laura Secord

The legend says that Laura Secord overheard some American officers planning an attack on the British colonel, Fitzgibbon, at a place called Beaver Dam. The Americans were discussing their activities in Laura's house, their temporary headquarters. Laura was determined to inform the British. The legend says that she walked, using a cow to help her escape past the American sentries (the sentries would think she was taking the cow to pasture). She travelled on foot through swamps and forests and fields, past watchful American guards and howling wolves. It took many hours to travel to the British lines. But Laura's timely warning allowed Fitzgibbon to prepare a defence and defeat the Americans. The legend inspired poets and painters to praise Laura and her brave deed.

Then the legend was attacked! Did Laura really walk all day and all night? How far did she go? When, exactly, was her famous walk? And did her warning make any difference at all in the Battle of Beaver Dam?

Unlucky Laura. Historians checked and rechecked her story. They had doubts about it. Some tried to show that her walk had not helped the British. Professor John Moir may have the last word. He says that Laura did provide helpful information after walking about nineteen kilometres on a very hot day. Laura may have saved the day after all. Poor Laura. She hadn't intended to worry a lot of historians! She just wanted to help defeat the Yankees.

1. Write a paragraph defending Laura's legend.
2. Why are such legends needed? What do people learn from them?
3. Write a newspaper account of Laura Secord's story.
4. Write a diary entry for Laura Secord for the day and night of her walk.

Other important events took place outside Canada. In 1814 a large British force captured and burned Washington, D.C. An attempted invasion from Lower Canada was turned back by the Americans at Plattsburg, New York. And a few weeks after peace had been declared, an American force defeated British attackers in the Battle of New Orleans.

1. A map will show that much of the heavy fighting in the war took place along the Niagara Peninsula. What reasons might the Americans have had for choosing to attack that part of Canada?

2. Where would an attack from the United States be most effective? Devise a plan to attack Upper Canada from the south.

The War Comes to York

On the morning of April 27, 1813, fourteen ships of the United States navy landed 1700 troops on the beaches west of the village of York (population 600). The town, capital of Upper Canada, was defended by Major-General Sir Roger Sheaffe. He led about 300 British regulars, 300 York militiamen, and 100 Indians.

The Americans attacked and drove the defenders back from the weak fort. A powder magazine blew up, killing and wounding many Americans. Among those killed was their leader, General Pike. The American attack pushed the defenders back toward York. As the British forces retreated, Major-General Sheaffe's orders to blow up the fort's main powder magazine were followed. Again many on both sides were killed or wounded. Major-General Sheaffe led his regular troops back through York and on to Kingston, leaving the York militia, Indians, and citizens of the town in American hands.

It had been a rough fight. Sixty-two British regulars were killed and seventy-six wounded; an unknown number of Indians were dead; five militiamen were killed and five wounded. By dusk the Americans were in possession of the town. They stayed four days, during which time several important buildings were burned (in-

The Fort York barracks on the shore of Lake Ontario. Would the fort be easy to defend against attack? Suggest reasons why the fort was built so close to the lake.

cluding the Upper Canadian parliament buildings). Some looting took place, and important military equipment was lost. The citizens of York were glad to see the invaders sail away on May 2 to continue the war on the Niagara frontier.

A closer look at the capture of York reveals some very interesting stories. ...
a) Part of a letter from Stephen Moore of Baltimore, to his brother:

Niagara, 5th May, 1813
I have to inform you now of the result [of our attack on York] which has been victorious and glorious to the American arms, although peculiarly unfortunate to me. The enemy sprung a mine upon us, which destroyed about 60 of their men, and killed or maimed about 130 of our men. This horrible explosion has deprived me of my left leg and otherwise **grievously** wounded me. I was taken from the field, and carried on board the commodore's ship, where my leg was amputated, and I am now likely to recover.[1]

1. What was the "mine" that exploded, wounding Moore? Why did he think it was a mine?
2. Why might the numbers of casualties be wrong?

b) Ely Playter was a member of the York militia. His diary was not forgotten, even during the tense days of the American occupation of York.

April 28th. Walked down to the back of the Town, met Young Debtlor who told me his father was Dead, was wounded in the leg, had it cut off and Died soon after.

April 29th. At Home packing up my things and hideing them. D. Brooks passed on his way to Kingston, and many others also. An (American) officer and some men came to my house, broke the Door and took many things away. We watched them till dark.

April 30th. I went to the Garrison and signed my parole and got a pass.* I spoke to General Dearborn of his men plundering my house. He said it was Contrary to his orders. The appearance of the town and garrison were dismal, the latter shattered and rent by cannonballs and the explosions of the Magazine, not a building but shows some marks of it. The Town thronged with the Yankees, many busy, the Council office with every window broke and pillaged of everything, the Government Building, the Block House and the buildings adjacent all burned to Ashes.[2]

1. Draw a picture to illustrate something from Ely Playter's diary.
2. Does Playter seem upset about the plunder of his home by the Americans?
3. Why would the U.S. army release the militiamen, instead of keeping them prisoner?

c) Many citizens of York had good reason to feel hostile towards "the Yankees." Here is one reason:

I certify that during the possession of York by the Enemy, I met Mrs. Givens, wife of James Givens, Indian Agent, in great Distress having been driven from her house by a party of plunderers who had threatened her life. That one of them was apprehended in my presence loaded with plunder and from whom a silver cup and mirror was taken.
Wm. D. Powell, Oct. 3, 1815[3]

Mrs. Givens's home was the target of looters who took more than a silver cup and mirror. They also helped themselves to carpets, curtains, teapots, sheets, lamps, silver cutlery, wine, and all of the wearing apparel of Mrs. Givens and her seven children. The looters were presumed to be American soldiers.

*Canadian militiamen were paroled by the U.S. army if they handed in their weapons and agreed to return to their homes.

grievously: seriously

1. *What reasons might the Americans have had for looting the house of the man who was the local Indian agent?*
2. *What feelings would the Givens family and their neighbours likely have towards the United States after the War of 1812?*

d) Losses at York, April, 1813.
—two main government buildings burned
—one naval ship, one merchant ship destroyed
—one unfinished naval vessel burned by the British
—library, office of the Executive Council looted
—thirteen homes, five stores looted
—some tools stolen, livestock taken

e) Bishop Strachan and the Yankees
There was one man who seemed to relish the American occupation of York, for it gave him a chance to dis-play his leadership abilities. The man was Reverend John Strachan. His position as rector of York made him a sort of "guardian angel" of the town. Strachan was conspicuous in helping to arrange better conditions for the defeated militia and better protection for the town from looters. His courage was appreciated by the townspeople. They felt that he had stood up to the Yankees and had taken charge of affairs when the British left.

1. *Write a diary page describing conditions at York on April 30, 1813. Write another page for May 5.*
2. *Draw a picture story of the defeat of York.*
3. *Explain why the citizens of York would be anti-American after the war.*
4. *Both York and Washington were burned during the war. Why would these events make each side more determined to win the war?*

Chapter 41

THE WAR IN THE ATLANTIC COLONIES

No fighting took place in Nova Scotia, New Brunswick, Prince Edward Island, or Newfoundland. But the War of 1812 did have an impact on the Atlantic region. Trade increased, as did shipbuilding, since ships from Nova Scotia were used to carry goods to Britain and the West Indies. The timber trade also grew during the period of the British wars with Napoleon. The British navy needed ships to maintain control of the seas. Spars and masts from New Brunswick crossed the Atlantic to become part of the Royal Navy. Timber markets opened up, resulting in the growth of many small sawmills and the clearing of many hectares of forest.

Privateering

One activity was enjoyed by many in the Atlantic region: privateering. Privateering meant that private ship owners were granted permission to capture American merchant ships. Ships set out from Halifax, Saint John, or St. John's in search of American merchant ships loaded with cargo. Cheers rang out when these "prizes"

Halifax enjoyed prosperity during the War of 1812. Ships such as the Lady Hamilton, pictured here, put Halifax in the centre of the British maritime war effort.

were towed back to harbour. Some captains made a lot of money privateering. The champion was Joseph Barss of the *Liverpool Packet*. This small ship with a crew of forty-five fishermen captured fifty prizes, mostly from the Massachusetts coast. There was always a ready market for the captured cargoes. Everything from rum to silks to champagne could be sold by the privateers.

Although the war was not fought in their region, many men from the Atlantic provinces were directly involved. They served, voluntarily or otherwise, with the Royal Navy. A regiment of militia from New Brunswick walked to Lower Canada to help defend Canada from American attack. It was a gruelling winter march. Other Maritimers served in their local militia forces. Governor John Sherbrooke led a force from Halifax in a raid against American villages on the Maine coast in 1814. The Nova Scotians together with the British fleet captured a long stretch of the coast and held it until the war ended. Money collected in customs houses in Maine by the occupying British forces was later used to begin a new college (now Dalhousie University) at Halifax.

The area prospered because of the privateering, the trade, and the increased British spending. The navy always had money to spend. Merchants sold food and supplies; tavern keepers were busy.

The end of the war brought a new feeling of pride to the Atlantic colonies. They felt pleased about the successful campaigns in the Canadas and were aware of a shared experience with the Canadians.

1. What part did the Atlantic provinces play in the War of 1812?
2. List the benefits that the war brought to the region.
3. Why would Maritimers be happy that the Canadas had done well in the war against the American invaders?

After boarding and capturing the USS Chesapeake, British sailors from the Shanon sailed their prize to Halifax, where they received a warm welcome.

Chapter 42

THE WAR NOBODY WON

Peace: December 24, 1814

By December, 1814, both Britain and America were tired of war. Even more tired of it were the Canadians who lived in the Niagara region, at York, and along the shores of Lake Erie. Their homes, barns, and fields had been devastated by battles and fires and plundering raiders. Their families had been threatened, their farms pillaged, their animals slaughtered. The end of this war would not come too soon for them.

Both America and Britain realized the futility of continuing a war that seemed to lead nowhere. The leaders on both sides had made mistakes, and victory seemed far away. Negotiators met to work out acceptable peace terms. The Treaty of Ghent showed the truth about this strange war. There was no clear-cut victory for the United States or Britain. All territory held at the end of the war went back to its former owner. The problems that had caused the United States to declare war were ignored. They would have to be dealt with later.

Results of the War

One important part of the peace settlement was the Rush-Bagot agreement of 1817. The United States and Britain agreed to limit warships on the Great Lakes. There was also agreement on the boundaries between the United States and British territories west of Upper Canada: the forty-ninth parallel would divide them as far as the Rocky Mountains.

The outcome of the war? The British promptly forgot that it had occurred, although British regular troops and the Royal Navy had played a large part in the war, doing most of the fighting. The young United States felt that it had fought a second "war of independence," proving that it had a right to exist. The war served to unite Americans, and left them with a new song—"The Star-Spangled Banner."

For Canadians, the war was an important event. It brought them together in a new spirit of unity. In Upper Canada, a feeling of anti-Americanism that was very strong had developed as a result of the American raids on farms and villages. Canadians were proud of the successful defence of their lands against the American invaders, for both French and English had fought American armies to save their country. Upper Canadians were determined to preserve the links between Britain and their province. The Loyalists had brought their allegiance to Britain with them to Canada. The War of 1812 had helped to make this allegiance even firmer.

1. What evidence is there that nobody won the War of 1812?
2. What did the war do for the United States? For Canada?

The War Nobody Won

The War of 1812 was the war that nobody won. Both Canadians and Americans felt that they were victorious. If nobody won, then maybe everybody won.

The British did not devote all of their energies to defeating the Americans. They had a bigger headache—Napoleon. Large numbers of British troops were not available to fight in North America until very late in the war. For Britain, defending Canada was all they could manage.

The Americans had other reasons for not winning the war. They were poorly prepared, poorly led, and disorganized. Their leaders were unable to devise a strategy that would effectively hurt Canada. There were many in the United States who opposed the war and refused to support it with the men and materials needed for victory.

The armies on both sides faced a great enemy—nature. The backwoods of the United States and the Canadas did not make moving thousands of men and tonnes of equipment an easy task. Transportation on land was a great problem for the generals. Slogging through swamps and hacking trails into the bush did not make men rested and ready to fight. It just wore them out. Winter was no fun either, although transportation was possible along the ice of the St. Lawrence River.

1. List the reasons why the British side did not "win" the war.
2. List the reasons why the American side did not "win" the war.
3. What advantages are there to a war that nobody, or everybody, wins?

Kingston's Warships: Where Are They Now?

During the War of 1812, the town of Kingston was a shipbuilding centre where more than 1200 men worked overtime to construct warships for use on the Great Lakes. They had no time to waste. Just forty-five kilometres away, the Americans at Sacket's Harbour were as busily building ships.

The largest battleship in the world at the time was launched in September, 1814. The mighty *St. Lawrence* was a great achievement for the shipyards at Kingston.

At the war's end, there were two uncompleted ships, eight large warships, and several gunboats in Kingston. What became of them has been the subject of a long search. Historians such as Dr. R. A. Preston have examined old paintings, British navy documents, newspaper accounts, travellers' stories, and private papers in order to discover the fate of the ships. Divers have probed the waters around Kingston Harbour, Navy Bay, and Deadman Bay looking for evidence on the numerous wrecks that lie beneath the waves.

Their conclusions? The old fleet was kept in Kingston's dockyard until the ships were in such bad condition that they had to be sold or abandoned. The *St. Lawrence*, the pride of the fleet, was sold at auction for £25 and used as part of a pier for a Kingston distillery. She finally sank. Some ships were scuttled. Their timbers are still there, to be explored by curious divers looking for clues to Canada's past.

1. Why would Dr. Preston look for clues about the warships in so many different places?
2. What part did the divers play in solving the mystery of the warships?
3. Why was the fleet not used after the War of 1812 a) on the Great Lakes? b) anywhere else?

The HMS St. Lawrence mounted 102 cannons. It was considered more handsome and better finished than American ships. Of course, it took more time to build and was far more expensive to build than American ships. What advantages would there be in having such a large ship in the British navy?

Unit Four
SOCIAL LIFE IN UPPER CANADA

Chapter 43

THE GREAT MIGRATION, 1815-1850s

A Deadly Cargo

Cholera, diphtheria, and typhus were diseases caused and spread by foul water. These diseases were often lumped together in the nineteenth century, though each has its own symptoms. Cholera brought vomiting, diarrhea and fever, followed by death, sometimes within a few hours of its first appearance. In its earliest stages, cholera was identified by a coating on the tongue of its victims.

The Plague Year

The small rowboat moved easily toward the sailing ship. The oarsman looked over his shoulder at the motionless ship and made a minor adjustment in his rowing to let the current carry him. The passenger nervously examined the contents of his small black leather bag.

Aboard the sailing ship, rows of immigrants lined the rail, watching the approaching rowboat. Some passengers were pale and obviously frightened, others seemed to be numb to what was happening.

Over their heads, high in the ship's rigging flapped the dreaded plague flag.

It was May 17, 1847. The place was Grosse Isle, about fifty kilometres from Quebec City. The ship was the *Syria*, just arrived from Liverpool, England with 241 Irish passengers on board. During the voyage, typhoid fever had broken out among the passengers. Nine had died before reaching Canada. A further 84 showed signs of having the illness.

The rowboat was bringing a doctor to examine the passengers. Those showing signs of illness would not be allowed to land upriver at Quebec, but would have to remain at Grosse Isle until they were cured or dead.

1847 came to be known as the Plague Year. Of the nearly 100 000 immigrants who passed through Grosse Isle, more than 5 000 died on the island. Another estimated 15 000 died from typhus, cholera, diphtheria, or their after effects in the new land. At least 17 000 died aboard the ships carrying them over the Atlantic and were buried in the sea.

Who were these desperate people? Why were they prepared to risk such dreadful odds to come to Canada?

Arrivals at the Port of Quebec
From Britain   1829-1859   000's

from England: ———
from Ireland: - - - - - - -
from Scotland: ++++++++++++

What group contributed the most immigrants to Canada?
What year marked the high point of immigration?
In what year did the fewest immigrants come? Why?

Diphtheria was also caused by contaminated water. Its main sign was extreme swelling in the throat accompanied by fever. It often resulted in death.

Typhus, or typhoid fever, was also the product of foul water. It produced a high fever and death.

All of these diseases spread rapidly once they took hold. Once a ship's water was contaminated, everyone was exposed to the disease because everyone drank the water. In the early 1800s, there was little that doctors could do to prevent the spread of such illnesses or to cure their victims. Many immigrant ships had no trained doctor, in any case.

Why People Left Their Homes

Between 1815 and 1850 about 800 000 people left the British Isles to come to Canada. There were many reasons for this remarkable surge of people.

The End of the War

For nearly two decades before 1815, Britain had been involved in a long, costly, and bloody war with France. During this period, many men were needed for the army, navy, and war industries. There was almost no unemployment of any sort. In fact, the navy often resorted to "impressment," a sort of legal kidnapping to get enough able-bodied men for its ships.

The defeat of France's emperor, Napoleon, at the Battle of Waterloo in 1815, finally brought peace to Britain. It also brought an end to many of the government contracts for the production of weapons, uniforms, and other war supplies. Soldiers and sailors returning home from the wars joined the growing ranks of the jobless. It was from these that a number of immigrants came.

The Industrial Revolution

A second source of immigrants was to be found among the skilled workers and craftspeople who were losing their jobs to the new machines. In what was called the "industrial revolution," machinery powered by water wheels and steam engines began to replace the traditional hand labour of weavers and other skilled workers. With a power loom, or better still, a factory full of looms, a few unskilled and low-paid workers could produce more cloth than dozens of highly paid hand weavers. The jobless workers sometimes moved to the new factory towns to take lower-paying jobs. Conditions in these towns were often unpleasant. The famous nineteenth century English writer, Charles Dickens, described one of the factory towns in his novel *Hard Times*:

THE LAND THEY LEFT BEHIND

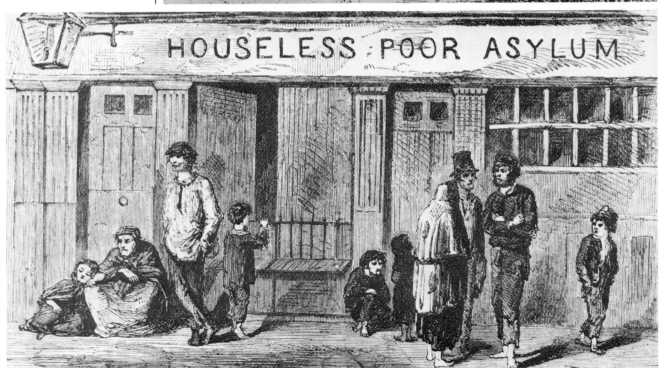

counterpart: duplicate

interminable: endless

monotonously: without change

melancholy: sad

It was a town of red brick, or of brick that would have been red if the smoke and ashes had allowed it; but as matters stood it was a town of unnatural red and black. ....

It was a town of machinery and tall chimneys, out of which **interminable** serpents of smoke trailed themselves for ever and ever, and never got uncoiled.

It has a black canal in it, and a river that ran purple with ill-smelling dye, and vast piles of buildings full of windows where there was a rattling and a trembling all day long, and where the piston of the steam-engine worked **monotonously** up and down, like the head of an elephant in a state of **melancholy** madness. It contained several large streets all very like one another, and many small streets still more like one another, inhabited by people equally like one another, who all went in and out at the same hours, with the same sound upon the same pavements, to do the same work, and to whom every day was the same as yesterday and tomorrow, and every year the **counterpart** of the last and the next.[1]

It is not surprising that people living in conditions such as these might consider moving to a new land.

In rural England and Scotland, small tenant farmers who rented farm land from landlords found conditions were changing. For centuries these farmers had worked the same small plots of land that their fathers and grandfathers had before them. Often they came to regard the land as their own. The landlords received, as rent, part of the crop grown. As property taxes rose to help pay for the war costs, many landlords were unhappy with the rental arrangements.

The new factories in industrial England offered a solution to the landlords' problems. The power looms could weave far more cloth than was being produced. A new source of wool was urgently needed. Landlords who evicted their tenants could turn the land over to sheep grazing and receive cash payments for their wool from the woollen factories.

Thousands of "crofters" as the tenant farmers were called, were turned off the land and sent on their way. This was done on a large scale in Scotland where the rocky glens were almost completely emptied of people. They called it the "Highland Clearances." Many displaced crofters came to Canada.

Famine in Ireland

Perhaps the most desperate of all the people restlessly on the move at this time were the Irish, including the passengers of the *Syria*. The main food source for most poor Irish was the potato. In the 1840s, the crop had failed for several years in a row. Extremely damp weather combined with disease to prevent the seed potatoes from growing in the soil. The result was famine and starvation for the Irish poor. Faced with this disaster, the government in 1847 turned over the

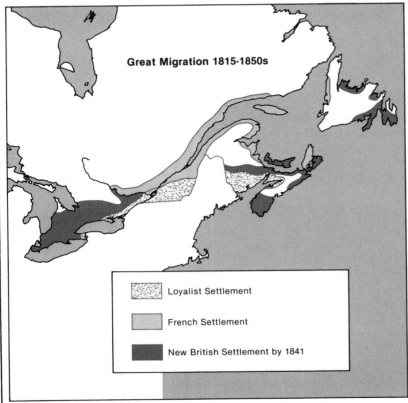

Great Migration 1815-1850s

Loyalist Settlement

French Settlement

New British Settlement by 1841

care of the poor and starving to local authorities. These local authorities were usually the wealthy and important people in the area, often the large landlords. Since they were not receiving rents from their tenants because of the potato failure, they were often unwilling to provide help for the poor. In many cases, they evicted their tenants and burned the thatch roofs of their homes so that the tenants would not be able to go back to them. The roads of Ireland in 1847 were filled with wandering beggars in search of food and shelter.

Britain in the first half of the nineteenth century was bulging with people who wanted out.

1. What groups of people in Britain would most want to leave at this time? Why?
2. Why would landlords and the government encourage these people to leave?
3. Who was responsible for creating the large number of poor and homeless people at this time?

POPULATION OF UPPER CANADA

Event	Year	Population
Upper Canada created	1791	10 000
Early settlement and road construction	1809	60 000
War of 1812	1812	70 000
	1822	126 000
Canada Land Company formed	1823	
Lachine Canal opened	1824	
	1828	240 000
Welland Canal opened	1829	
Rebellion of 1837	1837	396 000
Irish potato famine began	1846	
	1848	726 000
First daily newspaper in Kingston	1849	
St. Lawrence and Atlantic	1851	952 000
Railway began operations		

Examine these figures carefully.

1. What time period shows the largest increase in the number of people in Upper Canada?
2. What time period shows the greatest percentage increase in Upper Canada's population?
3. What time period shows the least population growth?
4. Can you suggest any reasons why population growth is not always the same?

Encouragment of Immigrants

Although Britain was crowded, there was empty land in Upper Canada. To some government officials, this was the obvious answer to the problem of Britain's homeless and jobless poor. Many of the poorest people were encouraged to immigrate to Canada. They were given help in paying their passage costs by the government or by charities. In some cases, the very landlords who had turned out their crofters, loaned them the needed money.

There was also some concern about growing American influence in Upper Canada. This was due to the large number of "Late Loyalists" who had acted on Lieutenant-Governor Simcoe's advertising campaign. They were interested in good, cheap farm land rather than loyalty to the British Crown. This had been apparent during the War of 1812 when numbers of the "Late Loyalists" had refused to fight for Britain. Some had openly aided the Americans in that war.

If large numbers of new immigrants loyal to Britain came to Upper Canada, the threat of this American influence might be reduced.

Information for Immigrants

There were a number of sources of information about life in Upper Canada to help the immigrants. A flood of books and magazines contained all sorts of useful and helpful information. The climate, soil, plants, wildlife, condition of roads, quality of hotels and their beds, costs of needed products, and even the manners of Canadians were carefully listed.

These guides for settlers were written by English visitors who had travelled to the new colony, and in some cases, settled there. The most famous of these authors were two remarkable sisters, Susanna Moodie and Catharine Parr Traill. They came to Canada with their husbands in the 1830s and helped to carve new farms from the dense forest. In a series of books and

articles, they described the many sides of pioneer life. In addition to the chores of raising children, chopping wood, feeding pigs, and baking bread, they found time to write about their new lives with skill and care. Mrs. Traill sketched many of the wild plants and flowers of Upper Canada and described them with scientific accuracy. She also found time to write children's stories.

Our knowledge about life in this period would be much less detailed without these sources.

Food and Drink on the Ship

The quantities of **provisions** which each passenger, fourteen years of age and upwards, is entitled to receive on the voyage to America are:[2]

British Law

3 quarts [3.4 L] of water	daily
2½ lbs. [1.1 kg] of bread or biscuit	weekly
1 lb. [0.4 kg] wheaten flour	weekly
5 lb. [2.2 kg] oatmeal	weekly
2 lb. [0.9 kg] rice	weekly
1½ lb. [o.6 kg] sugar	
2 oz. [113 g] tea	
or 4 oz. [56 g] coffee or cocoa	weekly
2 oz. [56 g] salt	weekly

American Law

3 qts. [3.4 L] of water	daily
2½ lb. [1.1 kg] navy bread	weekly
1 lb. [0.4 kg] wheaten flour	weekly
6 lbs. [2.7 kg] of salt pork	weekly
(free from bone)	
½ lb. [0.2 kg] sugar	weekly
2 oz. [56 g] tea	weekly
8 oz. [226 g] of molasses and vinegar	weekly

What to Take

As to furniture..., I would by no means advise the emigrant to burden himself with such matters. ... Good clothing and plenty of good shoes and boots, are your best stores. ...[3]

Canadian Winters

The frost commences about Christmas, and continues until near April ... during which time if plenty of snow falls, the inhabitants enjoy sleigh riding with safety, well wrapt up in buffalo robes, bear skins, &c.[4]

The Soil

Indeed, were it not for the ... richness of the soil, which **yields** ... almost without cultivation, the settlers could not obtain a **subsistence** from their farms until after many years occupation. In sowing wheat, they use the small **proportion** of one bushel, and one bushel and a half to the acre. In England, three are required.[5]

yields: produces

subsistence: living

proportion: part

Where to Settle

... The **most eligible** part of Canada for emigrants desiring to buy **wild** land is the western portion of the upper province that lies between the great waters of Lakes Ontario, Erie, Huron, and the smaller Lake Simcoe. Railroads and public works are being carried on in this part of the country; the land is of the richest and most fertile description.[6]

most eligible: best
provisions: food and drink
wild: uncleared

Problems with Servants

They demand the highest wages, and grumble at doing half the work, in return, which they cheerfully performed **at home**. They demand to eat at your table, and to sit in your company, and if you refuse ... they tell you that "they are free ... that you may look for another person to fill their place as soon as you like". ...[7]

at home: in England

The Future

It is a good thing for those who grow up with a new place; they are sure to become rich men.[8]

1. What made Canada a good place to come to?
2. What problems would an immigrant have to deal with?
3. Who would be most likely to read the settlers' guides? Who would be unlikely to read them?
4. If you were thinking of coming to Canada in the early 1800s, what sorts of information would you want before you made your decision?

Chapter 44

THE VOYAGE TO CANADA

How They Travelled

Immigrants who could afford to pay the cost of cabin accommodation aboard a passenger ship found the voyage to Canada pleasant and exciting. Most immigrants were not so fortunate. The minimum cost per person of five pounds was more than many workers earned per year. For the jobless and homeless poor who were anxious to start new lives in Canada, such costs were far too expensive. For these immigrants the voyage was in "steerage."

"Steerage" was the crowded and stuffy area below the deck. There were no portholes, few sanitary services, and almost no privacy. Many ships were old and unseaworthy. Some had been built to carry timber and were roughly converted to carry passengers.

In the early years of the Great Migration, there were few laws to protect immigrants. Ships were sometimes dangerously overloaded. Dishonest captains lied about the true length of the voyage. When passengers ran out of food, they had to buy extra supplies from the captain and crew at high prices. In some ships, the crew felt free to rob the passengers and to abuse the women. Some passengers formed volunteer committees to stay awake at night to prevent this.

The Perils of the Sea

Few passengers were prepared for the sudden fury of an Atlantic storm. When one struck, the passengers were herded below decks and locked there until it passed. Conditions below decks were often terrible. Many passengers were seasick. They had no toilets. Storms sometimes lasted several days. Some passengers went mad in the cramped, crowded, and smelly conditions.

Occasionally the storms were so violent and the ships so unseaworthy that shipwrecks occurred. There were rarely enough lifeboats for everyone on board. The case of the *John* provides a shocking example of what sometimes happened.

The *John* left Plymouth Sound in England on May 3, 1855, bound for Quebec. It carried 149 adult passengers and 114 children. The *John* was wrecked on rocks the very day it sailed. The captain and crew were apparently drunk and seized the few lifeboats, leaving the passengers aboard:

... [T]he sea broke heavily over the vessel, ... each wave carrying its victims into eternity amidst the most terrific shrieks of the rest, expecting every moment to meet the same doom. One hundred and ninety-six men, women, and children were swallowed up, and about eighty saved. ... Not a seaman perished.[1]

The captain was convicted of manslaughter.

The Terror of Disease

Perhaps the most feared danger that immigrants had to face was disease. The deadly cholera, typhus, and diphtheria struck with little warning. No one knew who would be the next victim once a ship became disease ridden. There seemed to be nothing that a passenger could do to escape. A Scottish immigrant described the effect of an epidemic on his ship:

One got used to it—it was nothing but

splash, splash, all day long—first one, then another. There was one Martin on board, I remember, with a wife and nine children.... Well, first his wife died, and they threw her into the sea and then he died, and they threw him into the sea, and then the children, one after t'other, till only two were left alive; the eldest, a girl about thirteen who had nursed them all, one after another, and seen them die—well, she died, and then there was only the little fellow left. ... He went back, as I heard, in the same ship with the captain.[2]

To many passengers, arrival at Quebec must have been less the beginning of a new dream than the end of a nightmare.

1. List the problems that passengers might experience at this time.
2. Who was responsible for these problems?
3. What qualities would an immigrant need to have, to undertake a voyage in steerage?

Encounter with an iceberg off the Grand Banks. What would happen if the ship and the iceberg collided?

Chapter 45

FROM QUEBEC TO UPPER CANADA

The relief of immigrants who had safely "made it" across the Atlantic Ocean must have been mixed with concern when they realized how far they still were from their final destinations: their lots. Quebec was hundreds of kilometres from Upper Canada, and Upper Canada was a large province with few passable roads. Many days of travel lay ahead for pioneer families.

There were various ways for immigrants to travel from Quebec to Upper Canada. The most convenient method of travelling to Montreal was by **steam packet**. Several of these ran regularly between Quebec and Montreal. Immigrants had to travel overland, around the rapids, from Montreal to Lachine. Wagons and carts were available to carry people and their belongings. From Lachine west, stagecoaches or steamships provided uncomfortable but reliable service for those with money to spend for fares. The poorer travellers went on foot. There were plenty of inns and farmhouses along the route, which followed the north shore of the St. Lawrence River. Tired immigrants were welcomed.

steam packet: a small passenger ship

A steamboat wharf in Montreal in 1832 was a busy place. Immigrants could comfortably travel between Quebec and Montreal on their way to Upper Canada.

Into the Bush

People whose chosen area of settlement was in the back country, inland from the more populated areas of Upper Canada, faced further transportation problems. They may have made it safely to Brockville, or Cobourg, or York, but they still had to travel to their lots. This was often a troublesome trip. Water transportation was preferred, because of the poor roads. The trip of Mr. and Mrs. Thomas Langton, and their daughter, Anne, introduced the family to travel in Upper Canada. They were on their way from York to the Peterborough area. Here is Mrs. Langton's description:

August 4, 1837. We embarked [at York] about 10 o'clock in the evening in the steam packet for Port Hope. No sleep during the whole night; at 6 o'clock (a.m.) we disembarked and went to a disagreeable damp old inn for breakfast, and found that we had some hours to wait for the stages to convey us for about 9 miles [14 km] to Rice Lake.

The stage is a kind of wagon with 2 seats slung across, and over good roads would not be unpleasant. Some part of the road was good, other parts very shaking and uneasy. We had 2 hours to wait for the steamer [for crossing Rice Lake]. At last we saw a **ponderous** body slowly approaching us—it was certainly the most **uncouth** steam packet we had ever seen. We dined on board, a comfortable clean dinner. It was quite dark before reaching the place of disembarking, and we had then to be rowed up the [Otonabee] River about a mile [1.6 km] before reaching Peterborough.

The family waited several days at Peterborough before continuing on their way. A ten-kilometre trip on horseback behind her. Mrs. Langton's description of the trip continued....

August 14th. We proceeded to the boat stationed ready for us on Mud

THE UPPER CANADA COACHES leave MONTREAL EVERY DAY except *Saturday* and *Sunday*, at FOUR o'clock, A.M. Montreal, May 3, 1832.   d

LAKE ONTARIO.

Lake. We were rowed by 3 gentlemen and an assistant. In about 4 hours we stopped to eat our **provisions**. We re-embarked, and in something more than 2 hours, arrived at Bobcaygeon. We had to walk more than half a mile [1 km] over a wretched unmade road in the wood to our sleeping-place, a nice clean log house with a nice clean hostess. We had a comfortable cup of tea.

August 15th. The morning was wet and very unfavourable-looking; a party of young men arrived [with 2 rowboats]. We embarked. At six o'clock [in the evening] we were rowed to the landing place. John [her son] led me up a most rugged path, seemingly very happy and proud to welcome his parents to his little habitation in the backwoods.[1]

1. Try to calculate how long it took the Langtons to travel from York to their backwoods home.
2. Make a flow chart to show the different kinds of transportation the Langtons used on their trip. Your flow chart could be done with sketches.
3. What evidence is there that some conveniences were available for travellers, even in the backwoods?

Notices were published in Quebec and Montreal papers, advertising coach and steamboat schedules so that travellers could plan their journeys.

provisions: lunch

ponderous: heavy

uncouth: awkward

Chapter 46

SETTLING THE PROVINCE

Land for Settlers

The people who flocked to Upper Canada in the first half of the nineteenth century wanted two things—a new life and land. The British government had plans, too. It sought a settled colony in Upper Canada, income to pay the province's bills, and a suitable way of dealing with the thousands of people in Britain who were suffering from unemployment, poverty, and a lack of opportunity. Various land-granting methods were tried.

In the earliest days of the colony, free land was granted to Loyalists, soldiers, and servants and friends of the government. Land was also granted to settlers who could obtain proof of ownership of their lots by performing various settlement duties. These duties included building a small house, clearing and fencing two hectares, and clearing part of the roadway in front of their lot. Many people were settled on farms by this method, but the system had severe drawbacks.

Explain in your own words why so many people who wanted farms in Upper Canada became squatters.

Land for Speculators

Thousands of hectares of land were granted to people who had no intention of settling on them. These people were speculators who hoped to keep their land and sell it for a profit as the colony developed. Other land was held in reserve for the Crown, and to support a "Protestant clergy," according to the Constitutional Act of 1791. This reserved land was to be rented or sold. The Crown and Clergy Reserves amounted to 2/7 of every township in the province.

Huge blocks of land were left unoccupied, making life difficult for settlers. They were often very isolated, separated from each other by hectares of wilderness. They resented the failure of the owners of the unoccupied lands to clear roads or fields. Pioneers who had to do compulsory road building were unhappy about landowners who had no such duties. People who wanted to farm were also unhappy to find that much of the best land had already been granted to someone who was holding it for selling later, not for farming.

Townships were surveyed before land could be granted for settlement. Two-sevenths of the lots in every township were reserved. The rest of the land was open for settlers.

A Typical Township in Upper Canada

Crown Lots
Clergy Lots
Lots for Settlement

14 km
19 km

Concessions: 14th, 13th, 12th, 11th, 10th, 9th, 8th, 7th, 6th, 5th, 4th, 3rd, 2nd, 1st, Broken Front

Lots: 1–24

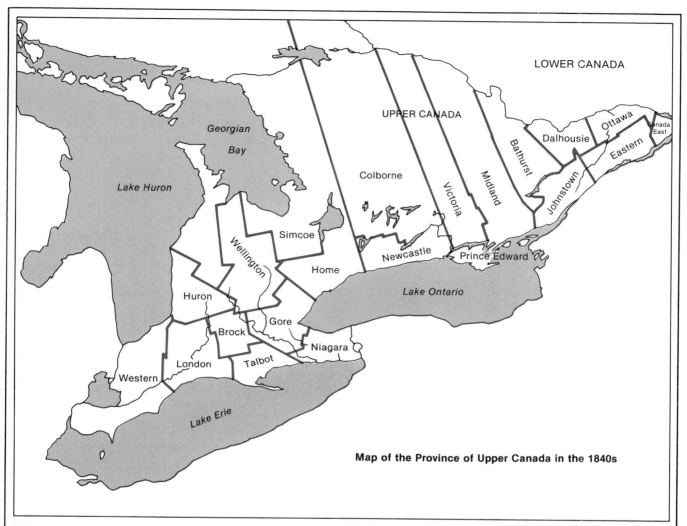

Map of the Province of Upper Canada in the 1840s

Map of Upper Canada showing the districts in the 1840s.

Land Sales by Auction

To remedy some of these problems, the British government decided, in 1826, to sell land in Upper Canada by auction. This method involved serious problems, too. Settlers still faced uncertainties about getting their lots. They were expected to find isolated land offices and bid on lots that were offered for sale. Settlers often arrived at land offices to find that good lots had already been sold to speculators who could afford to pay high prices. Many frustrated settlers still could not satisfy their main desire—to obtain land to farm. As a result, many immigrants continued their search for land elsewhere (in the United States). Others became squatters. They simply chose a piece of unoccupied land and began to clear and farm it.

Settlement Schemes

The lands of Upper Canada were settled by people from all walks of life and through many different settlement schemes. The British government tried a policy of "assisted emigration" for a few years. Agents of the government gathered large groups of people in Britain and brought them to settle in chosen parts of the province. After 1825 the government no longer provided direct aid for emigrants, but other groups in Britain did. Local parishes or private groups of individuals pooled their money and sent emigrants to Canada. Companies were formed to bring settlers. And individuals who had determination and a little money managed to find their own way across the Atlantic to Upper Canada. The vast majority of these people were from England, Ireland, and Scotland.

1. List the different methods by which immigrants could be settled on land in Upper Canada.
2. How is real estate bought and sold today? What procedures must a buyer follow? How does this differ from the way Upper Canadian settlers obtained land?

Indians and Reserves in Upper Canada

As settlers pushed their way into the Upper Canadian forest, the people who had lived there for hundreds of years faced the prospect of drastic change. The British government developed ways of dealing with the possible conflict between settlers and native peoples. Only the Crown could obtain land directly from the Indians. This was done by various treaties as settlement advanced. Indians were left reserved lands for their own use and were given payment and presents in exchange for their lands.

Many government officials, as well as Christian missionaries and teachers, hoped that the Indians would use their reserve lands to farm, as the pioneers around them were doing. Roads, farms, schools, and villages would be located on reserved lands. Soon the Indian lands would look no different from the townships of the immigrant settlers. This did not happen quickly. Indian lands would look no different from those of the British policy makers. Government Indian agents lacked funds to carry out road building and other plans for development.

Why might the Indians not wish to become settled pioneer farmers?

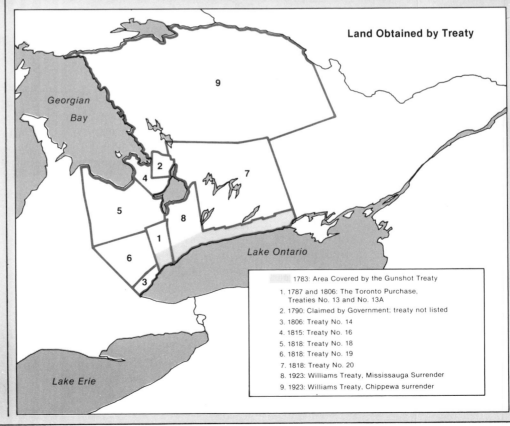

Land Obtained by Treaty

Georgian Bay

Lake Ontario

Lake Erie

1783: Area Covered by the Gunshot Treaty
1. 1787 and 1806: The Toronto Purchase, Treaties No. 13 and No. 13A
2. 1790: Claimed by Government; treaty not listed
3. 1806: Treaty No. 14
4. 1815: Treaty No. 16
5. 1818: Treaty No. 18
6. 1818: Treaty No. 19
7. 1818: Treaty No. 20
8. 1923: Williams Treaty, Mississauga Surrender
9. 1923: Williams Treaty, Chippewa surrender

Land was obtained by treaty from the Indians. Each treaty provided some reserve land for the Indians' use.

SURVIVING THE NEW LAND

Chapter 47

Getting Land

For most settlers, getting a block of land was just the start of a long and difficult struggle. Those able to buy land that had already been cleared had a real advantage. Those who were granted a "location ticket" to undeveloped Crown land didn't know what they were getting. It might be swamp or useless scrub land. Often it was covered with thick forest when its owner arrived to take possession of it.

The location ticket stated a number of tasks that settlers had to do before the land became theirs. Here is a typical list of duties:

... to clear and fence 5 acres [2 ha] for every 100 acres [40 ha] granted; to erect a dwelling house of 16 feet [5 m] by 20 feet [6 m]; and to clear one half of the road in front of each lot. The whole to be performed within two years of the date of the ticket.[1]

Survival Skills

Some settlers faced serious problems in their first few years. Often they had spent all their money on the passage to Canada. They expected to be able to grow their own food at once. If their land was heavily forested, this was impossible. Some had to take work clearing other settlers' land in order to buy food for their families. Later, as the colony developed, jobs in lumber camps and towns offered opportunities for poor settlers. Sometimes settlers were unable to fulfil the duties on their location tickets because they had to work for cash. Sometimes they lost their land.

Superintendent's Office,
Perth, U.C. 17 *April* 1816

THE BEARER, *Peter McPherson Enright* is Located to the *West half* of Lot No. *Twenty-seven* in the *Tenth* Concession of the Township of *Elmsley* County of *Leeds* — and District of *Johnstown*

THE CONDITION of this Location is such, That if the above named *Peter McPherson* is not residing upon, and improving the above described Lot, clearing and putting in crops at least four acres yearly, then this Title to be void and of no effect, and subject to be immediately re-granted.

N. B. After Location no exchange can take place, nor is this certificate of any value but to the original Grantee.

By Order,

D. Daverne Esq.

Superintending Settlers.

A location ticket from 1816. How do the conditions described in this location ticket compare with those in the one given in the text? Why would there be differences in the wording of such documents?

Clearing the land. A group of Irish workers felling timbers to be used in the construction of a shanty.

A farm in the bush. Many first homes were similar in appearance to this one. What evidence is there in the picture to suggest that this farm has not been occupied for long?

The long hours of back-breaking labour needed to clear the land often took a physical toll. Few of the new settlers were competent woodsmen. Accidents were common and sometimes fatal. William Singer, a brick-layer turned farmer and lumberman, may have been more unlucky than many other settlers in his efforts to learn the necessary new skills:

I have been very unfortunate. I've cut myself four or five times: I cut my hand in the summer while mowing ... I cut my foot very bad four weeks ago, it's not well yet. I cut two of my toes off: Mr. Silcog sewed them on again: they seem to be getting on very well. ...[2]

It is not surprising that the number of would-be settlers who abandoned their new homes in the wild lands was fairly high.

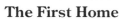

The First Home

The first challenge to the settlers' survival skills was the creation of a shelter that would enable them to survive the harshness of a Canadian winter. The first primitive hut or shanty was not usually intended to house the settlers for more than a year or two. It would then be replaced by a larger and better-built home, often erected with the help of neighbours. Until such time as a real house could be constructed, living conditions could be worse for the settlers' families than for their livestock. Mrs. Traill described one such farm that she saw on

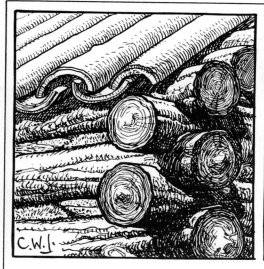

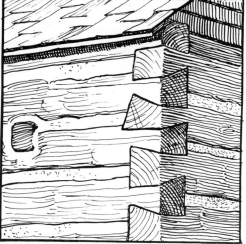

Log-house construction. Which of these types of construction would be the simplest to build? Why? Why have no nails been used in these buildings? What makes the roof watertight?

her travels through Canada:

I actually once saw a patchwork quilt, pegged up in front of the shed where the cows were stabled, though from the appearance of the dwelling-house, I should have supposed it could ill have been spared from the children's beds, but the cow must be sheltered whoever else suffered from the cold wind and snow.[3]

Early homes sometimes resembled stables or pigsties more than the houses the settlers had left behind them in Britain. The purpose of the first house was to be snug and warm during winter storms. Such dwellings often had to be built very quickly. Despite this, they could be fairly comfortable, if the description given by Major Strickland is to be believed:

On the 16th of May, 1826, I moved with all my **goods and chattels**, which were then easily packed into a single-horse waggon, and consisted of a plough-iron, six pails, a sugar-kettle, two iron pots, a frying-pan with a long handle, a tea-kettle, a few cups and saucers, a chest of carpenter's tools, a Canadian axe, and a cross-cut saw.

My stock of provisions **comprised** a parcel of groceries, half a barrel of pork, and a barrel of flour. ...

My friends in Douro turned out the next day and assisted me to put up the walls of my shanty and roof it with basswood troughs, and it was com-

pleted before dark. ...

I was kept busy for more than a week chinking between the logs, and plastering up all the **crevices**, cutting out the door-way and place for the window-**casing**, then making a door and hanging it on wooden hinges. I also made a rough table and some stools ....

Four thick slabs of limestone placed upright in one corner of the shanty, with clay packed between them to keep the fire off the logs, **answered** very well for a chimney, with a hole cut through the roof above to vent the smoke.

I made a **tolerable** bedstead out of some ironwood poles, by stretching strips of elmwood bark across, which I **plaited** strongly together to support my bed, which was a good one and the only article of luxury in my possession.'[4]

With such a luxurious bedstead, a settler might escape the pain and monotony of long hours spent swinging an axe. The promise of the new land was coming true.

1. Explain the reasons for the duties listed in the location ticket.
2. What circumstances could lead to settlers failing to keep their land?
3. What personal qualities would help settlers to succeed in establishing a new farm?

crevices: cracks

casing: frame

answered: worked

tolerable: fairly good

plaited: wove

goods and chattels: property

comprised: included

Chapter 48 | PEOPLE FOR A PROVINCE

Perth, 1816: The Soldier-Settlers

We came through so much to settle here in Upper Canada. We don't regret it, but it's been a hard, hard journey. It all began when we beat Napoleon. When the war ended, we returned home to Scotland. There was no work, our families were suffering, and we needed help.

Then a Mr. Campbell came to our valley. He said we could go to Upper Canada. The British government would pay our way and we'd get free land, food, and axes. We'd be able to buy farm tools cheaply. Jenny and I talked it over and it seemed like the answer to our prayers—a new life in a new land. We'd not be starving any longer.

Well, we signed up with Mr. Campbell. Then began the waiting time. At last a message came to our village. We were to sail on July 12. Jenny and I gathered a few belongings. We said goodbye to our beloved Scottish hills, and walked to Glasgow.

On September 16, we arrived at Quebec. Then it was up the St. Lawrence River to Montreal, and on to a village called Cornwall. We began a wretched winter in the barracks there. The roof leaked and snow blew in through cracks in the walls. Scotland, at its worst, seemed better than this. But our boy, William, was happy, for he was in Mr. Holliday's classes at the school there. A little plaster, a few shingles, and some planks did wonders for our leaky barracks. By Christmas, we'd settled in.

In February, Captain Ferguson set off to buy the land for our settlement from the Chippewa and Mississauga Indians. We were to be settled in the country far back from the St. Lawrence River. We had to protect the province in case the Yankees should ever invade again, as they did in the War of 1812. We're to be north of the Rideau River.

Spring came to Cornwall at last. And spring in our new land was a wonderful time. At the beginning of April we travelled up the St. Lawrence River to the village of Brockville. Then began the slow journey by wagon along Mr. Sherwood's new road. We passed through endless forests, unbroken except for the rivers and lakes, and a few tiny clearings.

Finally we reached Perth, the name given to our settlement's village. Perth's name reminded us of home. But it was not yet a village. We found only a clearing with one cabin for the supplies and another for Mr. Sherwood, the surveyor, and Mr. MacDonnell, the settlement superintendent.

We got a location ticket from Mr. MacDonnell and found our lot. By the end of June, our cabin was built. We knew we'd not be able to grow enough food for the coming months. But the government provided enough to keep us well, and so did the forest.

And now, we're settling in. Our second winter in Canada will be spent in our own home.

Andrew MacLean
Perth, 1816

On October 16, this report was written about the Perth settlement:

In the village of Perth there are 20 houses and in its immediate vicinity there are 250 houses which will be ready for occupation before the winter. Amongst the settlers there are 80 head of cattle and 800 bushes [2912 L] of fall wheat now in the ground. At present

there are 840 men, 207 women, and 458 children.[1]

The Perth soldier-settlement was on its way. Other soldier-settlements were begun in 1818 at Richmond, in Carleton County. The settlers there received more help from the government than the Perth group had. Each family received food for a year, as well as these things:

axe	scythe
broadaxe	hammer
mattock	nails
pickaxe	saw
spade	twelve panes of glass
shovel	putty
camp kettle	blanket
hoe	

and a set of carpenter's tools for all members of the settlement.

1. Why were the soldiers brought by the British government to settle in Upper Canada?
2. What problems had Andrew MacLean's family overcome by the time he told his story?
3. Find out how pioneers used the tools listed. Find a picture of several and sketch them.

Lanark, 1820: The Poor Scots Weavers

The end of the wars with Napoleon brought severe hardship to the weavers of Glasgow, Scotland. They were unemployed, and their families were hungry. The British government decided to send 1200 weavers' families to Upper Canada. These were the terms:

sixty hectares of free surveyed land,

free passage from Quebec to the settlement,

seed grain and tools supplied at cost,

loans of money on arrival in Canada to help settlers get established.

Emigrants were expected to pay for their passage across the Atlantic Ocean. Since few could afford this, money was collected in London. The weavers left for Upper Canada in the summer of 1820.

Settler Alex Watt wrote a letter to a friend in Glasgow:

Perth, October, 1820

I am 7 miles [10 km] from Lanark. I am well pleased with my land. It is nearly covered with sugar maple, beech, and ash trees. I have a small swamp for grass, and a fine meadow. I could keep a cow on it. I have got very good neighbours. There are 3 lots on the north side of mine not yet taken up. Prices for food are very high.

We are going out tomorrow to cut roads and build our houses. We have gotten rations from the government since we came from Quebec. We have gotten a good blanket apiece; we are to get cooking utensils, farm implements and assistance of every kind over and above our money. There are 3 or 4 children dead since we left Montreal, but I was never in better health.[2]

What differences were there between the arrangements and terms of settlement for the Perth soldier-settlers and the Lanark group?

New Lanark

By December, 1820, New Lanark, as the settlement was named (after a county in Scotland), had begun to look like a village. Several homes were ready, the first schoolhouse had been planned, and a group of settlers had begun plans for a church. There were three stores in the village, and a mill was under construction. By May, 1821, nearly 2000 people were settled in the New Lanark area. They were joined by 1800 more Scottish immigrants a few months later.

James Dobbie sums up his feelings about his Upper Canadian home.

Lanark, April 24, 1826

I and my family are still taking well with this country, and I really do bless God every day I rise that He was ever pleased to send me and my family to this place.

My stock of cattle consists of 1 **yoke** of oxen, 3 milk cows, and 3 young ones. I have got up a very handsome new house, with the assistance of 15 young men. It was raised in 1 day.[3]

What reasons do James Dobbie and Alex Watt give for being pleased about moving to Upper Canada?

yoke: pair

Pioneer farmers looked forward to the day when their land showed cleared fields, neat fences, and a large house and barn. Locate this pioneer farm's original log house.

226

Peterborough, 1825: Farms for the Irish

Life in Ireland was harsh. Farms were poor: there were too few jobs, too many people, and too little food.

In 1825 Peter Robinson, the Upper Canadian agent of the British government, was authorized to help. He gathered together over 2000 poor Irish people and explained his plan: they would be settled in Upper Canada. Their passage to the province would be paid by the government. On arrival in Upper Canada, the immigrants would be taken to their new farms. Each family would receive sixty hectares of land. On this lot would be a log shanty. Each family would receive food for eighteen months—pork and flour. Farm tools and household equipment were part of the bargain, too. Each family received a cow, an axe, an auger, handsaw, nails, a hoe, a kettle, a frying pan, an iron pot, seed potatoes, and Indian corn. The plan seemed too good to be true. It meant escape from the misery of Ireland, and a chance for the poor to become landowners.

Many people rushed to join the group that journeyed from Cork County, Ireland. Their travels ended in Peterborough, a county surveyed for their settlement. It was named after Peter Robinson.

They received their lots and set to work to build farms. Most succeeded, although a few drifted away from the area, to settle in York, or the United States. A few traded their farm tools and food for the plentiful whisky available in the village of Peterborough. Most of the Irish immigrants settled in and began the work of all pioneers. After a few years, the area was home. Nobody doubted that they were better off in Peterborough than they had been in Ireland.

By 1838 Peterborough boasted 150 houses and was home to 900 people. There were four churches, a school, stores, inns, a circulating library, a post office, and several distilleries. Other settlers followed the Irish pioneers, working to make Peterborough a thriving Upper Canadian community.

1. *What did the Irish, whom Peter Robinson settled, receive from the British government? Why do you think the government was so generous with these people?*
2. *Write a letter home to your mother in Ireland, describing your first year in the Peterborough settlement. Explain why you are or are not pleased to have immigrated.*
3. *Summarize, in chart form, the various measures taken by the British government to assist immigrants in settling in Upper Canada.*

THE CANADA COMPANY,
Have nearly One Million Acres of Land,
OF THE FINEST DESCRIPTION,
For Sale, in the Huron Tract,
And persons desirous of purchasing can obtain all the necessary information, as to prices, situation of vacant Lots, and mode of application, from the *Land Agents*, appointed for that purpose, at the Company's Offices in,

Goderich, Stratford, & Hay.

The object which the Canada Company have principally in view in appointing those Agents, is that they may afford this information, for they have not been empowered to receive Money; persons, therefore, having to make payments, either on account of credit Instalments falling due, or first Instalments on new purchases, may lodge the money with the Bank of Upper Canada Agency in the *Town of London*, on account of the Canada Company, who will give them a Receipt for the same, which may be remitted to the Commissioners in Toronto as Cash, and by return of Post its receipt will be acknowledged; or should there be no Bank Agency in the neighbourhood, they may retain the money till the arrival of one of the Commissioners, who will attend at each Agency every second month, for the purpose of receiving money and issuing Location Tickets to purchasers; or they may forward the amount, at their own risk, by the Post from *Stratford* or *Goderich*, and which leaves the latter place twice each week for Toronto.

No person will be allowed to take up Land who is not prepared to *pay the first Instalment in Cash*, either by remittance in the manner here pointed out, or to the Commissioner on his periodical visits, and should this regulation not be complied with, the Lands will be immediately held as open for re-sale; nor will any person be allowed to hold Land who has not made a regular application for it through the Land Agent, and received his written permission to take possession of it on the terms here stated.

Canada Company's Office,
Toronto, 1st May, 1836.

Printed at the U. C. Gazette Office.

Canada Company broadsides encouraged settlement. Why would so much information be included in a broadside?

Guelph was founded for the Canada Company. It was a bustling town in the 1840s.

Prosperous farms grew up in the Guelph area. What evidence is there that these farms are very successful?

Guelph: The Canada Company Brings Settlers

Direct government aid to immigrants ended with the Peterborough Irish in 1825. The next year, a land settlement company called the Canada Company was created. It bought a large amount of Upper Canadian land (about 1 000 000 ha), brought in settlers, and sold land to them to make a profit. John Richards joined the thousands who settled in the Guelph area. He explains:

Emma and I arrived at Quebec in the spring of 1832. We met the Canada Company agent, Mr. Johnson, and soon arranged for our trip to Guelph. We had decided while still in England that Guelph would be our next home. Impressive **broadsides** and pamphlets given out by a Canada Company agent in London had helped us choose Guelph. The agents were so helpful. We were shown pictures of roads, mills, even a small village. The Company's advertisements were very encouraging.

Our passage from Quebec to York was paid by the Canada Company. It was a small saving for us. We didn't have to bother making the travel arrangements as the Company did that for us. From York, the Company wagons brought us to Guelph. We were surprised to see that the Canada Company's pamphlets hadn't betrayed us. The town of Guelph was bigger than it had been when the artist drew his pictures. We strolled through the village, past shops, a distillery, a school, a brewery, a blacksmith's shop, a sawmill, grist mill, three churches, and five inns. Roads had been built, as well as a school and mills, even before the first settlers arrived in 1827.

The Company planned well in order to attract settlers. A Settlers Savings Bank is located here for us. Of course, the Canada Company sends our letters home to England, free of charge. Emma and I are glad we chose Upper Canada, and we're glad we chose the Canada Company's settlement.

John Inglis agreed with Emma and John Richards. Here is part of a letter he wrote back home to Scotland:

February 26, 1831
I would not return to Scotland, though anyone would pay my passage back and give me £20 [about $50.] a year. I could never have the prospects for my family in Britain that I here have; only one thing is to be remarked. No one need come here in prospect of doing well unless he intends to work hard. He who does so will, in the course of seven or eight years, feel independent.[4]

1. What measures did the Canada Company take to bring settlers to the Guelph area?
2. Why do you think the Canada Company did so much to encourage the Guelph settlers?
3. What is the main reason for John Inglis's happiness about having settled in Canada?

On Their Own

There were immigrant groups that received government help, groups that came because of the advertisements of the Canada Company, and groups that were specially chosen to settle in Upper Canada. But there were also thousands of other people who left Britain on their own to settle in the new land. Here is the story of one of those individuals, as told by a descendant. It's the story of John Miller.

In 1835 John Miller crossed the Atlantic Ocean and made his way to Markham Township to work for his uncle.

In 1839, John Miller drew his wages for his 4 years' labour: 2 cattle and 4 sheep. With his Irish bride, Margaret Whiteside of Scarborough, he came to the 200 acre [80 ha] farm, called Thistle Ha', in the Township of Pickering.

Now began the enormous task of turning this wilderness into a farm. He encountered huge maple trees with only his brawn [muscle] and an axe to fell them. More discouraging was the fact that the ground was full of stones of all sizes.

The first crops were barley and peas, sown by hand and reaped by scythe. Starvation was sometimes near at hand and there is a story of one spring when this pioneering family had to turn the cattle out in the woods and then pick for their own use the plants the cattle ate. The few potatoes that were saved for planting were dug up a few days later to eat. Flour was obtained by carrying through the woods a sack of wheat the many miles [kilometres] to the grist mill in Markham.

Gradually the forest was cleared. Trenches were dug around the big stones and the boulders were heated by burning wood in the trenches. Cold water was then thrown on them to shatter them into pieces that could be dragged by oxen or horse teams.[5]

The Miller family grew as the years passed, until twelve children lived at Thistle Ha'. In 1855 a large, beautiful stone house was built on the farm. Hard work, determination, and intelligence helped make many settlers like the Millers, builders of Upper Canada.

1. What reasons might John Miller have had for coming to Upper Canada?
2. How did John and Margaret keep from starving? How did they deal with the huge stones in their fields?
3. There is a different story for every pioneer family that came to Upper Canada. Make a chart showing similarities and differences between John Miller's story and that of one of the soldier-settlers, the weavers, the Peterborough Irish, the Canada Company settlers.

Chapter 49 | EVERYDAY LIFE AT HOME

Farming: Elizabeth Fraser's Story

Peter and I came to Upper Canada to farm. We've spent twenty years raising our five children and working our land. When we first unloaded our few belongings from the wagon, this farm was only a forest. But we got to work.

Our first cabin was small and uncomfortable, but it was all we had. A chopping gang helped us clear our first few hectares of land. We burned the brush in the fall of that year, 1828 it was, and planted some fall wheat. All winter, we planned and dreamed. Peter found time to make a bit of furniture for us, and I learned all about baking bread and serving salt pork.

Well, the years flew by. Peter and I worked hard. The children have always done their share of the chores, too. Nobody has been idle. We've done

better than Joe Hunter on the next road. Why, he's still got his family in their old log house, after ten years. And little land cleared. Too much drinking, they say. None of that for us. You can see how we've prospered.

Our new two-storey brick house is a beauty. We've got glass in the windows, rugs on the floors, cedar shingles on the roof, and a beautiful iron cookstove. Peter even bought me a fine new corner cupboard from the cabinet-maker in town. I'd like a piano next.

The animals are in new "houses," too. The first shelter for our yoke of oxen and a few pigs was pretty crude. It barely kept the bears away from the piglets. And there was no cover for the hay. Now, in our new barn, there's room for cows, sheep, horses, and plenty of storage space for hay and grain. There haven't been any bears

Large brick bake ovens were heated by wood fires. Why might a woman want to use an oven outside her house?

around for years. The hens, geese, and turkeys have their own little houses.

My gardens are looking better every year. In August, the flowers are wonderful. We've a lawn, too.

The vegetable garden in the early days was hard to locate. It was just a few precious seeds scattered among the stumps in our clearing. We always had trouble with nibblers—deer, rabbits, mice, and birds all loved to taste our vegetables or seeds. Now, I have a large, fenced vegetable garden, a potato patch, and a herb garden. I tend the gooseberry and current bushes, and remember the exciting day when Peter brought home the apple and pear trees from the nursery in town. That was eight years ago. Now we have lots of fruit for eating in the fall, and for drying. And, of course, I take Andrew, Matthew, and Mary off to the berry patches in June and July. Pails of strawberries or raspberries, and bright red stains on the children's fingers always come back from a berry-picking afternoon. We even have a small sugar bush to supply our maple sugar.

Our farm has come a long way in the twenty years since 1828. We've cleared nearly ¾ of our 100 ha of land. We'll leave the trees on the rest. We need lots of firewood, and the sugar bush has to be kept up. Our crops have been good.

We don't have to use as much muscle as we did in the early days. Farmers

A village scene in Upper Canada. Note the Conestoga wagon. In what ways is this village scene different from a village scene of today?

Corn was grown on many farms. Pioneers learned about corn from the Indians, who had cultivated it long before Europeans came to North America.

Blacksmiths were important to farmers. What is the blacksmith doing here? What things might a blacksmith shop provide for settlers?

now have help with their work: better ploughs, a mechanical hay mower, and two strong teams of horses help Peter and the older boys get their crops planted and harvested. We don't have to make our own crude implements any more. Peter once used pine roots to make a harrow. Now we can buy a good steel one in town. We've seen many changes. ...

1. Make an 1828 and an 1848 chart to summarize the changes and improvements that have been made by Elizabeth and Peter. Include houses, barns, animals, food, gardens, furniture, farm methods, and tools.

leavening: something that makes bread rise

2. Most families today do not have the opportunities (or necessity) to work together, as Elizabeth, Peter, and their children did. What advantages and disadvantages might there have been for a pioneer farm family that always had to work together to prosper? Would you like to live in a society where such a working arrangement was possible? Explain why or why not.

Women

- A settler's wife should be active, industrious, ingenious, cheerful, not above putting her hand to whatever is necessary to be done in her household, nor so proud to profit by the advice and experience of older portions of the community.
- She must become skilled in the arts of sugar-boiling, candle and soap-making, the making and baking of huge loaves [of bread], cooked in the bake-kettle, unless she be the fortunate mistress of a stone or clay oven.
- She must know how to manufacture hop-rising or salt-rising for **leavening** in her bread, salting meat and fish, knitting stockings and mittens and comforters, spinning yarn in the big wheel, and dyeing the yarn when spun, to be manufactured into cloth, making clothes for herself, her husband and children.
- The management of poultry and the dairy must not be omitted.[1]

Some pioneer women were ready to tackle almost any job:

Two young sisters from Galway [in Ireland] earned local **renown** as axewomen; they could match most men in the bush and were seen walking 17 miles [27 km] to the store, returning each with a full sack of flour or 90 pounds [40 kg] of potatoes on the shoulder.[2]

Many very interesting pioneer women lived in Upper Canada and wrote of their experiences in the backwoods of the province. The list begins with Elizabeth Simcoe, the wife of Upper Canada's first lieutenant-governor. She painted and sketched and wrote of life in the province's earliest days. Others followed Mrs. Simcoe. Their reminiscences, drawings, letters, and diaries are a gold mine of valuable information, providing present-day readers with a look at pioneer life. Women such as the remarkable sisters Catherine Parr Traill and Susanna Moodie; Anne Langton, and Frances Stewart have helped students of Upper Canadian history to appreciate everything from the unusual wild flowers of the wilderness to the unusual habits of some pioneers.

1. What qualities, besides those mentioned, would help make a successful pioneer wife?

2. Pioneer women like the ones described here wrote about life in Upper Canada. Suppose that you had to write about life in Ontario today. Make a list of ten topics you would choose to write about, and explain your choices.

Pioneer children enjoyed their toys just as much as children do today. This woman is making corn-husk dolls. Based on what you can see in the picture, write a set of instructions for making a corn-husk doll.

renown: fame

Food

Upper Canadian pioneers lived, at first, on an endless diet of salt pork,

Mrs. Moodie's sketches and books were popular. This sketch shows workers at the Marmora iron mine in the 1820s. Workers pickaxed iron ore for wages of twenty-four dollars a month in 1826.

potatoes, corn, and bread. When they could grow vegetables, or barter, or buy other food, they could vary their menus. Fortunately, the wilderness was home to "food" as well as to pioneers. Deer, rabbit, fish, wild fruits, berries, maple sugar, and edible wild plants were available.

Pioneer gardens produced crops of potatoes, turnips, cabbages, onions, pumpkins, and squash. No settler's garden was without its herbs, for seasoning and medicinal uses. Orchard trees could be purchased in the towns, and most settlers included apples in their diet.

Settlers relied on cows for a good part of their food supply: milk, butter, cheese, and meat.

Some food was imported to Upper Canada to be sold in town and village stores. Raisins, sugar, chocolate, nutmeg, ginger, rice, and molasses were among the items available to pioneer shoppers in the Niagara region.

Tea and Coffee

Real tea, coffee, and chocolate were hard to get in pioneer times. The settler found many substitutes. Different kinds of plants and flowers made an acceptable tea:

Balm or bee balm made Oswego tea.

Sweet gale and sweet fern made a good tea, as did young leaves of wintergreen, or dried flower head of white clover.

The settler also had substitutes for coffee. The roasted grains of rye, the nut-like seeds of goose grass, and the roots of dandelion and chicory, roasted and ground, made acceptable coffee. However, roasted barley was considered the best substitute.[3]

Coffee made from corn was also used by the settlers. Whole ears of corn were dried and roasted. Then they were boiled. The resulting liquid was sweetened with maple sugar.

Mrs. Traill's Recipe for Making Coffee from Dandelion Roots

Prepare the dandelion roots by washing thoroughly, but do not scrape off the outer brown skin ... cut up in small pieces and dry (slowly) until crisp enough to grind in the coffee mill.[4]

AT SCHOOL

Chapter 50

No School for Me

"Billy, you can't go to school today—or tomorrow either. Now that spring is here, you must help your brother Daniel and me with the planting. You're twelve now—old enough to do your share."

My father's words made me grin—no more school! The farm work is tiring, but at least I won't be trudging through the forest to school. I only went for three months this year. My friend James Edwards has never been to school. He can't even read or write his name yet.

Our little log schoolhouse sits in a clearing by the Wells road. There are benches around the walls of the schoolroom. There's a stove sitting in the middle of the room, and Mr. Sherwood has a small desk near the stove.

There are twenty-eight of us trying to remember Mr. Sherwood's lessons, learning to read and write, and do our arithmetic. We had a cold week in January, when John Gordon's father refused to send his share of the wood supply for our stove. Mr. Sherwood had to ask Robert Hart's father to bring extra wood.

Mr. Sherwood is a minister for the Church of England at Johnstown, when he's not teaching us at school. I'm not sorry I won't be seeing him again for a few months—maybe not till next October. I guess Catherine will be staying home now, too. Mama has lots of chores for my sisters, just as father has for us boys.

List three ways that "school" for Billy is different from "school" for you.

Pioneer schoolhouses were a lot like pioneer homes in the early days — small log buildings in tiny clearings in the forest.

Inside a backwoods schoolhouse. What differences are there between this class and yours?

Early Schools

Many schools in Upper Canada were like the one described by Billy. They were called common schools. Parents grouped together, donating their time, tools, labour, and building materials to construct a log schoolhouse. Then they set about hiring a teacher. The government helped to pay some of the costs of the school: money was granted for part of the teacher's salary and for buying textbooks. However, the main responsibility for the school rested with the parents. Those parents who did not wish to send their children to school, or who could not afford it, kept their families at home. There was no feeling that schools should be free and compulsory for all children.

Many schools, especially in the country, were badly equipped. Money was scarce, so there were few textbooks, globes, atlases, or other necessities. Many Upper Canadians complained that too many textbooks used in the schools were American. These books contained ideas which people did not think were appropriate for Upper Canada and, too often, ignored British North America completely.

There were other problems with the early system of education. The province set up eight grammar schools that were like high schools. Most children from rural areas found it impossible to attend grammar schools, since they were all in towns. Students from outside the towns had to move to town to go to school. Naturally, many parents complained. They wanted their children to go to school, but transportation problems, lack of money, and the difficulties of organizing a school, and finding a teacher, frustrated many people.

The government passed several education acts to improve the situation. A provincial board of education was created to supervise the schools, control the money that was granted, approve textbooks, and train teachers. Roman Catholic parents were permitted to establish separate schools for their children. In later years, education was paid for by school taxes. School became free and compulsory. Every child in the province could attend school.

Colleges were established in the 1830s and 1840s, the University of Toronto in 1849. Those who sought further education could obtain it in Upper Canada, instead of having to travel to Britain or the United States.

1. What factors often prevented Upper Canadian children from attending school?
2. Many Upper Canadians complained about the over-use of American books in schools. Some Canadians today worry about the American "invasion" of our lives through books, TV shows, movies, magazines, etc. Is this "invasion" good or bad?

Private Schools

The first schools in Upper Canada were private, run by individuals, and served only a few boys. Many common schools were built after 1816, but private schools continued to attract students, especially in towns such as York. This advertisement for a private girls' school appeared in a York newspaper in 1822:[1]

Mrs. Cockburn

Respectfully announces that she will commence her school duties on the First Monday in June.

Terms per quarter:
For Education in the English Language, Grammar, History, Geography, use of Globes, with Plain and Fancy Needlework *£2.00*
Writing and Ciphering *0.10*
French Language *1.00*
Drawing and Painting on Velvet *1.10*
For Board and Lodging . . . *8.10*
Music, Dancing, Flower and Card-Work are also taught in the school.

Every Lady to provide a Table, a Teaspoon, Knife and Fork, Sheets and Towels, and to pay for her own washing.

1. What subjects at Mrs. Cockburn's school are not taught at your school?
2. Which subjects would you choose if you were a student at Mrs. Cockburn's school? Did the prices influence your decision? What subjects would you omit from your own timetable if you had to pay for them?
3. Did you supply any of the books or equipment you use at school? Do you think students should provide their own books or other equipment? What did the students at Mrs. Cockburn's school have to supply?

Teachers

Let's meet Mr. Anderson, an Upper Canadian teacher.

Dear Jonathan:

What will you say if I tell you I am keeping a School. I still live at Mr. Bottums. My School House is Mrs. Sherwood's old House. I have 31 Scholars. Miss Maria Jones and Miss Sophia Sherwood is 2 of the number. I have **2/6 per month** for each Scholar, I don't wish to let my Father know what I get per Month.

E. Anderson
Prescott, May, 1805[2]

Other teachers had "school" in their own homes in the early days. Anne Langton, a pioneer in the Peterborough area, wrote:

I had Menzies' 2 little girls for a lesson today [Jan. 2, 1839]. I have lately begun to teach them a little. They come for about an hour 3 times a week; as yet we are not all perfect in our letters, and I sometimes feel that I shall not accomplish much.[3]

1. Find the punctuation and grammar errors in Mr. Anderson's letter.
2. Why might Mr. Anderson not wish his father to know his salary?
3. What was Anne Langton teaching her students? What advantages and disadvantages would there be in going to a school in a house such as the Langtons'?

Well-qualified teachers were often hard to find. It seems likely that there were as many good teachers as bad ones, as many strict ones as lax ones, as many conscientious ones as lazy ones. Parents of school children hired the best teachers they could find and afford. As the province's population grew, and teachers came under the supervision of the provincial government, teacher training improved.

Do you think that free, compulsory education is a right or a privilege? What did some Upper Canadians think about free, compulsory education?

quarter: quarter of a year

2/6 per month: 2 shillings, 6 pence

Chapter 51

AT CHURCH

The church was the centre of many activities for rural Upper Canadians. It was the first building settlers planned and constructed, after their log houses were built. Settlers brought with them firm Christian religious beliefs, and most wished to continue worshipping as they had at home. Their religion was a great comfort to many pioneers who were suffering from isolation or loneliness, homesickness or regret. It also served to bring people together.

Isolated settlers gathered in someone's house to hold services and make plans to build a church and hire a clergyman. **Bees** were held to put up the church building. People donated labour, food, shingles, planks, logs—everything needed to complete the church. There were congregations of every sort in Upper Canada: Church of England, Presbyterians, Methodists, Roman Catholics, Quakers, Mennonites, and Baptists.

Saddlebag Preachers and Camp Meetings

For settlers who were very early pioneers, and cut off from their neighbours, a visit from an **itinerant** minister was a welcome event. The Methodists sponsored many "saddlebag" preachers in Upper Canada. These were men who travelled on horseback to isolated farms, to bring a Christian message to families. They carried Bibles and religious books in

bee: a neighbourly gathering for work

itinerant: travelling

A saddle-bag preacher travelling on horseback.

The Blue Church, located near Prescott. The first church was built on this site in 1790. This picture shows the third church built on the same spot in 1845.

their saddlebags. Reverend Nathan Bangs, an itinerant preacher in the Bay of Quinte region, went from house to house and introduced himself with this greeting: "I have come to talk with you about religion, and to pray with you. If you are willing to receive me for this purpose, I will stop; if not, I will go on."[1] Most people gladly welcomed the visitor.

Large groups of worshippers gathered periodically at camp meetings. These religious get-togethers lasted several days and required people to "camp-out." They prayed, sang familiar hymns, and listened to rousing preachers. As many as 5000 people, and 10 or 12 preachers arrived on horseback, or in wagons. Camp meetings were a welcome opportunity for pioneers to escape their loneliness, isolation, or boredom, as well as to worship together.

1. Why do you think saddle-bag ministers were so welcome in many pioneer homes?
2. Why do you think camp meetings were popular? Are there similar religious gatherings today? What form do they take?

The Clergy Reserves

There was conflict in Upper Canada over the question of the Clergy Reserves. These were the lots reserved by the Constitutional Act of 1791 for the "support of a Protestant clergy." The Clergy Reserves amounted to 1/7 of the land in each township.

Members of the Church of England felt that the Clergy Reserves had been set aside for the benefit of that church alone. They wanted the Church of England to receive any money that was derived from renting or selling Clergy Reserve land. Other churches objected to this, and asked the British government to use Clergy Reserve money to support education in the province. Many people resented Church of England leaders, such as

Bishop John Strachan, who felt that the Church of England should hold a favoured position in the province because it did in Britain, and Upper Canada was a British colony. The Clergy Reserves issue was not satisfactorily solved until 1854, when the Canadian Parliament passed a law stating that money from the sale of Clergy Reserve lands should go to communities in the province.

Too Much Whisky

Church leaders in Upper Canada were concerned about a common social problem in the province—alcohol. Cheap whisky was too easy to buy. Inns and taverns were built in every tiny village settlement in the province, and tavern keepers were always busy serving thirsty visitors. To encourage people to drink less (or nothing) many **temperance** societies were formed, often with church support.

1. Find out more about one of these religious groups: Mennonites, Quakers, Dunkers, Children of Peace. Write a brief report.
2. Explain the Clergy Reserves conflict in your own words.
3. Find out more about the temperance movement and why it became popular.

This group of Scots settlers gather for a service of worship in their new land.

temperance: avoidance of alcohol

Chapter 52

FOR BODY AND MIND

Sheep provided warm woollen clothing for Upper Canadians. What is this man doing?

dearth: shortage

The wool was "carded" to straighten out the fibres before spinning. Why was this necessary?

The Clothes on Your Back

What did Upper Canadians wear? How did they obtain their clothing? Here's one modern historian's description:

Those who could afford to had regular supplies [of clothing] sent from Britain. In Otonabee Township [near Peterborough] Mrs. Stewart, a woman who cheerfully did much for herself, found a **dearth** of wearing apparel and sent to Ireland "for a chest of useful material every year. These consignments were various and wonderful; among the contents being cloth for men's clothing, material for winter and summer dresses, linen, flannel, boots, shoes, stockings...." There were many cases like this but curiously few references to shopping expeditions in the towns where a var-

iety of material was available.

The poorer settlers had no money for purchases abroad and seldom saw the towns where they might have bought clothes in exchange for farm products. ... For everybody to some degree and for many people almost entirely clothes were made at home. In some cases a family would perform every stage from processing flax and making cloth in a loom to cutting and sewing garments. For those who raised sheep and had a spinning wheel woollen clothes could be added. One set of precious buttons might be transferred from a discarded garment to its **successor**. Many women and men treasured "party" clothes but the average rural costume was simple and famed more for its warmth and endurance than for style.[1]

It is clear that pioneers in Upper Canada could find many different articles of clothing and fabric, in stores in the towns, from the earliest days. These items were listed for sale, in shops owned by various merchants, in the Niagara region between 1791 and 1840:

Textiles: cambric, muslin, gingham, canvas, cotton, flannel, cashmere, woollens, linens, velvets, corduroy, ribbons, laces

For the Gentlemen: stockings, gloves, shirts, suspenders, knee buckles, boots (and boot repair kits of sole leather, shoe knives, awls, thread)

For the Home: towels, woollen blankets, cotton wool for quilts, thread, yarn, buttons, needles, scissors, bed ticks (for mattresses)

1. What differences were there between the way the poorer settlers and wealthier ones dressed and obtained their clothing?
2. Find some pictures of Upper Canadian costumes.

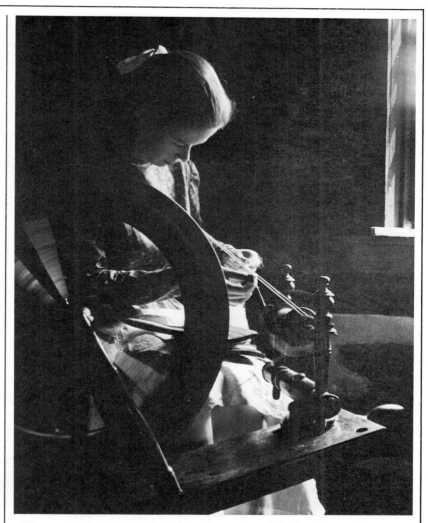

Spinning the wool into yarn.

successor: follower

Staying Healthy

Diseases and accidents were common in Upper Canada. People in town, village, and countryside faced many threats to their health and safety. Sanitation was usually crude, sewers rare, and garbage carelessly treated. Infectious diseases like typhus and cholera were common. Children were frequently the victims of disease, and many infants died from exposure, disease, or unsanitary conditions.

People were often expected to be skilled at first aid, especially in isolated farms. Here's a pioneer story:

When Thomas Mason of Haliburton was crushed by a falling tree, his left leg was broken and his throat ripped open, exposing the windpipe. Mrs. James Hewitt, a neighbour, took her darning needle and thread and sewed up the throat and Mason survived past his 102nd birthday.[2]

ague: malarial fever

Some cures used in pioneer days:
— sassafras tea or brandy to combat **ague**
— red-clover tea to cure bronchitis
— alder-bark tea to cure constipation
— burdock-leaf tea to purify the blood
— smartweed steeped in vinegar to soothe bruises
— crushed leaves of plantain to help sore feet
— an onion applied to the sting to cure a bee sting

The Company was noted far and wide for several different remedies. Horse Condition Powder, the Canadian Vegetable Anti-Bilious or Poor Man's Pill, Burdock Blood Bitters, and Egyptian Salve, were four of the medicines made in the factory.[3]

1. Try to imagine the uses of some of the medicines made in the Brougham Pill Factory.
2. Design a medicine-bottle label for a remedy such as those made at the Brougham Pill Factory.

By the 1830s, "drugstores" and medicine factories began to appear in villages and towns. Here's a description of the Brougham Pill Factory. It opened in the early 1840s and was typical of many others in small villages.

Nelson Woodruff and William Bentley manufactured pills, powders and salves. They employed 5 or 6 girls and a manager. In addition, a travelling salesman was employed to deliver the remedies in a horse and light wagon.

A settler's grave. How is this grave site different from burial places today?

Doctors

Doctors and surgeons had been in Upper Canada since the days of Lieutenant-Governor Simcoe, but in the early pioneer period there were few qualified medical men or nurses. Doctors were often prevented from visiting isolated patients by the poor roads and slow transportation methods. Many settlers were suspicious of "doctorin" methods that were new to them, and few farmers could pay a doctor anything but farm produce. As

An outside view of a courthouse in the backwoods of Upper Canada. What might the men in the foreground be discussing?

a result, doctors were often discouraged from practising their trade. As the population increased and the colony developed, more doctors served more people.

Public Health

Public health was of great concern to people living in towns in Upper Canada. Towns like Kingston and Brockville faced special problems, for newly arrived immigrants passed through these towns on their way to other settlements. Immigrant travellers often stayed for a few days and left cholera or typhus behind.

Sanitary conditions were very bad in many towns. In Kingston, water was sold by carters who filled their barrels from the St. Lawrence River or Lake Ontario. If the water looked clean, it was considered safe. Sewage was dumped on the harbour ice in winter and outside of town in summer.

Immigrants often camped on the wharves of Kingston before travelling inland. Their drinking water was from the harbour, their toilets were primitive, and the immigrants were often in a weakened physical condition. It's not surprising that many people became ill or that diseases spread in the town. To help prevent the spread of disease, stricter health and sanitation regulations were passed in the 1830s.

Citizens of Kingston decided to work together to help solve the health problems posed by the waves of immigrants who passed through or stayed in their town. The Kingston General Hospital was built in 1832. Public hospitals were rare in Upper Canada. A hospital had been built at York in 1829. Other towns were slower to build and support hospitals.

1. How would improved sanitary conditions in a town help prevent the spread of diseases like typhus or cholera?
2. Make a list of possible sanitary regulations to help "clean up" a town and prevent the spread of disease.

Law and Order

Upper Canada was served by British law. Courts were set up soon after 1791 to enforce the law and maintain order. Local magistrates, called **justices of the peace,** had authority to deal with lawbreakers. Criminal laws in the early part of the 1800s provided very harsh penalties in Upper Canada, as they did elsewhere. The death penalty was decreed for many crimes, including horse stealing and forgery. Many convicted criminals knew the agony of the lash. People who couldn't pay their bills were sometimes put in jail. Fines were also imposed for many crimes. Assault was the most common

justice of the peace: magistrate

An inside view of the same backwoods courthouse. Which man is the justice of the peace? Which man is the accused? Where is the jury?

An inside view of the same backwoods courthouse. Which man is the justice of the peace? Which man is the accused? Where is the jury?

valise: hand luggage

offence, due in part to the easy availability of cheap whisky. Drinking often led to quarrelling and fighting.

Courts were expected to be conducted by the justices of the peace in an orderly, respectable manner, even if held in a log cabin in the woods. Trial was by jury. As the province grew, large impressive courthouses were built in chosen towns.

1. In what ways did punishment in Upper Canada differ from punishment today for similar crimes?
2. Find out more about early justices of the peace. Are there such justices now? What is their job?

They Read It in the Paper

Newspapers were special in Upper Canada. Books were scarce, but newspapers were available in many towns beginning in 1810, the year the Kingston *Gazette* was founded. Early newspapers contained a lot of world news copied from papers from Britain and the United States. There was also a great deal of advertising for people to read. Personal notices and advertisements, as well as business and government messages, were published in early papers. News stories were often very long and detailed. The papers usually were eight pages long. Most were published weekly, some less often.

Here is a modern historian's description of the Brockville *Recorder* for May 15, 1830. ...

Here is a picture of a saddle, illustrating the ad of A. W. Graves, Brockville, "Saddle, Harness, Trunk and **Valise** Maker." S. and S. Skinner announce that they are in the Wagon-Making and Blacksmithing business. Daniel Fields announces that his "Fashionable Hat-Store" in Prescott has just received "The Spring Fashions. Ladies' and Gentlemen's Hats made to the latest and most approved style."

Then there is William Harvey of Perth, who has lost a yoke of steers "strayed from Mr. Chamberlain's Tavern, Elizabethtown."[4]

1. In what ways were newspapers in Upper Canada different from today's newspapers? In what ways are they similar?
2. Write an ad for one of the products made at the Brougham Pill Factory, to be placed in an Upper Canadian newspaper.
3. Do some detective work to find the names of some early newspapers in your community. Are they still published?

GETTING TOGETHER

Chapter 53

Getting the Mail

Isolated settlers, far from friends and families in their homelands, often longed for news. Susanna Moodie explains:

After breakfast, Moodie [her husband] rode into the town and when he returned at night, brought several long letters for me. Ah! Those first kind letters from home! Never shall I forget the **rapture** with which I grasped them, the eager, trembling haste with which I tore them open, while the blinding tears which filled my eyes hindered me for some minutes from reading a word which they contained.[1]

Pioneers sent letters on single sheets of paper that were folded and sealed with wax; no envelopes were used. Mail was charged according to the number of sheets, so one sheet usually had to do. It was crammed with the sender's tiniest handwriting. Postage was paid by the receiver. Because of this, the poorest pioneers often could not afford to pick up their mail at all. Some crafty people arranged to hear the news anyway.

A former postmaster at Oakville told of an Irishman who, finding a letter for him, asked that it be read aloud twice. Having heard it thoroughly, he announced that it was not intended for him and went away, thus saving 7 shillings [the price of the letter].[2]

The postal system suffered serious problems in the early days. Travel by land and sea was as slow for mail as it was for people. Settlers wanted mail and sent petitions to the British government asking for more post offices. They complained about poor service and high postal rates. People often had to travel long distances to the nearest post office, or count on travellers to bring them their mail.

rapture: joy

Despite problems, people sent lots of mail.

In 1851 the British government turned control of the postal service over to the government of Canada. This move brought many changes and improvements. More post offices were built, rates were lowered, and service improved. The first Canadian postage stamp was issued in 1851. It was a red stamp with a beaver design.

Design a postage stamp for Upper Canada that shows something about conditions in the province.

Working Together: Bees

Lack of machinery or even horse or ox-power meant that pioneers had to work together, using their own strength, to build houses, barns, churches, and schools. Gatherings of people for a big job were called bees. Bees were held for such tasks as chopping, logging, house building, barn raising, and harvesting. Women had quilting bees to make quilts and exchange news. Bees were a chance for isolated settlers to do two things: help a neighbour and enjoy an outing.

Susanna Moodie and her husband had a logging bee. She described the scene:

Thirty-two men were invited to our bee, and the maid and I were engaged for 2 days in baking and cooking for our guests. It was a burning hot day towards the end of July when our loggers began to come in.

Our men worked well until dinner-time, when, after washing in the lake, they all sat down to the **rude board** which I had prepared for them, loaded with the best fare. Pea soup, legs of pork, venison, eel and raspberry pies, with plenty of potatoes, and whisky to wash them down, besides a large iron kettle of tea, were served.

The dinner passed off tolerably well; some of the Irish settlers were pretty far gone [drunk]. The men went back to the field.

After the sun went down, the logging-band came in to supper, which was all ready for them. Those who remained sober ate the meal in peace, and quietly returned to their own homes, while the vicious and drunken stayed to brawl and fight.

I was so tired with the noise, the heat, and the fatigue of the day, that I went to bed.[3]

1. Why were bees held?
2. Mrs. Moodie's view of bees was very negative. Why do you think she felt this way? What things about bees did she not like?
3. Write a description of the Moodie logging bee from the point of view of a logger.

Playing Together

Most Upper Canadians had little leisure time, but they still managed to have lots of fun. People in the country made sport out of many activities that were also part of their working day: ploughing matches, chopping contests, and hay-mowing competitions. Ploughing matches were great occasions for mixing competition and beer drinking. Country "sports" also included wrestling matches and organized fist fights. Dancing was a favourite social activity for early settlers. They also enjoyed weddings, funerals, and bees.

In towns and villages, people got together for many different sports and games. Curling clubs were organized in the 1820s; hockey was played on the ice of Kingston harbour in the 1840s. Players on ponds and lakes all over the province soon took up the new game. Skates were metal runners strapped onto ordinary boots.

Outdoor sports included horse racing, fishing, hunting, rifle shooting, lacrosse, snowshoeing, and canoeing. Cricket became popular during the 1830s. Teams which organized games away from home always had a tough time meeting their schedules. A team from Sherbrooke in Lower Canada spent nearly two weeks in 1835 travelling on foot, horseback, stagecoach, and steamboat to play a few cricket matches in Hamilton and York.

Indoors, a big favourite was checkers (called draughts). Teams of players challenged other teams to fiercely contested matches. The betting was often active. People also played cards, billiards, and quoits.

People also found time to read. Homes of prosperous settlers often contained libraries. Books were sent from relatives in Britain to eager readers in Upper Canada. Lending libraries were organized by individuals and some towns had public libraries from which readers could borrow books, magazines, and newspapers.

1. Find out more about some Upper Canadian sports or games that you aren't familiar with (quoits or cricket or ploughing matches). Write a brief report.
2. Find out more about the rules or uniforms of early team sports and games such as hockey, cricket, curling, and lacrosse.

A painting of a quilting party.

Chapter 54 | THE COLONY DEVELOPS

Changes

In 1791 Upper Canada was little more than an idea in the mind of John Graves Simcoe. Its population was very small. Its tiny settlements were separated from one another by vast areas of wilderness and bad roads. Its settlers were living off the land, dependent on Britain and other countries for most manufactured products, luxuries, and necessities.

By the 1850s, conditions had changed dramatically. Small villages had grown into towns. Roads and canals had opened up much of the colony to travel and trade. Businesses and manufacturing operations produced a variety of products. Newspapers brought news of the outside world as well as details of events in the colony to readers in the towns and the countryside. The gaps in the map were gradually filling in with the settlers of the Great Migration.

The pioneer age was coming to an end.

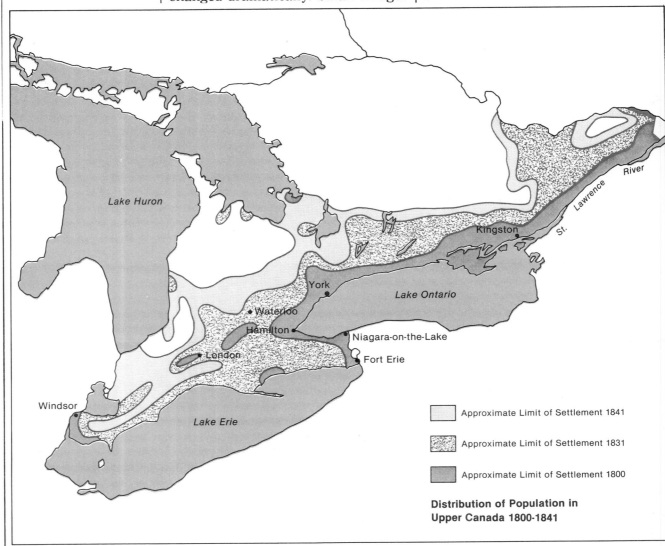

Lake Huron

Lake Ontario

St. Lawrence River

Kingston

York

Waterloo

Hamilton

Niagara-on-the-Lake

London

Fort Erie

Windsor

Lake Erie

Approximate Limit of Settlement 1841

Approximate Limit of Settlement 1831

Approximate Limit of Settlement 1800

Distribution of Population in Upper Canada 1800-1841

Examine the map entitled "Distribution of Population in Upper Canada: 1800-1841" before answering these questions.

1. What areas of Upper Canada were settled by 1800?
2. What pattern can you see in the way new areas of settlement opened up after 1800?
3. What reasons can you think of to explain the east-west rather than north-south settlement pattern?

Those Awful Roads

Almost every traveller to Upper Canada in the early nineteenth century agreed on one thing: the roads were terrible. In the words of one such observer:

The great leading roads of the Province had received little improvement beyond being graded, and the swamps made passable by laying the round trunks of trees side by side across the roadway. Their supposed resemblance to the ... cloth gained for these crossways the name of corduroy roads. The earth roads were passably good when covered with the snows of winter, or when dried up in the summer sun; but even then a thaw or rain made them all but impassable. The rains of autumn and the thaws of spring converted them into a mass of liquid mud, such as **amphibious** animals might delight to **revel in** ...

amphibious: water-going
revel in: delight in

In 1825, William L. Mackenzie described the road between York (Toronto) and Kingston as among the worst that human foot ever trod, and ... "the travellers in the Canadian stage coach were lucky if, when a hill had to be **ascended**, or a bad spot passed, they had not to alight and trudge ankle deep through the mud. ... In spring, when the roads were water-choked and rut-gullied, the rate might be reduced to two miles an hour. ... The coaches were **liable** to be

ascended: climbed

liable: likely

On the road between Kingston and York about 1830. Who might these people be? Imagine their thoughts as they trudge along this road? What is the road made of?

What is happening here? What season of the year is this? Imagine you are one of the passengers in the coach. Write a letter to a friend describing the trip you have just made.

embedded: stuck

embedded in the mud, and the passengers had to dismount and assist in prying them out by means of rails obtained from the fences."[1]

Nineteenth-century wagons and coaches did not have springs or shock absorbers. When we read descriptions of painful trips over corduroy roads and in and out of potholes, we can understand why complaints about roads were clear in every traveller's memories of Upper Canada.

There were attempts to build good roads in the colony. In the 1790s, major arteries such as Yonge Street and Dundas Street were begun. These helped to open up some of the land-locked areas. However, the laws made the construction and repair of roads the responsibility of the landowners living next to them. This caused problems. No one was paid for this labour. One man's ideas of a well-maintained road was very frequently different from another man's view. Settlers who were anxious to get their farm land cleared and into production cared little for bogged-down travellers.

In the eyes of most settlers, the main problem was the Clergy Reserves land. This was land set aside to support the Protestant churches financially. Because of argument over who should get the money from its sale, most of it remained unsold for some time. Often these reserve lands separated one stretch of road from another. Until the land was sold and settled, no one was going to build a road across it.

1. Why were roads in Upper Canada in such bad shape for much of the time?
2. Who was responsible for these roads? Is this an efficient way of looking after them?

Lakes and Rivers

The first highways in Upper Canada were the waterways. The navigable rivers and lakes had been used by the native peoples, fur traders, and explorers. Some of them, especially the St. Lawrence and Great Lakes routes, were used by the settlers as well. Many of the first settlements were on the shores of lakes or the banks of rivers. No one was more aware of the advantages of travel by water than those early travellers who had to use the roads.

But there were serious difficulties in relying on the waterways. In places, rapids or waterfalls prevented passage of boats. Some rivers that were both broad and deep in the spring became shallow by late summer. Navigable rivers shrank in depth as land clearing lowered the water table of nearby land. Winter ice made travel by boat impossible.

Canals

Some of these difficulties were solved by the construction of a series of canals to link together the main centres in Upper Canada.

Although they were much more expensive to build than roads, canals were thought to be a better means of transportation. Heavy cargoes such as timber and grain were almost impossi-

Canals

0   100   200 km

ble to move by road. They could be transported by boat or barge much more easily.

As a result, a network of canals was built including the Lachine canal on the St. Lawrence River in 1824 and the Welland canal which by-passed Niagara Falls in 1829. The most complicated of the canals was the Rideau canal. It ran nearly 200 km from Kingston to Bytown (Ottawa). Its planning grew out of the War of 1812 where the difficulty of protecting the St. Lawrence route from the Americans had become obvious. The canal was intended to allow troops and supplies to travel safely, away from the Americans.

Lieutenant-Colonel John By of the Royal Engineers was given the job of constructing the Rideau canal in 1826. He extended the size of the proposed project from the small dimensions that would only allow small troop barges to pass through to a larger size that would enable commercial cargoes to be carried. The locks he designed were thirty-eight metres long, ten metres wide with a draft of two metres. The locks and dams were built of stone. Thousands of labourers, many of them recently arrived Irish

and Scots immigrants, slaved to help complete the project by 1832.

Working conditions on the Rideau project were highly dangerous as this description by John MacTaggart shows.

... [T]he [men] receive dreadful accidents; ... they have to ... dig beneath the roots of the trees, which ... fall down and smother them. ... Some of them ... would take jobs of **quarrying** ... never thinking that they did not understand the business. Of course, many of them were blasted to pieces by their own **shots**, others killed by stones falling on them. I have seen heads, arms, and legs, blown in all directions. ...[2]

No one is sure how many men died of accidents such as these or from the outbreaks of cholera which swept through the workers' camps.

The success of the Lachine, Welland, and Rideau canal systems led some business and government leaders to dream of a St. Lawrence seaway that would make it possible for ships to travel from Europe to the Great Lakes. One of these men, William Hamilton Merritt, described such a plan as "worthy of *great minds* ... future ages will applaud the wisdom of ... [those] who commenced the St. Lawrence Canal on a sufficient scale to insure its full and complete usefulness. ..."[3]

Few of Merritt's partners shared this vision. The St. Lawrence Seaway was not constructed until the mid-twentieth century.

1. How did the lakes and rivers influence the way Upper Canada developed?
2. What were the advantages of using lakes, rivers, and canals as transportation routes?
3. What were the disadvantages?

A covered sleigh travelling between York and Kingston. Compare this means of travelling with the coach in the other picture. Which is the more comfortable? Which would probably be faster?

quarrying: using blasting powder to blow up large rocks

shots: charges

Chapter 55

ECONOMIC GROWTH

A Knife for Andrew

Twelve-year-old Andrew Farquarson stumbled as he hurried towards the waiting wagon.

"Careful," he muttered to himself. It would be disastrous if he broke his eggs. His father grumbled at Andrew to hurry along. There were a number of errands to attend to in Embro. They didn't go to the village every week, so when they did go, there was a lot to do.

Andrew wondered if Mr. Fraser remembered that this was the day. Earlier that spring when he had been to the store, Andrew had spotted the knife—a treasure.

"Real Sheffield steel, from England," old Fraser had purred as he turned the slim blade in his hands.

It was the sort of knife any boy would have prized.

Andrew didn't have the price of five pence. Few people in Embro did. He had asked Mr. Fraser if he could pay for the knife in eggs, since he had his own hens.

Fraser wasn't sure. He had to think about it for awhile. Finally he had reluctantly agreed. The number of eggs to be paid had been agreed on after some careful bargaining.

Today's eggs marked the final payment. Andrew would have his own knife at last.

1. Why didn't Andrew try to borrow the price of the knife?
2. Why did Andrew have to wait until he had paid the entire price before he got the knife?
3. Why would a knife be an important and valued possession to a pioneer boy?

Money Problems

In the early years, Upper Canada's economy looked rather strange. Most prices were quoted in British pounds, shillings, and pence. However, in many parts of the colony, American dollars were most commonly used. There was a serious problem of a lack of money in circulation. Unusual substitutes such as flattened brass buttons, Spanish, French, or Portuguese coins and paper money issued by private banks or towns were sometimes used.

For some pioneers, even these forms of money were useless. Their problem was that they had spent all their money on their passage, land, livestock, and equipment. They had no cash.

The Barter System

Since there were many people with this same problem, a system of barter

Paper money issued by the village of Cobourg in 1848. Why would a village issue its own money? Were there any risks involved in accepting this sort of money? Why has the bill been issued by the Board of Police?

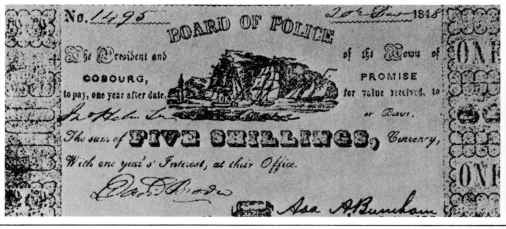

exchange developed. Quite simply, this meant that one person would trade something that was not needed (such as a pig) for something that was needed (such as a new axe). Merchants in small towns realized that unless they bartered they would be unable to do business with many customers. Merchants sold not only the goods listed on their signs, but also those that had been bartered to them.

Barter also meant trading work for an object. A farmer took a load of grain to be ground into flour to the grist mill or a load of logs to be sawn at the sawmill. Instead of paying fees to the millers for their services, he gave them part of the flour or lumber. In the same way, a man might agree to help his neighbour to clear land in return for a cow. In the barter system everyone involved gained something, though no money changed hands.

Fairs began partly to allow widespread bartering to take place. Some objects bartered at fairs were livestock of all types, leather, wool, yarn, cloth, linen, and farm products such as butter and maple sugar.

The barter system served the needs of a simple economy and helped to overcome the problem of a lack of money.

1. What substitutes for money were used in pioneer times? Why?
2. What substitutes for money are often used today?
3. What are the advantages of a barter system? What are its disadvantages?
4. Can you think of any examples of the barter system at work today?

Making Potash

The two young men looked tired. Their faces were caked with a mixture of dust, ashes, and grime that would have given them the look of corpses except for the streams of sweat that poured from their brows. Stripped to the waist, they ignored the black flies that swarmed around them. All of

Making potash. Is this a large or a small-scale operation? How can you tell?

their concentration was on the long-handled metal ladles with which they stirred the contents of the large iron pots.

To a visitor from another country it might have looked like a scene from some artist's vision of hell. In truth, there were times when the men must have felt that hell was exactly where they were.

They were making potash.

Potash

Potash was the first export product for most early settlers in Upper Canada. Its manufacture was simple, requiring only large amounts of ash, a few implements, and a great deal of patience and energy.

The ash came from the settlers' land clearing. By using a "slash and burn" technique, the pioneers cut off lower branches of trees and uprooted small shrubs and bushes. Once this brush had dried, it was set afire to clear the land. The trees killed by the fire were easier to fell than live ones.

Women and children often were given the task of collecting the ashes

255

from these fires. When they had enough ashes, the special kettles and ladles were brought out of storage or rented from the nearest owner.

Water was added to the ashes to produce lye, a solution rich in natural chemicals. Sometimes water was diverted from a stream through a trough to do this. The lye was put in a large tank, usually of double-thick planks. The lye was ladled from the tank into the heavy iron kettles. These would become red-hot once the process began.

Fires under the kettles boiled the lye. As the mixture thickened in the kettle, it had to be stirred continually. If only one kettle was used, it took a week of monotonous, numbing labour to make one barrel of potash.

The Potash Industry

Potash was exported to Britain and Europe where it had a variety of uses in the newly developing chemical industries. It was used in the manufacture of glass and soap, in the preparation of woollen cloth for dying as well as for fertilizer.

Potash was shipped in large oak barrels weighing about 250 kg. Depending on its quality, it would bring from $80 to $120. On average, one barrel was produced from each acre [1/3 ha] of timber cleared and burned. Since the wood had to be cleared before farming began, it is easy to see why so many pioneers made potash.

Potash as a Staple

Potash became the first important staple product of Upper Canada. The fishing industry had been the staple of Newfoundland and New England. The fur trade had provided the economic stimulus for New France. Now potash was the staple that brought much-needed cash to Upper Canada. Without it, the pioneers could not have imported products. Without potash, many could not have paid their debts. New immigrants often got their first job working on a potash crew and picked up useful skills as well as coins for their pockets.

The problem with potash was that it was not a renewable resource. Once the land was cleared and burned off it could not produce more potash.

1. Why was making potash important to the pioneers of Upper Canada?
2. Describe potash making. Would you want to make it?
3. What is a "staple"? Why is a staple important to a country. What are some Canadian staples today?
4. What is a renewable resource? Give an example of both a renewable and a non-renewable resource that is important today.

The Timber Trade

The timber trade was the second important staple for Upper Canada. Like potash, it too rose to great heights, only to fade out later. Few nineteenth-century woodsmen believed it would ever end. The forests seemed to go on forever.

Square timber is the product of the woodsman's adze, a special type of axe with its blade shaped like a hoe. Perfect specimens of tall, straight, knot-free pine were carefully shaped by master craftsmen to form square and true edges. This was to fit the maximum amount of useful timber into the holds of the timber ships. Rounded edges wasted valuable space.

The Start of the Timber Trade

Britain had begun to rely on the forests of North America for timber during the wars with Napoleon's France. The forests of the Maritimes were closer to Britain and were the first ones to be harvested. However, since the loggers were only looking for perfect specimens, they did not worry about the damage they were doing to surrounding trees. They left large piles of brush and debris in their path, with forest fires as a common result.

Life aboard the large log rafts. At What stage in the movement of the timber to the timber ships is this? What would happen next?

Life in the Lumber Camps

By the 1820s and '30s, timbering had reached the Ottawa valley and northern parts of Upper Canada. It peaked in the 1850s when thousands of young men spent their winters in the shantees of the lumber camps. Their hours were spent in back-breaking labour followed by the devouring of huge meals. Where it was allowed, alcohol was drunk in large quantities. Gambling and fighting appear to have been the most common forms of amusement in these camps.

The whole operation ended in the spring with the rafting of the logs downriver to the timber ships. The exploits of these often reckless dare-devils steering their stubborn and unpredictable rafts at breakneck speeds through dangerous rapids is one of the more colourful chapters of Canadian history. Unfortunately few other Canadians thought of the lumbermen as heroes.

Their moral character, with few exceptions, is dishonest and worthless. I believe there are few people in the world, on whose promises less faith can be placed, than on those of a lumberer. In Canada, where they are longer bringing down their rafts, and have more idle time, their character, if possible, is of a still more shuffling and rascally description. Premature old age, and shortness of days, form the inevitable fate of a lumberer. ...[1]

Running the rapids with a log raft. Do these raftsmen have any safety gear to help them in case they upset?

Seeding by hand. This method was called broadcasting because the seed was thrown in broad sweeps or casts of the arm to cover the stretch of ground in front and on both sides of the sower. What other meaning does the word "broadcasting" have?

sickle: a long-bladed knife with a curved edge
sheaves: bundles
flail: a weighted, flexible stick used in threshing
winnow: to separate the wheat grain from the outer husks
chaff: outer husk of grain

The Collapse of the Timber Trade

Like the potash industry, the timber trade was to prove short-lived. Its collapse was partly the result of the wasteful cutting methods employed by the lumberers but also the result of other changes. As conditions in nineteenth-century Europe changed after the Napoleonic wars, many businessmen reopened contacts with the timber-producing region of Scandinavia. Timber from this area could be imported more cheaply than Canadian timber, except that there were special taxes to be paid on it. These businessmen eventually pressured the British government into allowing the import of Scandinavian timber without a penalty. The Canadian timber trade never recovered. The timber trade was becoming less important also because of the shift in ship building from wooden ships to the new steel-hulled craft. Within a few years the sound of falling pines would echo less often through the northern woods.

1. Why were the lumbermen so particular in choosing trees for square timbers?
2. What was life like in the lumber camps? Can you suggest why it was like this?
3. What sort of reputation did the lumbermen have? Did they deserve it?
4. What led to the collapse of the timber trade?

Growing Wheat

The third economic staple of the young colony was wheat. Many farmers were already growing wheat and other grains such as oats and barley at the same time that they were making potash. Farmers often found it more difficult to sell their grain, due to the problems of transporting a large and bulky cargo over inadequate roads. The methods used in the growing of grain also placed limits on the size of the crop. The following description of early farming techniques illustrates some of the problems involved:

SOWING THE GRAIN

Formerly the farmer in sowing his grain had a sack tied around his body and as he walked over the ground he scattered the seed with a sweep of his hand. ... It is interesting to hear some of the old folks tell how first the grain was sown, cut, threshed, and got ready for the mill. It was frequently planted in the stumpy ground with a hoe or rake. When ripe it was cut with the **sickle**, bound in **sheaves**, and taken to the threshing-floor, ... where, by means of the **flail**, ... the heads were pounded until the grain was all threshed out. It was then "**winnowed**," or cleaned, ... until it was free of the **chaff**, after which several bags were put across a horse's back and sent to the mill—often fourteen or fifteen miles [24 or 32 km] or more distant—to be ground into flour, the farmer having to wait patiently his turn for this to be done, ... which sometimes kept him from home for several days. ... The first mills were situated on some stream or creek, where water-power could be obtained, ...

258

MOWERS AND REAPERS

CRADLING THE GRAIN

Following the sickle came the cradle, which consisted of a framework ... for gathering the grain together as it was being cut, fixed to the **scythe**, ... The farmer, with a sweeping stroke of his **brawny** arms, would cut down a **"swath"** of from four to six feet [1 to 2 m] in width. The binders (men and women) would follow with their rakes and, ... bind up the bundle. An expert cradler could cut as much as three or four acres [1 1/3 to 1 2/3 ha] of good standing grain in a day, about as much as three or four men could bind. After the grain had been bound it was gathered together and stood on end, ..."

THE REAPING MACHINE

The cradle was **superseded** by the reaping machine, which has [had] many improvements ... since its introduction in 1831, when a man walked behind and raked the grain off the table as it was being cut. In 1845 a seat was made for this man at the rear of the machine, and in 1863 a self-raking attachment was added, until ... we have machines which not only cut the grain but also bind it into sheaves as well ....[T]he reaping machine is a striking illustration of the truth of the old saying, "Necessity is the mother of invention."[2]

Some wheat farmers did not understand the problems involved in agriculture. They were sometimes reluctant to rotate crops, not knowing the harm that could be done to farm land through the repeated growing of the same crop on the same fields. As a result, some of the areas first cleared lost their fertility within a decade or so. This land was abandoned as farm land and only much later was some of it reclaimed for the growing of tobacco. Settlers were paying the price of their lack of knowledge of wheat farming.

Even experienced farmers could do little against the fearsome diseases such as wheat rust and smut which could destroy whole fields of apparently healthy grain. They were helpless to do anything until tougher strains of grain were developed later in the century. Even in a new land bright with promise, there could be problems.

1. How was grain grown and harvested in pioneer times?
2. How did the farming methods that were used limit the amount of wheat produced?
3. Why was getting grain ground into flour sometimes a problem?
4. How did agricultural tools and machinery change during the 1800s?
5. What does the statement "necessity is the mother of invention" mean? Do you agree with this?
6. What problems were part of wheat farming in Upper Canada?

scythe: a long-handled cutting tool

brawny: strong and muscular

swath: area cut

superseded: replaced

Chapter 56 | THE GROWTH OF TOWNS

Bryce's Mill

Amy Bryce loved the old mill. Whenever she could, she spent hours in its loft. She lay back on the sacks of grain and closed her eyes. She knew every sound by heart: the regular soft "whoosh" of the water wheel as it slowly turned, the gentle creaking of the huge wooden gears, the soft "scrunch" of the stone grinders. From

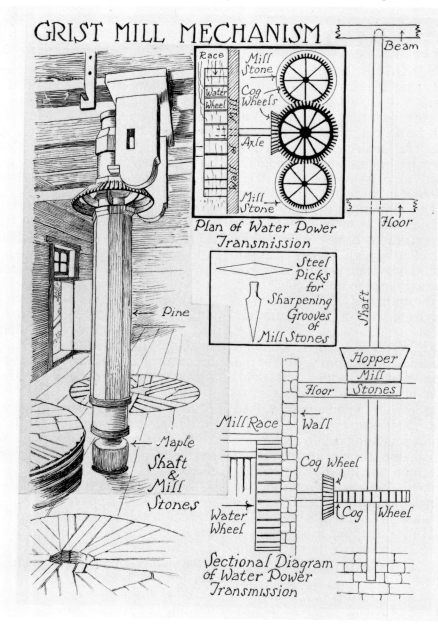

GRIST MILL MECHANISM

Beam

Race
Mill Stone
Water Wheel
Cog Wheels
Axle
Mill Stone
Floor

Plan of Water Power Transmission

Steel Picks for Sharpening Grooves of Mill Stones

Pine

Shaft

Maple
Shaft & Mill Stones

Hopper
Mill Stones
Floor

Mill Race
Wall
Cog Wheel
Water Wheel
Cog Wheel

Sectional Diagram of Water Power Transmission

time to time these sounds were interrupted by the sudden rush of grain dropping from the bin on its way to be ground to flour.

To Amy, the mill was a magic place. It had a special smell all its own. A mixture of flour, dust, dried wood, leather, and grease tickled her nose. When she opened her eyes, tiny specks of dust seemed to dance in the dim shafts of light.

She heard her grandfather's step on the stairs and seconds later his head emerged from the trap door.

"So this is where you are," he said.

"Tell me again about the mill when it was new," Amy urged.

"Well, that was thirty-five years ago, in 1822. There wasn't a soul within miles of here. But I knew the minute I saw this stretch of river that this was the place for a mill. The river's narrow here with steep banks—easy to dam.

"It took my father and I three years to build it. When the mill was finished, it was the best one in three counties."

"What happened then?" Amy asked.

"Well, the first years were slow. There were times when we weren't sure if we had made a good choice, but in time more settlers came and opened up the township. Then Sam Cuthbert decided this was a good place to open up a general store. Frank Dawson opened a tavern here that same year. Later, after the fire, he rebuilt it as a hotel and tavern. Why in no time we had a cozy little settlement here, all because of this old mill.

"Next thing you know, Reverend Carter made this part of his circuit, and before long we had a church too. And all the time more folks were coming and building more houses, more shops, a school. The place really took off after Zach Peters started his sawmill downriver a bit."

"How did they decide on the name, Grandfather?" Amy asked.

"Well, everybody agreed that the mill was what made the town possible. It had to be named after it."

1. How was the location for the mill picked?
2. List the order of construction of the other buildings in Bryce's Mill.
3. Can you explain why the settlement developed the way it did?

Bryce's Mill does not really exist. It never did. However, the pattern of growth described for it was typical of many villages and towns in Upper Canada.

The period from 1791 to the 1850s saw a tremendous growth in urban centres. From Brockville in the east, to Sandwich in the west, towns and villages seemed to mushroom.

Why Did Towns Develop?

Some towns grew up around military garrisons like Kingston, Newark (Niagara-on-the-Lake), and York. Others, like Cobourg, sprang up around excellent natural harbours. Many town sites followed the pattern of the mythical Bryce's Mill in selecting the location of a mill as a nucleus. Brantford is an example of this sort of settlement.

Most towns of this period shared a number of features. There was usually a variety of stores ranging from grocery and provisions stores to farm-equipment suppliers to dry goods and clothing stores. Most towns could boast at least one splendid church. Most towns had local industries such as tanneries, breweries, distilleries, cabinet making, wagon works, glass works, smithies, or ship building. There was a steady movmeent of people from the countryside to the towns to take advantage of the jobs being created. Unsuccessful or unhappy farmers now had an alternative.

1. What different factors led to towns growing up in various places?
2. Why did towns attract people from the countryside?

THE GROWTH OF TORONTO

Muddy York

Perhaps the most impressive, as well as the most puzzling, example of urban growth was the town of York (Toronto).

With its large harbour and series of rivers and fertile valleys, Toronto had been the site of Indian villages for hundreds of years before the coming of Europeans. The French had constructed a series of forts and trading posts within the boundaries of present-day Toronto although none were con-sidered to be major positions. The last of these, Fort Rouillé, was burned by the French in 1759, rather than have it fall into the hands of the British.

From then until Lieutenant-Governor Simcoe's decision to make it the capital of the province, Toronto remained little more than a clearing on the edge of the wilderness. Even Simcoe's decision to move the capital to Toronto was supposed to be temporary. He planned eventually to build a new city on the forks of the Thames River in the heart of the colony to be named after the British capital, London. However, in 1796 there were problems in obtaining the needed money, and York remained the capital, at least for the time being.

York suffered considerably from the War of 1812. It was occupied by American forces and many buildings were burned in 1813.

By 1815 its population still numbered only about 700 people. Yet by 1851, some 30 000 individuals had flocked to it, making it the largest settlement in the colony, passing rivals such as Kingston.

Growth of York

Some clues to the growth of York may be obtained from this description of the town in 1831, three years before it became a city under its first mayor, William Lyon Mackenzie. The description is part of a longer passage written in 1831 by an English traveller in a book called *The Emigrant's Guide, or Canada as it is*:

York is fast becoming a place of considerable importance. The **situation** is central, between a great extent of inland navigation and a very large **tract** of well settled country. All the supplies, for above a hundred and fifty miles [240 km] above it, are drawn from York. There are already many considerable establishments in its neighbourhood, such as paper makers, hatters, **parchment** makers, potteries, and many other branches. ...

The trades of York appear to be more distinctly **classed** than are to be observed in many other towns in Canada. There are **drapers** who appear to keep only those goods in their immediate line. ... Here are grocery and spirit stores, selling nothing but spirits, and wines. ... There are in York iron**mongers**, silversmiths, druggists, stationers, & c., ...

There have been for the last two or three years, three large steam-boats running constantly between Prescott and Niagara,—the splendid new steamer, the Great Britain, now makes the fourth. ...

The improvements in the town of York are making **inconceivable** progress. Both public and private buildings, of the most substantial kind, are being erected in all directions. They are mostly of brick, of which article there is now an immense quantity made near the town. **Mechanics** of all grade **obtain** ready employment. ... In fact, the prosperity and growth of the capital seems to keep pace with the general improvement of the Province. ...

There is great encouragement for mechanics in and about York. The wages of smiths and carpenters are seven shillings and six pence a day; masons about the same. Most other trades are well paid. They certainly may live very much cheaper here than at home; and if they are sober men, they have a chance of saving money. Shoe makers, hatters, and tailors, get the highest wages in York, for such is the gaiety of this **thriving** town, that their respective trades are well encouraged. Here are advertising boot makers from **"Hoby's,"** tailors from **"Bond-street,"** **milliners** and dress makers from the **"West End;"** in fact, here is a London in miniature. The place is yet too small to support a regular theatre; although they have occasionally some travelling performers.[1]

It seems apparent from the words of George Hume, that for York, as well as for the colony as a whole, the years of challenge were coming to a close. The years of change were about to begin.

1. What advantages did York's location give it as a town site?
2. List the jobs mentioned in York in 1831. How many of them still exist?
3. What seems to have been the most important industry located in York at this time? Explain the reasons for your answer.
4. How was life in York different from life in the rural areas of Upper Canada?

Documents

Unit One

CHAPTER 2

1. Adapted from, Karl H. Schlesier, *The Beaver*, Spring, 1973.

2. William E. Coffer, *Spirits of the Sacred Mountains* (New York: Van Nostrand Reinhold, 1978).

3. *Maclean's Magazine*, November 29, 1976.

4. Adapted from, William E. Coffer, *Spirits of the Sacred Mountains* (New York: Van Nostrand Reinhold, 1978).

5. W.A. Kenyon, *Some Bones of Contention* (Toronto: Royal Ontario Museum, 1978).

CHAPTER 3

1. Adapted from, James Houston, *The White Dawn: An Eskimo Saga* (Scarborough: Signet, 1971).

2. Adapted from, Peter Such, *Riverrun* (Toronto: Clarke, Irwin & Company, 1973).

CHAPTER 4

1. Adapted from, Maurice Metayer ed., *Tales from the Igloo* (Edmonton: Hurtig Publishers, 1972).

2. Adolph Hungry Wolf, *The Blood People: A Division of the Blackfoot Confederacy* (New York: Harper & Row, Publishers, 1977).

3. Ibid.

4. E.S. Rogers, *The Beaver*, Summer, 1970.

CHAPTER 5

1. Charles Hoffmann, *Drum Dance: Legends, Ceremonies, Dances and Songs of the Eskimos* (Agincourt: Gage Publishing, 1974).

2. Adapted from, Christie Harris, *Raven's Cry* (Toronto: McClelland and Stewart, 1966).

3. Kent Gooderham, ed., *I Am an Indian* (Toronto: J.M. Dent & Sons, 1969).

CHAPTER 6

1. Adapted from, Allan A. Macfarlan, *Fireside Book of North American Indian Folktales* (Harrisburg: Stackpole Books, 1974).

2. Adapted from, Adolph Hungry Wolf, *The Blood People* (New York: Harper and Row, Publishers, 1977).

3. John G. Neihardt, *Black Elk Speaks, Being the Life Story of a Holy Man of the Oglala Sioux* (Lincoln: University of Nebraska Press, 1961).

Unit Two

CHAPTER 7

1. Timothy Severin, "The Voyage of Brendan" *National Geographic*, vol. 152, no. 6, Dec. 1977

2. Tryggvi Oleson, *Early voyages and northern approaches, 1000-1632* (Toronto: McClelland and Stewart, 1963).

CHAPTER 8

1. *The Voyages of Jacques Cartier*, ed. H.P. Biggar (Ottawa: The Queen's Printer, 1924).

2. Cameron Nish, *Canadian Historical Documents Series, vol. 1, The French Regime* (Scarborough: Prentice-Hall, 1965).

3. *The Voyages of Jacques Cartier*, ed. H.P. Biggar (Ottawa: The Queen's Printer, 1924).

4. W.A. McKay, *The Great Canadian Skin Game* (Toronto: Macmillan of Canada, 1967).

CHAPTER 9

1. D.C. Smith, *Colonists at Port Royal* (Toronto: Ginn and Company, 1970).

CHAPTER 10

1. W.L. Grant, trans., *History of New France* (Toronto: Champlain Society, 1907-14).

CHAPTER 12

1. *The Works of Samuel de Champlain*, ed. H.P. Biggar (Toronto: Champlain Society, 1922) vol. 2.

2. Ibid.

CHAPTER 15

1. *The Jesuit Relations and Allied Documents, Travels and Explorations of the Jesuit Missionaries in New France*, ed. R.G. Thwaites (Cleveland: Burrows Brothers, 1896-1901) vol. 5

2. Ibid. vol. 8.

3. A.G. Bailey, *The Conflict of European and Eastern Algonkian Cultures, 1504-1700* (Toronto: University of Toronto Press, 1969).

4. *The Jesuit Relations and Allied Documents*, ed. R.G. Thwaites (Cleveland, 1897) vol. 5.

CHAPTER 16

1. Ibid. vol. 4.

2. Father C. LeClerg, *New Relation of Gaspesia*, trans. W.F. Ganong (Toronto: Champlain Society, 1910).

3. *Word from New France: The Selected Letters of Marie de l'Incarnation*, trans. and ed. Joyce Marshall (Toronto: Oxford University Press, 1967).

4. William Toye, *The St. Lawrence* (Toronto: Oxford University Press, 1959).

CHAPTER 17

1. Marcel Trudel, *The Beginnings of New France* (Toronto: McClelland and Stewart, 1973).

CHAPTER 18

1. Mère Marie de l'Incarnation; *Lettres* ed. l'abbé Richaudeau-Tournai, 1876 vol. 2.

2. William Toye, *The St. Lawrence* (Toronto: Oxford University Press, 1959).

3. Cameron Nish, *Canadian Historical Documents Series Vol. 1,* (Scarborough: Prentice-Hall, 1965).

CHAPTER 19

1. W.J. Eccles, *Canada Under Louis XIV* (Toronto: McClelland and Stewart, 1964).

2. Y.F. Zoltvany, *The French Tradition in America* (New York: Harper & Row, 1969).

3. S.D. Clark, *The Social Development of Canada* (Toronto: University of Toronto Press, 1942).

4. Ibid.

5. Cameron Nish, *Canadian Historical Documents Series, vol. 1* (Scarborough: Prentice-Hall, 1965).

6. W.J. Eccles, *The Canadian Frontier* (New York: Holt Rinehart and Winston, 1969).

CHAPTER 21

1. C. Jaenen, *The Role of the Church in New France* (Toronto: McGraw-Hill Ryerson, 1976).

2. Louis Franquet, *Voyages et Memoires sur le Canada* (Quebec: A Coté et cie, 1889).

CHAPTER 27

1. Cameron Nish, *Canadian Historical Documents Series, vol. 1* (Scarborough: Prentice-Hall, 1965).

CHAPTER 28

1. Quoted in, W.J. Eccles, *The Order of New France* (Toronto: CBC International Service, 1969).

2. Ibid.

Unit Three

CHAPTER 33

1. Bart McDowell, *The Revolutionary War* (Washington: National Geographic Society, 1967).

2. W. Neidhardt, *Struggle for the 14th Colony* (Toronto: Clarke, Irwin, 1972).

3. Bart McDowell, *The Revolutionary War* (Washington: National Geographic Society, 1967).

Documents

CHAPTER 35

1. Catherine Crary, *Price of Loyalty: Tory Writings from the Revolutionary Era* (New York: McGraw-Hill, 1973).

2. Thomas Jones, *History of New York During the Revolutionary War, & of the Leading Events in the Other Colonies at that Period, vol. 2* (New York: Arno Press, 1968).

CHAPTER 36

1. Catherine Crary, *Price of Loyalty* (New York: McGraw-Hill, 1973).

2. W.O. Raymond, *The Founding of Shelburne, vol. 3* (St. John: New Brunswick Historical Society, 1908).

3. John McGregor, *British America, vol. 2* (London, 1832).

4. Catherine Crary, *Price of Loyalty* (New York: McGraw-Hill, 1973).

5. W.O. Raymond, *Winslow Papers* (St. John: New Brunswick Historical Society, 1901).

6. P. Campbell, *Travels in North America* (Toronto: Champlain Society, 1937).

7. P.C. White, *Lord Selkirk's Diary* (Toronto: Champlain Society, 1958).

CHAPTER 37

1. J.W. Lydekker, *The Reverend John Stuart, vol. 2* (New York: Historical Magazine of the Protestant Episcopal Church, 1942).

2. Gerald M. Craig, *Early Travellers in the Canadas, 1791-1867* (Westport: Greenwood Press, 1976).

CHAPTER 38

1. J.J. Talman, *Loyalist Narratives from Upper Canada* (Toronto: Champlain Society, 1946).

CHAPTER 40

1. C. Compton-Smith, *The Capture of York: A Collection of Documents & Records* (Scarborough: McGraw-Hill, 1968).

2. Ibid.

3. Ibid.

Unit Four

CHAPTER 43

1. Charles Dickens, *Hard Times* (New York: Norton, 1966). Originally published in 1908.

2. Catherine Parr Traill, *The Canadian Settler's Guide*, 1855 (Toronto: McClelland and Stewart, 1969).

3. Ibid.

4. William Cattermole, *Emigration: The Advantages of Emigration to Canada*, 1831 (Toronto: Coles Publishing Company, 1970).

5. John Howison, *Sketches of Upper Canada*, 1821 (Toronto: Coles Publishing Company, 1970).

6. Catherine Parr Traill, *The Canadian Settler's Guide*, 1855 (Toronto: McClelland and Stewart, 1969).

7. Susanna Moodie, *Roughing It in the Bush, or Forest Life in Canada*, 1852 (Toronto: McClelland and Stewart, 1962).

8. Catherine Parr Traill, *The Canadian Settler's Guide* 1855 (Toronto: McClelland and Stewart, 1969).

CHAPTER 44

1. Edwin C. Guillet, *The Great Migration* (Toronto: University of Toronto Press, 1937).

2. Ibid.

CHAPTER 45

1. H. Langton ed., *A gentlewoman in Upper Canada, the Journals of Anne Langton* (Toronto: Clarke, Irwin & Company, 1950).

CHAPTER 47

1. W.A. Fisher, *Legend of the Drinking Gourd* (Barrie: 1973).

2. Edwin C. Guillet, *The Great Migration* (Toronto: University of Toronto Press, 1937).

3. Catherine Parr Traill, *The Canadian Settler's Guide* (Toronto: McClellnd and Stewart, 1969).

4. Ibid.

CHAPTER 48

1. Andrew Haydon, *Pioneer Sketches in the district of Bathurst* (Toronto: Ryerson Press, 1925).

2. Ibid.

3. Ibid.

4. Canada Company, Report of the court of directors to the proprietors for 1831.

5. Robert Miller, *The Ontario Village of Brougham* (Brougham 1973).

CHAPTER 49

1. Catherine Parr Traill, *The Backwoods of Canada* (London: Charles Knight, 1836).

2. W. Morton and L. Hannon, *This land, these people* (Toronto: Gage Publishing, 1977).

3. Eustella Langdon, *Pioneer Gardens* (Toronto: Holt, Rinehart and Winston of Canada, 1972).

4. Ibid.

CHAPTER 50

1. D.A. Lawr and R.D. Gidney, *Educating Canadians: a documentary history of public education in Canada* (Toronto: Van Nostrand Reinhold, 1973).

2. R. Mackenzie, *Leeds and Grenville* (Toronto: McClelland and Stewart, 1967).

3. H. Langton ed., *A gentlewoman in Upper Canada: the Journals of Anne Langton* (Toronto: Clarke Irwin & Company, 1950).

CHAPTER 51

1. H.H. Walsh, *The Christian Church in Canada* (Toronto: Ryerson Press, 1956).

CHAPTER 52

1. G.P. Glazebrook, *Life in Ontario, a social history* (Toronto: University of Toronto Press, 1968).

2. W. Morton and L. Hannon, *This land, these people* (Toronto: Gage Publishing, 1977).

3. Robert Miller, *The Ontario Village of Brougham* (Brougham, 1973).

4. R. Mackenzie, *Leeds and Grenville* (Toronto: McClelland and Stewart, 1967).

CHAPTER 53

1. Susanna Moodie, *Roughing It in the Bush* (Toronto: McClelland and Stewart, 1962).

2. G.P. Glazebrook, *Life in Ontario, a social history* (Toronto: University of Toronto Press, 1968).

3. Susanna Moodie, *Roughing It in the Bush* (Toronto: McClelland and Stewart, 1962).

CHAPTER 54

1. Adapted from, Caniff Haight, *Country Life in Canada Fifty Years Ago* (Toronto: Hunter Rose & Co., 1885).

2. Raymond Reid, *Footprints in Time: A Source Book in the History of Ontario* (Toronto: J.M. Dent and Sons (Canada) 1967).

3. Harold A. Innis and Arthur R.M. Lower, *Select Documents in Canadian Economic History, 1783-1885* (Toronto: University of Toronto Press, 1933).

CHAPTER 55

1. J. McGregor, *Historical and Descriptive Sketches of the Maritime Colonies of British America* (London: Longman, Rees, Orme Brown and Green, 1928).

2. Adapted from, *Pen Pictures of Early Pioneer Life in Upper Canada* (Toronto: William Briggs, Coles Canadiana Collection, 1905).

CHAPTER 56

1. George Henry Hume, *The Emigrant's Guide; or, Canada as it is* (Quebec: William Gray & Co., 1831).

Illustrations

Archives Nationale du Québec, pp. 64; 66; 73, GH971-99; 85, top, GH971-88; 85, bottom, GH971-82; 86, N673-50; 94, top, N673-51; 101, bottom; 117, bottom, GH 27018; 118, top, GH470-116; 118, middle, GH872-32; 118, bottom, GH872-31; 133, GH272-72; 148, GH970-659; 150, top left, GH-47012; 150, middle left, GH470-133; 152, bottom, GH-470108. Art Gallery of Ontario, p. 247. *Artscanada*, Dec. 73-Jan. 74, p. 42. *The Beaver*, Summer 1970, p. 32, bottom. Daphne Beavon, p. 3, no. 8. Bibliotheque Nationale du Québec, pp. 61; 78; 80; 82; 90, top; 100; 101, top; 102, top; 105, bottom; 111, bottom; 112, top left; 113, top right; 127, top; 128; 139; 141. Black Creek Pioneer Village, pp. 225, bottom; 230, bottom; 231, top; 231, bottom; 232; 233, top; 236; 240, top and bottom; 241. British Museums, pp. 208, 209. Canadian Broadcasting Corporation, p. 3, nos. 10 and 11. Canadian Historical Association, 1968, p. 210. City of Bristol Museum and Art Gallery, p. 56. Confederation Centre Art Gallery & Museum Permanent Collection, Charlottetown, p. 176. Confederation Life Collection, pp. 75; 173, 52-267-4; 186. Dover Publications Inc., pp. 159, top; 161, top; 164, bottom left and bottom right; 165, top; 166. Editeur Officiel du Québec, p. 124, 5898-42. Glenbow Museum, 47, top left, P-1888-2; 47, top right, P-906-398. The Grimsby Independent Limited, pp. 12, 13. Lazare and Parker, p. 35, bottom. Library/Hudson's Bay Co. Archives, pp. 31; 112, top right, 66-8. Malak Ottawa, Ontario, p. 18, top. McClelland and Stewart, Toronto, pp. 248 (map redrawn from map appearing in *Patterns of Settlement in Southern Ontario*; reprinted with permission of The Canadian Publishers, McClelland and Stewart, Toronto); 137 (from *New France: The Last Phase*, by Stanley; reprinted by permission of The Canadian Publishers, McClelland and Stewart, Toronto). Metropolitan Toronto Library Board, pp. 189; 199; 216, JRR-2851; 235, JRR-333-8; 237, M1-16; 252, top; 253. Mika Publishing, pp. 160; 161, middle and bottom; 170; 171; 181; 186; 225, top. Miller Services, p. 2, no. 5. Molson Archives, p. 119, bottom. Tom Moore, Toronto, for Aggregation Gallery, Toronto, p. 8, top. Musée de la Province de Québec, p. 127, bottom, 2761-41. National Archives (U.S.), p. 162, 148-GW-439. National Army Museum, London, p. 165. National Film Board of Canada, pp. 50, top, 64-2290; 50 bottom, 64-2295; 51, S11057; 58, S-1661; 92, bottom, S2522; 93, top, S4278. National Gallery of Canada, Ottawa, pp. 180, 6275; 185, 5777. National Map Collection Public Archives, pp. 65, C111350; 121, C26219; 130, C22032. National Maritime Museum, p. 171, 3145(B). National Museums of Canada, pp. 4; 14; 18, bottom; 32, top, J5046; 37, top, N50918. National Photography Collection, pp. 3, no. 9; 6; 7, top and bottom; 21, PA42121; 27, top, C24486; 28, top, C20843; 28, bottom, C43526; 33, bottom, C24482; 34, C49476; 35, middle, PA45110; 36, C6791; 37, bottom, C20834; 38, C8220; 39, top, C38191; 43, C20857; 47, bottom, C26051. National Postal Museum, p. 245. Natural Science of Canada, Ltd., pp. 22, 23. Nelson, Foster & Scott, p. 33, top. Print reproduced courtesy of Thomas Nelson & Sons, Ltd., p. 258. New Breed, Feb.-Mar. 1977, p. 5. New Brunswick Museum, pp. 89, top; 149, bottom. Notman Photographic Archives, pp. 120, bottom, 3345; 122, bottom, 3617; 123, bottom, 3020; 125, top, 3237; 125, bottom, 3235; 126, top, 3292; 126, bottom, MP68/75. Office du Film de la Province de Québec, p. 129. Ontario Archives, Toronto, p. 227, P1812. Oxford University Press, p. 123. Parks Canada, p. 55. Public Archives, pp. 19, top left, middle left, bottom; 26, 81456; 48, 80026; 49, 77013; 61, bottom; GH971-95; 62, GH473-63; 63, C6680; 69, top, C98232; 69, bottom, C9711; 70, C9711; 74, C-5750; 76; 79, C-16952; 81, C70267; 84, C11232; 90, bottom; 98, C6325; 102, bottom; 103, C29486; 104, bottom; 107, top, C11013; 107, bottom, C22007; 108, top, C5746; 113, bottom left, C-1349; 114, C3686; 115, top, C47916; 115, bottom, C1735; 117, top, C-12504; 119, top, C-15784; 120, C352; 126, middle, C73589; 135, C70247; 136, bottom; 142, C70232; 147, top, C70235; 147, bottom, C4291; 149, top, C-20756; 151, top, C73434; 151, bottom, C-11043; 158, C17512; 167; 169, C-17509; 172, C-2381; 175, C40162; 177, top left; 177, top right, C1761; 177, bottom two photos, C-4746; 179, C001; 182, C11811; 183, C2401; 186; 189, bottom photo, C34334; 191, bottom, N1173-155; 192, middle, C16404; 192, bottom, C276; 193, bottom, C6487; 194, C8536; 196, C-11053; 197, C-14905; 201, C968; 212, all photos, C6556; 217, 123694; 221; 222, top, C72985; 222, bottom, C11774; 223, top, 73519; 226, C44625; 228, top, C32; 228, bottom, C44626; 233, bottom, C172; 238, top, C73660; 238, bottom, C23505; 239, C6886; 242, C38560; 243, C16523; 244, C16525; 246, C017; 249, C12632; 250; 252, bottom, C2367; 254; 255; 257, top, C2349; 257, bottom, C2384; 259, C69508; 260, C73410; 262, top, C2327; 262, bottom, C9725; 263, C16467. Royal Ontario Museum, pp. 27, bottom; 200, 968147-8; 203, 967-1061. Courtesy of Sainte-Marie among the Hurons, Midland, Ontario, pp. 94, bottom; 95, top left, top right, middle left, and middle right; 97. Ted Spiegel from Black Star, p. 174. State Historical Society of Wisconsin, p. 140. Today Magazine, p. 2, no. 3. Toronto Star Syndicate, p. 3, no. 6. Toronto Sun Syndicate, pp. 2, nos. 1, 2, and 4; 3, no. 7. Universitetets Oldsaksamling Oslo, p. 54. Webster Canadiana Collection, New Brunswick Museum, pp. 67; 104, top; 131; 143. Daniel Wiener, p. 136. Paul Wilson, p. 7, bottom left corner.

Cover photograph: Public Archives of Canada, C-2433.

Unit page photographs: Archives Nationale du Québec, p.53, N673-43. Public Archives of Canada, pp. 1, C26051; 53, C276; 205, C-17.

Index

Index